GREATER BRUSSELS

W9-AYV-411

0 km 3

0 miles 3

THE UPPER TOWN
Pages 54–75
Street Finder maps 2, 3, 4

THE UPPER
TOWN

0 metres 500

0 yards 500

EYEWITNESS TRAVEL

BRUSSELS
BRUGES, GHENT & ANTWERP

EYEWITNESS TRAVEL

BRUSSELS

BRUGES, GHENT & ANTWERP

LONDON, NEW YORK,
MELBOURNE, MUNICH AND DELHI
www.dk.com

PRODUCED BY Duncan Baird Publishers
London, England

MANAGING EDITOR Rebecca Miles
MANAGING ART EDITOR Vanessa Marsh
EDITORS Georgina Harris, Michelle de Larrabeiti
DESIGNERS Dawn Davies-Cook, Ian Midson
DESIGN ASSISTANTS Rosie Laing, Kelvin Mullins
VISUALIZER Gary Cross
PICTURE RESEARCH Victoria Peel, Ellen Root
DTP DESIGNER Sarah Williams

Dorling Kindersley Limited
PROJECT EDITOR Paul Hines
ART EDITOR Jane Ewart
MAP CO-ORDINATOR David Pugh

CONTRIBUTORS
Zoë Hewetson, Philip Lee, Zoë Ross,
Sarah Wolff, Timothy Wright, Julia Zyrianova

PHOTOGRAPHERS
Demetrio Carrasco, Paul Kenward

ILLUSTRATORS
Gary Cross, Richard Draper, Eugene Fleury, Paul Guest, Claire Littlejohn,
Robbie Polley, Kevin Robinson, John Woodcock

Reproduced by Colourscan (Singapore)
Printed and bound by South China Printing Co. Ltd., China

First American Edition, 2000
09 10 9 8 7 6 5 4 3 2 1

Published in the United States by DK Publishing,
375 Hudson Street, New York, New York 10014

Reprinted with revisions 2003, 2005, 2007, 2009

Copyright 2000, 2009 © Dorling Kindersley Limited, London

Published in Great Britain by Dorling Kindersley Limited

ISSN 1542-1554
ISBN 978-0-75666-106-9

FLOORS ARE REFERRED TO THROUGHOUT IN ACCORDANCE WITH EUROPEAN
USAGE; I. E., THE "FIRST FLOOR" IS THE FLOOR ABOVE GROUND LEVEL

Front cover main image: The Grand Place with carpet of flowers, Brussels

---

We're trying to be cleaner and greener:

- we recycle waste and switch things off
- we use paper from responsibly managed forests whenever possible
- we ask our printers to actively reduce water and energy consumption
- we check out our suppliers' working conditions – they never use child labour

Find out more about our values and best practices at www.dk.com

---

**The information in this
DK Eyewitness Travel Guide is checked regularly.**

Every effort has been made to ensure that this book is as
up-to-date as possible at the time of going to press. Some details,
however, such as telephone numbers, opening hours, prices, gallery
hanging arrangements and travel information are liable to change.
The publishers cannot accept responsibility for any
consequences arising from the use of this book, nor for any material
on third party websites, and cannot guarantee that any website
address in this book will be a suitable source of travel
information. We value the views and suggestions of our readers very
highly. Please write to: Publisher, DK Eyewitness Travel Guides,
Dorling Kindersley, 80 Strand, London WC2R 0RL, Great Britain.

◁ The Grand Place, centre of the Lower Town, at night

CONTENTS

INTRODUCING BRUSSELS

Belgian heroes Tintin and Snowy

Revellers in colourful costume at a
festival in the Grand Place

Vista of a tree-lined path in the Parc du Cinquantenaire

Basilique National du Sacré-Coeur

Gilt statue on façade of a Guildhouse in Antwerp

Belgian chocolates

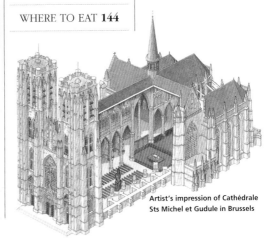
Artist's impression of Cathédrale Sts Michel et Gudule in Brussels

INTRODUCING
BRUSSELS

FOUR GREAT DAYS

The charms of Brussels, Antwerp, Ghent and Bruges are always agreeably understated. All are small enough to make walking the best means to get around. The pleasures lie in wandering, happening upon hospitable places to eat and drink, and visiting some of their

Notre Dame du Sablon, Brussels

rich and diverse collections of museums, galleries and churches. In best Belgian tradition, the way to approach such days is first and foremost to be unhurried. Be warned that almost all Belgian museums are closed on Monday. Prices shown include travel, food and admission.

BRUSSELS IN A NUTSHELL

- **The Grand Place, the city's magnificent centrepiece**
- **The Manneken Pis in all his glory**
- **Belgian art: wonderful and weird**
- **The historic sound of music**

TWO ADULTS allow at least 50 euros

Morning
The **Grand Place** *(see pp42–3)* is one of Europe's finest historic squares, and is a "must-see" sight. You could spend an hour just looking at the guildhouses, or dwell longer by settling into one of the bar-cafés on the square. Then walk along the Rue de l'Étuve to visit that famous icon of Brussels, the **Manneken Pis** *(see pp44–5)*.

Return to the Grand Place and the **Musée de la Ville de Bruxelles** to see its surreal collection of costumes and interesting exhibits on the history of the city. There are many places to find lunch in and around the Grand

Place, but choose carefully to avoid disappointment *(see pp152–55)*, especially around the tourist trap that is the Rue des Bouchers.

Afternoon
The afternoon can be spent in Brussels' best museums, which are up the hill, in the Upper Town. It is not far to walk, or you can take a bus to the **Place Royale** *(see p59)*. This is the location of Belgium's great national art collection, the **Musées Royaux des Beaux-Art** *(see pp62–7)*, which includes unmissable work by Rubens, plus the wonderful alternative art of the Belgian Symbolists. Also nearby is the excellent **Musée Instrumental** *(see p60)*, which has fine views over Brussels from its top-floor Café Du Mim. You could instead continue by tram or bus to the unique shrine to Art Nouveau, the **Musée Horta** *(see p82)*, stopping perhaps on the way back for some shopping in the upmarket boutiques of the Avenue Louise and **Avenue de la Toison d'Or** *(see pp168–71)*.

The gabled buildings of the Grand Place in Brussels

ANTWERP: FASHION, NEW AND OLD

- **Rubens' home, 17th-century seat of fashion**
- **High art from the age of Rubens**
- **A dynamic museum of modern fashion**
- **High-class boutiques**

TWO ADULTS allow at least 80 euros

Het Modepaleis, the principal boutique of Dries van Noten

Morning
First, get a glimpse of Antwerp's 17th-century golden age at the **Rubenshuis** *(see pp102–103)*. Then take a short walk, or a hop on a tram, to Antwerp's fine-art collection at **Koninklijk Museum voor Schone Kunsten** *(see pp100–101)*. Followers of fashion will want to see Ann Demeulemeester's shop, which shares Leopold de Waelplaats with the museum. From here it is just a short walk to the contemporary art collection at the **Museum voor Hedendaagse Kunst**, known as **MuHKA** *(see p99)*, and also the **FotoMuseum** *(see p99)*.

Afternoon

After lunch in one of the pleasant cafés located in the Grote Markt and the nearby streets *(see p164)*, visit Antwerp's museum of fashion, the **ModeMuseum** or **MoMu** *(see p98)*. Nearby is Het Modepaleis, the shop of designer **Dries van Noten** (Nationalestraat 16), and there are other good fashion-hunting grounds in the area. To seek refuge from all this high-octane fashion, head for the more stately charms of Antwerp's great cathedral, the **Onze Lieve Vrouwe Kathedraal** *(see p95)* and the old city square, the **Grote Markt** *(see p94)*.

GHENT: SACRED AND PROFANE

- Jan van Eyck's outstanding masterpiece
- One of Europe's best design museums
- Cutting-edge modern art

TWO ADULTS allow at least 80 euros

Morning

First, make a pilgrimage to Jan (and Hubert) van Eyck's exquisite panel painting, *The Adoration of the Mystic Lamb* in **St Baafskathedraal** *(see p114)*. Then walk to the Graslei and Korenlei *(see p115)*, stopping to admire the views from the St Michielsbrug bridge over the canal. Continue to **Design Museum Ghent** *(see p115)*, a superb museum tracing the history of interiors, furniture and furnishings. You could now take a 40-minute canal trip from the Korenlei, which gives an insight into the importance of the waterways in the city's medieval life. For lunch, there is a good choice of restaurants in the area *(see pp160–61)*.

The Korenlei on the bank of the River Leie in Ghent

Kerchovelaan and walk across the Citadelpark to the **Stedelijk Museum voor Actuele Kunst**, or **SMAK** *(see p117)*. This great collection of contemporary art is bound to leave an impression on you. Returning to the historic centre of the town, try an aperitif of jenever gin in one of the bars by the canal or in the Vrijdagmarkt.

BRUGES: MEDIEVAL GLORY

- A view of medieval Bruges
- Supreme art from its Golden Age
- A relaxing canal trip
- Beer "academies"

TWO ADULTS allow at least 100 euros

Morning

Start the day with an energetic climb up the 366 steps of the **Belfort** *(see p121)*, the city bell-tower, for some exhilarating views across Bruges. Now walk the short distance to the **Burg** *(see p120)*, a delightful square lined with historic buildings, including the **Stadhuis** *(see p120)*, and the double church of the **Heilig Bloed Basiliek** *(see p120)*. It is a short and pretty walk from here, along the canals, to the **Groeningemuseum** *(see*

Detail from *The Adoration of the Mystic Lamb*, Ghent

pp124–25), celebrated for its small but fabulous collection of late-medieval painting. There are plenty of places to eat nearby, especially around the Vismarkt back near the Burg, or by heading further west to Gruuthusestraat, Mariastraat and Walplein.

Afternoon

Start with a restful canal trip; tours last about 30 minutes and most start from landing stages near the Burg. Next, walk back along the canal called the Dijver to **Onze Lieve Vrouwekerk** *(see p121)*, one of Bruges' most attractive churches. On the other side of Mariastraat is the **Hans Memling Museum** *(see p123)*, a museum that combines a medieval hospital with a collection of late medieval paintings by Hans Memling. From here you could take a short walk to the **Gruuthuse Museum** *(see p122)* for a taste of medieval life.

Afternoon

Take a tram from the Korenmarkt to Charles de

The view of Bruges from the top of the Belfort

Putting Brussels on the Map

Brussels is the capital of Belgium and the centre of government for the European Union. Although one of Europe's smallest countries, covering 30,500 sq km (11,580 sq miles), Belgium has one of the highest population densities, with 10.5 million inhabitants (350 people for every square kilometre). Belgium is a bilingual country (Dutch and French). Although Brussels falls geographically in the Flemish (Dutch-speaking) half, it is largely French-speaking. Belgium's largest city, with almost one million inhabitants, Brussels is also the most visited, with around six million visitors a year, although 70 per cent of these come for business. Brussels' excellent communications make it an ideal place from which to explore historic Belgian cities such as Antwerp, Ghent and Bruges.

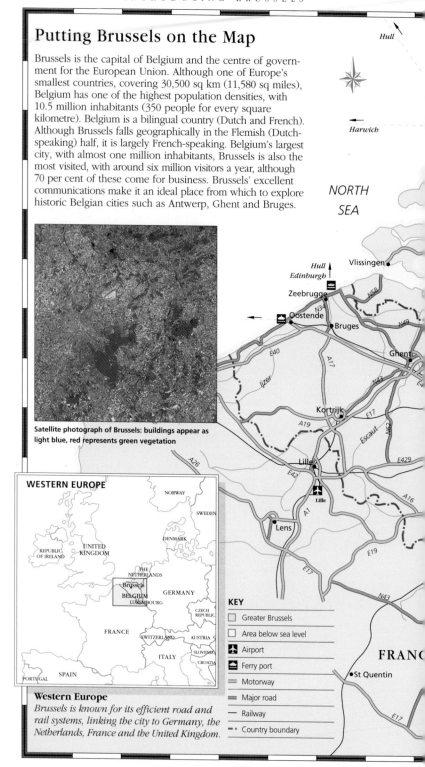

Satellite photograph of Brussels: buildings appear as
light blue, red represents green vegetation

Hull

Harwich

NORTH
SEA

Hull
Edinburgh

Vlissingen

Zeebrugge

Oostende

Bruges

Ghent

Ijzer

Kortrijk

Escaut

Lille

Lille

Lens

St Quentin

FRANCE

WESTERN EUROPE

NORWAY

SWEDEN

DENMARK

REPUBLIC
OF IRELAND

UNITED
KINGDOM

THE
NETHERLANDS

Brussels

BELGIUM

LUXEMBOURG

GERMANY

CZECH
REPUBLIC

FRANCE

SWITZERLAND

AUSTRIA

SLOVENIA

CROATIA

ITALY

PORTUGAL

SPAIN

KEY

☐	Greater Brussels
☐	Area below sea level
✈	Airport
⛴	Ferry port
═	Motorway
▬	Major road
—	Railway
‑‑	Country boundary

Western Europe

*Brussels is known for its efficient road and
rail systems, linking the city to Germany, the
Netherlands, France and the United Kingdom.*

BRUSSELS AND ENVIRONS

Mechelen

Aalst

Vilvoorde

Nationale

BRUSSELS

Leuven

Anderlecht

Woluwe

Halle

Wavre

Waterloo

Brussels and its Environs

*The sights in Brussels are covered in detail on pages 40–87
and a* Street Finder *map is provided on pages 188–93.
Attractions beyond Brussels can be found on pages 90–129.*

AMSTERDAM

Schiphol

Leiden

EN HAAG

Rotterdam

Hoek van
Holland

Rotterdam

Dordrecht

NETHERLANDS

Breda

Möenchengladbach

ANTWERP

Antwerpen

Albert Kanaal

GERMANY

Mechelen

Maastrict

Nationale

Maastricht

BRUSSELS

Leuven

Aachen

Waterloo

BELGIUM

Liège

Verviers

Namur

Charleroi

Dinant

Bastogne

LUXEMBOURG

Charleville-
Mézières

Arlon

Luxembourg

Luxembourg

0 km   20

0 miles   20

Central Brussels

Central Brussels is divided into two main areas, each of which has its own chapter in the guide. Historically the poorer area where workers and immigrants lived, the Lower Town contains the exceptional 17th-century heart of the city, the Grand Place, as well as the cosmopolitan Place de Brouckère, and the historic workers' district, the Marolles. The Upper Town, traditional home of the aristocracy, is an elegant area which encircles the city's green oasis, the Parc de Bruxelles. Running up through the area is Rue Royale, which ends in the 18th-century Place Royale, home to the city's finest art museums.

Hôtel de Ville
The focus of the Grand Place, Brussels' historic Town Hall dates from the early 15th century. Its Gothic tracery façade features the famous needle-like crooked spire (see pp44–5).

KEY

▮	Major sight
P	Parking
🛈	Tourist information
🚓	Police station
✚	Hospital
🚌	Bus terminus
🚊	Tram stop
🚉	Train station
M	Metro station
✝	Church

La Bourse Façade
Just behind the Grand Place on busy Boulevard Anspach in the Lower Town, Brussels' Stock Exchange was built in 1873 in ornate style (see p47).

Place du Petit Sablon
*This square is a jewel
of the Upper Town.
Originally a horse market,
the central area became
a flower garden in 1890,
surrounded by wrought-
iron railings decorated
with stone statuettes.
Each figure represents a
medieval trade or craft
that brought prosperity
to the capital (see
pp68–9).*

Palais Royal
*The official home of the
Belgian monarch, this is one
of the finest 18th-century
buildings in the Upper Town.
A highlight of Neo-Classical
architecture, it overlooks Parc
de Bruxelles (see pp58–9).*

0 metres 500
0 yards 500

Brussels' Best: Architecture

Reflecting Brussels' importance in the history of
northern Europe, the city's architecture ranges from
grand medieval towers to the glittering post-modern
structures of European institutions. With a few
examples of medieval Brabant Gothic still on show,
the capital of Europe has the best Flemish Renaissance
architecture in the world in the Baroque splendour
of the Grand Place, as well as elegant Neo-Classical
churches and houses. The quantity and quality of Art
Nouveau *(see pp18–19)*, with its exquisite interiors and
handmade features, are highlights of 19th- and 20th-
century residential building. The cutting-edge designs
in the Parliament Quarter, planned by committees of
European architects, take the tour up to date.

Basilique du Sacré-Coeur
*Begun in 1904 and only
completed in 1970, this huge
Art Deco edifice is the world's
fifth-largest church (see p85).*

BASILIQUE DU
SACRÉ-COEUR

Grand Place
*Almost entirely rebuilt by merchants
after French bombardment in 1695,
this cobbled square is one of the world's
best Baroque ensembles (see pp42–3).*

Palais de Justice
*Bigger in area than St Peter's in
Rome, the city's law courts
were built in Neo-Classical
style using the profits of
colonialism, and com-
pleted in 1883 (see p69).*

Lower Town

Porte de Hal
*This imposing 14th-
century tower is the
only remaining trace
of the city's solid, thick
second perimeter wall.
It owes its survival to its
use as an 18th-century
prison and latterly as a
museum (see p83).*

| 0 metres | | 500 |
| 0 yards | | 500 |

Cathédrale Sts Michel et Gudule
The white stone façade from 1250 is an outstanding example of Brabant Gothic style (see pp70–71).

Palais de la Nation
The home of the Belgian Parliament since the country's independence in 1830, this magnificent building was constructed in the late 18th century by the Neo-Classical architect Guimard, who also designed the expansive stone façade and many of the surrounding state buildings.

Upper Town

Palais d'Egmont
This ducal mansion bears the name of a Flemish count executed for defending his countrymen's civil rights in 1568 (see p69).

European Parliament
Nicknamed "Caprice des Dieux" ("Whim of the Gods"), this postmodern building serves more than 700 politicians.

Belgian Artists

Belgian art rose to the fore when the region came under Burgundian rule in the 15th century. Renaissance painters produced strong works in oil, characterized by intricate detail and lifelike, unidealized portraiture. The quest for realism and clarity of light was heavily influenced by the new Dutch schools of art. Yet, in contrast, Belgium's second golden artistic age, in the 20th century, moved away from these goals, abandoning reality for surrealism in the challenging work of artists such as René Magritte.

Belgium is justifiably proud of its long artistic tradition. Rubenshuis in Antwerp (*see pp102–103*), Brussels' Musée Wiertz (*see p72*) and Musées Royaux des Beaux-Arts (*see pp62– 7*) are fine examples of the respect Belgium shows to its artists' homes and their works.

Portrait of Laurent Froimont **by Rogier van der Weyden**

THE FLEMISH PRIMITIVES

Art in Brussels and Flanders first attracted European attention at the end of the Middle Ages. **Jan van Eyck** (c.1395–41) is considered to be responsible for the major revolution in Flemish art. Widely credited as the creator of oil painting, van Eyck was the first artist to use the oil medium to fix longer-lasting glazes and to mix colour pigments for wood and canvas. As works could now be rendered more permanent, the innovation spread the Renaissance fashion for panel paintings. However, van Eyck was more than just a practical innovator, and can be seen as the forefather of the Flemish Primitive school

with his lively depictions of human existence in an animated manner. Van Eyck is also responsible, with his brother, for the striking polyptych altarpiece *Adoration of the Mystic Lamb*, displayed in Ghent Cathedral (*see p114*).

The trademarks of the Flemish Primitives are a life-like vitality, enhanced by realism in portraiture, texture of clothes and furnishings and a clarity of light. The greatest interpreter of the style was Rogier de la Pasture (c.1400–64), better known as **Rogier van der Weyden**, the town painter of Brussels, who combined van Eyck's light and realism with work of religious intensity, as in *Lamentation (see p66)*.

Many in Belgium and across Europe were schooled and inspired by his work, continuing and expanding the new techniques. **Dirk Bouts** (1415–75) extended

the style. With his studies of bustling 15th-century Bruges, **Hans Memling** (c.1430–94) is considered the last Flemish Primitive. Moving towards the 16th century, landscape artist **Joachim Patinir** (c.1480–1524) produced the first European industrial scenes.

THE BRUEGHEL DYNASTY

In the early years of the 16th century, Belgian art was strongly influenced by the Italians. Trained in Rome, **Jan Gossaert** (c.1478–1532) brought mythological themes to the art commissioned by the ruling Dukes of Brabant.

But it was the prolific Brueghel family who had the most influence on Flemish art throughout the 16th and 17th centuries. **Pieter Brueghel the Elder** (c.1525–69), one of the greatest Flemish artists, settled in Brussels in 1563. His earthy rustic landscapes of village life, peopled with comic peasants, are a social study of medieval life and remain his best-known work. **Pieter Brueghel the Younger** (1564–1636) produced religious works such as *The Enrolment of Bethlehem* (1610). In contrast, **Jan Brueghel the Elder** (1568–1625) painted intricate floral still lifes with a draped velvet backdrop, becoming known as "Velvet Brueghel". His son, **Jan Brueghel the Younger** (1601–78) also became a court painter in Brussels and a fine landscape artist of note.

The Fall of Icarus **by Pieter Brueghel the Elder**

Self-portrait by Rubens, one of many from his lifetime

THE ANTWERP ARTISTS

In the 17th century, the main centre of Belgian art moved from the social capital, Brussels, to Antwerp, in the heart of Flanders. This move was largely influenced by **Pieter Paul Rubens** (1577–1640), who lived in Antwerp. He was one of the first Flemish artists to become known through Europe and Russia. A court painter, Rubens was also an accomplished landscape artist and interpreter of mythology, but is best known for his depiction of plump women, proud of their figures. Rubens was so popular in his own time that his bold and large-scale works were translated by Flemish weavers into series of tapestries.

Anthony van Dyck (1599–1641), a pupil of Rubens and court portraitist, was the second Antwerp artist to gain world renown. The Brueghel dynasty continued to produce notable figures: Jan Brueghel the Elder eventually settled in Antwerp to produce art with Rubens, while his son-in-law, **David Teniers II** (1610–90) founded the Antwerp Academy of Art in 1665.

THE EUROPEAN INFLUENCE

The influence of Rubens was so great that little innovation took place in the Flemish art scene in the 18th century. In the early years of the 19th century, Belgian art was largely dominated by the influence of other European schools. **François-Joseph Navez** (1787–1869) introduced Neo-Classicism to Flemish art. Realism took off with **Constantin Meunier** (1831–1905) and Impressionism with **Guillaume Vogels** (1836–96). The Brussels-based **Antoine Wiertz** (1806–65) was considered a Romantic, but his distorted and occasionally disturbing works, such as *Inhumation précipitée* (c.1830) seem to have early Surrealist leanings. **Fernand Khnopff** (1858–1921) was influenced by the German Romantic Gustav Klimt. An early exponent of Belgian Symbolism, Khnopff's work is notable for his portraits of menacing and ambiguous women. Also on a journey from Naturalism to Surrealism, **James Ensor** (1860–1949) often used eerie skeletons in his work, reminiscent of Bosch. Between 1884 and 1894, the artists' cooperative **Les XX (Les Vingt)** reinvigorated the Brussels art scene with exhibitions of famous foreign and Avant Garde painters.

SURREALISM

The 20th century began with the emergence of Fauvism led by **Rik Wouters** (1882–1916), whose bright sun-filled landscapes show the influence of Cézanne.

Surrealism began in Brussels in the mid-1920s, dominated from the start by **René Magritte** (1898–1967). The movement had its roots back in the 16th century, with the phantasmagoria of Bosch and Pieter Brueghel the Elder. Fuelled by the chaos of World War I, much of which took place on Flemish battlefields, Magritte defined his disorientating Surrealism as "[restoring] the familiar to the strange". More ostentatious and emotional, **Paul Delvaux** (1897–1994) produced elegant, freakish interiors occupied by ghostly figures. In 1948 the **COBRA Movement** promoted abstract art, which gave way in the 1960s to conceptual art, led by installationist **Marcel Broodthaers** (1924–76), who used daily objects, such as a casserole dish full of mussels, for his own interpretation.

Sculpture by Rik Wouters

UNDERGROUND ART

Notre Temps (1976) by Expressionist Roger Somville at Hankar station

Some 58 Brussels metro stations have been decorated with a combination of murals, sculptures and architecture by 54 Belgian artists. Although none but the most devoted visitor to the city is likely to see them all, there are several notable examples. **Annessens** was decorated by the Belgian COBRA artists, Dotremont and Alechinsky. In the **Bourse**, surrealist Paul Delvaux's *Nos Vieux Trams Bruxellois* is still on show with *Moving Ceiling*, a series of 75 tubes that move in the breeze by sculptor Pol Bury. At **Horta** station, Art Nouveau wrought ironwork from Victor Horta's now destroyed People's Palace is displayed, and **Stockel** is a tribute to Hergé and his boy hero, Tintin *(see pp20–1)*.

Brussels' Best: Art Nouveau

Among Europe's most important architectural movements at the start of the 20th century, Art Nouveau in Belgium was led by Brussels architect Victor Horta (1861–1947) and the Antwerp-born interior designer Henry van de Velde (1863–1957). The style evolved from the Arts and Crafts Movement in England and the fashion for Japanese simplicity, and is characterized by its sinuous decorative lines, stained glass, carved stone curves, floral frescoes and elaborately curled and twisted metalwork. As new suburbs rose up in the 1890s, over 2,000 new houses were built in the style. Although many were demolished, details can still be seen in almost every Brussels street.

Hôtel Métropole
The high-vaulted lobby and bar of this luxurious 1894 hotel recall the city's fin-de-siècle heyday (see p49).

Old England
This former department store uses glass and steel rather than brick, with large windows and twisted metal turrets (see p60).

Hôtel Ciamberlani
Architect Paul Hankar designed this redbrick house in rue Defacqz for the sgraffiti artist Albert Ciamberlani, with whom he worked.

The Lower Town

Musée Horta
Curved window frames and elaborate metal balconies mark this out as the home and studio of Art Nouveau's best-known architect (see p82).

Hôtel Hannon
This stylish 1902 townhouse was built by Jules Brunfaut (1852–1942). One of its metal-framed windows has striking stained-glass panes (see p83).

Maison Cauchie
*Restored in 1989,
architect Paul Cauchie's
home in rue des Francs
has examples of sgraffiti,
a technique in which
designs are incised onto
wet plaster to reveal
another colour beneath.*

Maison Saint Cyr
*Horta's disciple Gustave
Strauven was keen to out-
do his mentor with this
intricate façade, only 4 m
(14 ft) wide* (see p72).

The Upper Town

Hôtel Solvay
*An early Horta creation
of 1894, this home was
built for a wealthy family.
Horta designed every
element of the building,
from the ochre and yellow
cast-iron façade columns
and glass front door to
the decorative but func-
tional doorknobs* (see p83).

| 0 metres | 500 |
| 0 yards | 500 |

Belgian Comic Strip Art

Tintin's dog Snowy

Belgian comic strip art is as famous a part of Belgian culture as chocolates and beer. The seeds of this great passion were sown when the US comic strip Little Nemo was published in French in 1908 to huge popular acclaim in Belgium. The country's reputation for producing some of the best comic strip art in Europe was established after World War II. Before the war, Europe was awash with American comics, but the Nazis called a halt to the supply. Local artists took over, and found that there was a large audience who preferred homegrown comic heroes. This explosion in comic strip art was led by perhaps the most famous Belgian creation ever, Tintin, who, with his dog Snowy, is as recognizable across Europe as Mickey Mouse.

demonstrated by his work before and during the war, where he expressed a strong sense of justice in such stories as *King Ottakar's Sceptre*, where a fascist army attempts to seize control of a central European state. Hergé took great care in researching his stories; for *Le Lotus Bleu* in 1934, which was set in China, he wrote: "I started… showing a real interest in the people and countries I was sending Tintin off to, concerned by a sense of honesty to my readers."

Spirou cover

Hergé at work in his studio

HERGÉ AND TINTIN

Tintin's creator, Hergé, was born Georges Remi in Brussels in 1907. He began using his pen name (a phonetic spelling of his initials in reverse) in 1924. At the young age of 15, his drawings were published in the *Boy Scout Journal*. He became the protégé of a priest, Abbot Norbert Wallez, who also managed the Catholic journal *Le XXe Siècle*, and was swiftly given the responsibility of the children's supplement, *Le petit Vingtième*. Eager to invent an original comic strip, Hergé came up with the character of Tintin the reporter, who first appeared in the story *Tintin au Pays des Soviets* on 10 January 1929. Over the next 10 years the character developed and grew in popularity. Book-length stories began to appear from 1930.

During the Nazi occupation in the 1940s *Tintin* continued to be published, with political references carefully omitted, in an approved paper *Le Soir*. This led to Hergé being accused of collaboration at the end of the war. He was called in for questioning but released later the same day without charge. Hergé's innocence was amply

POST-WAR BOOM

Belgium's oldest comic strip journal *Spirou* was launched in April 1938 and, alongside the weekly *Journal de Tintin* begun in 1946, became a hothouse for the artistic talent that was to flourish during the post-war years. Many of the country's best-loved characters were first seen in *Spirou*, and most of them are still in print. Artists such as Morris, Jijé, Peyo and Roba worked on the journal. Morris (1923–2001) introduced the cowboy parody, *Lucky Luke* in *Spirou* in 1947, a character who went on to feature in live-action films and US television cartoons.

Statue of Tintin and Snowy

COMIC STRIP CHARACTERS

Some of the world's best-loved comic strip characters originated in Belgium. *Tintin* is the most famous, but *Lucky Luke* the cowboy, the cheeky children *Suske en Wiske* and *The Smurfs* have also been published worldwide, while modern artists such as Schueten break new ground.

Tintin by Hergé

Lucky Luke by Morris

During the 1960s, the idea of the comic strip being the Ninth Art (after the seventh and eighth, film and television) expanded to include adult themes in the form of the comic-strip graphic novel.

PEYO AND THE SMURFS

Best known for *The Smurfs*, Peyo (1928–92) was also a member of the team behind the *Spirou* journal which published his poetic medieval series *Johan et Pirlouit*, in 1952. *The Smurfs* first appeared as characters here – tiny blue people whose humorous foibles soon eclipsed any interest in the strip's supposed main characters. Reacting to their popularity, Peyo created a strip solely about them. Set in the Smurf village, the stories were infused with satirical social comment. *The Smurfs* were a popular craze between 1983 and 1985, featuring in advertising and merchandising of every type. They spawned a feature-length film, TV cartoons and popular music, and had several hit records in the 1980s.

Modern cover by Marvano

WILLY VANDERSTEEN

While *Spirou* and *Tintin* were French-language journals, Willy Vandersteen (1913–90) dominated the Flemish market. His popular creation, *Suske en Wiske* has been translated into English and appears as *Bob and Bobette* in the UK, and *Willy and Wanda* in the US. The main characters are a pair of "ordinary" kids aged between 10 and 14 years who have extraordinary adventures all over the world, as well as travelling back and forth in time. Today, Vandersteen's books sell in their millions.

COMIC STRIP ART TODAY

Comic strips, known as *bandes dessinées* or *beeldverhaal*, continue to be published in Belgium in all their forms. In newspapers, children's comics and graphic novels the Ninth Art remains one of the country's biggest exports. The high standards and imaginative scope of a new generation of artists, such as Schueten and Marvano, have fed growing consumer demand for comic books. Both French and Flemish publishers issue

Contemporary comic-strip artists at work in their studio

over 22 million comic books each year. Today, Belgian cartoons are sold in more than 30 countries, including the US.

Larger-than-life cartoon by Frank Pé adorning a Brussels building

STREET ART

There are currently 18 large comic strip images decorating the sides of buildings around Brussels' city centre. This outdoor exhibition is known as the Comic Strip Route and is organized by the Centre Belge de la Bande Dessineé (the Belgian Centre for Comic Strip Art) *(see pp50–51)* and the city of Brussels. Begun in 1991 as a tribute to Belgium's talent for comic strip art, this street art project continues to grow. A free map of the route is available from tourist information offices, as well as from the comic museum itself.

***Suske en Wiske* by Vandersteen**

***The Smurfs* by Peyo**

Contemporary cartoon strip by Schueten

Tapestry and Lace

For over six centuries, Belgian lace and tapestry have been highly prized luxury crafts. Originating in Flanders in the 12th century, tapestry has since been handmade in the centres of Tournai, Brussels, Arras, Mechelen and Oudenaarde, while the lace trade was practised from the 1500s onwards in all the Belgian provinces, with Bruges and Brussels particularly renowned for their delicate work. The makers often had aristocratic patrons; intricate lace and fine tapestries were status symbols of the nobility and staple exports throughout Europe from the 15th to 18th centuries. Today Belgium remains home to the very best tapestry and lace studios in the world.

Lacemaker's studio sign

Tapestry weavers *numbered over 50,000 in Flanders from 1450–1550. With the ruling Dukes of Burgundy as patrons, weavers prospered, and hangings grew more elaborate.*

Tapestry designs *involve weaver and artist working closely together. Painters, including Rubens, produced drawings for a series of weavings of six or more on grand themes (detail shown).*

The texture of the weave was the finest ever achieved; often 12 threads to the inch (5 per cm).

Weavers working today *still use medieval techniques to produce contemporary tapestry, woven in Mechelen and Tournai to modern designs.*

TAPESTRY

By 1200, the Flemish towns of Arras (now in France) and Tournai were Europe-wide known centres of weaving. Prized by the nobility, tapestries were portable and could be moved with the court as rulers travelled their estates. As trade grew, techniques were refined; real gold and silver were threaded into the fine wool, again increasing the value. Blending Italian idealism with Flemish realism, Bernard van Orley (1492–1542) revolutionized tapestry designs, as seen above in *The Battle of Pavia 1525*, the first of a series. Flemish weavers were eventually lured across Europe, where ironically their skill led to the success of the Gobelins factory in Paris that finally stole Flanders' crown in the late 1700s.

The lace trade *rose to the fore during the early Renaissance. Emperor Charles V decreed that lace-making should be a compulsory skill for girls in convents and béguinages (see p53) throughout Flanders. Lace became fashionable on collars and cuffs for both sexes. Trade reached a peak in the 18th century.*

Battles and classical myths were popular themes for tapestry series.

Lace makers *are traditionally women. Although their numbers are dwindling, many craftswomen still work in Bruges and Brussels, centres of bobbin lace, creating intricate work by hand.*

Victorian lace *heralded a revival of the craft after its decline in the austere Neo-Classical period. Although men no longer wore it, the growth of the status of lace as a ladies' accessory and its use in soft furnishing led to its renewed popularity.*

Belgian lace *is bought today mainly as a souvenir, but despite the rise in machine-made lace from other countries, the quality here still remains as fine as it was in the Renaissance.*

BRUSSELS THROUGH THE YEAR

The temperate climate of Brussels is typical of Northern Europe and means that a range of activities throughout the year take place both inside and out. Mild damp winters and gentle summers allow the city's strong artistic life to flourish in historic buildings and modern stadiums alike. The Belgians make the most of their seasonal changes. Theatre, dance and film start their season in January, with evening venues

Revellers at Ommegang

that range from ancient abbeys lit by the setting sun to drive-in cinemas. The city's flower festival launches the summer in highly colourful style, with the Grand Place literally carpeted in millions of blooms every other August. Through the year, festivals in Brussels range from energetic, exuberant historic processions that have taken place yearly since medieval times, to innovative European experimental art.

SPRING

Brussels' lively cultural life takes off as the crisp spring days lengthen and visitors begin to arrive in the city. Music festivals take place in a wide variety of open-air venues. As the city's parks burst into bloom, the world-famous tropical greenhouses at Laeken are opened to the public and Brussels' chocolatiers produce delicious creations for Easter.

The Royal Glasshouse at Laeken, famed for its rare exotic orchids

MARCH

International Fantasy Film Festival *(middle fortnight)*. Lovers of the weird and wonderful will find new and vintage work here in cinemas all over the city.
Ars Musica *(mid-Mar to early Apr)*. This celebration of modern music is one of Europe's finest festivals, boasting famous performers and beautiful venues, often the Musée d'art ancien *(see pp62–3)*. The festival is now a must for connoisseurs of the contemporary music world.
Eurantica *(last week)*. The Baudouin Stadium at Heysel plays host to hundreds of traders and members of the public anxious for bargains in the world of antiques.
Easter *(Easter Sunday)*. The annual Easter Egg hunt, with eggs allegedly hidden by the bells of churches in Rome. Over 1,000 brightly coloured

Easter eggs are hidden by adults in the Parc Royal, and Belgian children gather to forage among the flowerbeds.

APRIL

Sablon Baroque Spring *(third week)*. The Place du Grand Sablon hosts new classical ensembles in a gathering of young Belgian talent performing 17th-century music.
The Royal Greenhouses at Laeken *(12 days, dates vary)*. The private greenhouses of the Belgian Royal family are opened to the public as their numerous exotic plants and cacti start to flower. Breathtaking 19th-century glass and wrought ironwork shelters hundreds of rare species *(see pp86–7)*.
Flanders Festival *(mid-Apr to Oct)*. A celebration of all things musical, this

classical medley offers more than 120 performances by internationally renowned choirs and orchestras.
Scenes d'Ecran *(third weekend)*. Over 100 new European films draw crowds in cinemas across the city.

MAY

Europe Day Festivities *(7–9 May)*. As the capital of Europe, Brussels celebrates its role in the European Union – even Manneken

Runners taking part in the Brussels Twenty-Kilometre Race

AVERAGE DAILY HOURS OF SUNSHINE

Hours

Jan Feb Mar Apr May Jun Jul Aug Sep Oct Nov Dec

Climate
Belgium has a fairly temperate Northern European climate. Although not often freezing, winters are chilly and a heavy coat is required. Summers are warmer and much brighter, though you will still need a jersey for the evenings. Rainwear is always a necessity.

Pis is dressed as a Euro-supporter, in a suit of blue, decorated with yellow stars.
Kunsten FESTIVAL des Arts *(9–31 May)*. This innovative festival covers theatre and dance and is the forum for much exciting new talent.
Les Nuits Botaniques *(mid-May)*. Held in the former greenhouses of the Botanical gardens, now the French cultural centre, this series of musical events is a delight.
Queen Elisabeth Music Contest *(May to mid-Jun)*. Classical fans will flock to the prestigious musical competition, now in its fifth decade. Young singers, violinists and pianists gather in front of well-known conductors and soloists to determine the champion among Europe's finest student players.
Brussels Twenty-Kilometre Race *(last Sunday)*. As many as 20,000 keen professional and amateur runners race round the city, taking in its major landmarks.
Jazz Marathon *(last weekend)*. Bistros and cafés are the venues for myriad small jazz bands, with some well-known artists playing anonymously.

SUMMER

The season of pageantry arrives with Ommegang in July, one of Europe's oldest and best-known processions, which takes place in the Grand Place and the surrounding streets. Multicultural music runs throughout the summer, with classical,

jazz and avant-garde US and European performers playing in venues ranging from tiny beer cafés to the great King Baudouin stadium in Heysel. Independence is celebrated on Belgian National Day. Families enjoy the Foire du Midi, the huge fairground over 2 km square (1 sq mile) covered with rides and stalls.

JUNE

City of Brussels Summer Festival *(early Jun to Sep)*. Classical concerts take place in some of the city's best-known ancient buildings.
Festival of Wallonia *(Jun–Oct)*. Covering Brussels and Flanders, this series of gala concerts showcases the best in young Belgian classical orchestral and soloist talent.
Brussels European Film Festival *(late Jun)*. Premières and film stars are adding weight to this European film showcase. **Couleur Café Festival** *(last weekend)*. Spread over three summer evenings in the Tour et Taxis

African drummer performing at the Couleur Café Festival

renovated warehouse, the fashionable and funky programme includes salsa, African drummers, acid jazz and multicultural music.
Fête de la Musique *(last weekend)*. Two days of concerts and recitals featuring world music take place in the halls and museums of the city.

JULY

Ommegang *(first weekend in July)*. This festival has been celebrated in Brussels since 1549, and now draws crowds from around the world.

The Ommegang pausing in front of dignitaries in the Grand Place

AVERAGE MONTHLY RAINFALL

Rainfall chart
*On the whole
Belgium is rather
a rainy country,
with Brussels expe-
riencing constant
low rainfall
throughout the year.
Spring is the driest
season, but
summers can be
damp. In winter,
rain may turn to
snow and sleet.*

Translated as "a tour", the procession revolves around the Grand Place and the surrounding streets. Over 2,000 participants dress up and become members of a Renaissance town; jesters, courtiers, nobles and soldiers; they go on to parade before Belgian dignitaries. Tickets have to be booked months in advance.

Brosella Folk and Jazz Festival *(second weekend).* Musicians from all over Europe play informal gigs in the Parc d'Osseghem in the shadow of the Atomium.

Festival d'Eté de Bruxelles *(Jul–Aug).* Classical concerts take place through the high summer in venues around the Upper and Lower Town.

Foire du Midi *(mid-Jul–mid-Aug).* Brussels' main station, Gare du Midi, is host to this month-long funfair, which attracts people in their thousands. Especially popular with children, it is one of the biggest fairs in Europe, and includes an enormous Ferris wheel.

Belgian National Day *(21 Jul).* The 1831 declaration of independence is com-memorated annually with a military parade followed by a firework display in the Parc de Bruxelles.

Palais Royal Open Days *(last week in Jul–second week of Sep).* The official residence of the Belgian Royal family, the opulent staterooms of the Palais Royal, including the huge throne room, are open to the public for six weeks during the summer *(see pp58–9).*

Costumed revellers at the Plantation of the Meiboom

AUGUST

Plantation du Meiboom *(9 Aug).* This traditional festival dates from 1213. Parading crowds dressed in huge puppet costumes parade around the Lower Town and finally reach the Grand Place where a maypole is planted as a celebration of summer.

Tapis des Fleurs *(mid-Aug,*

biennially, for four days). Taking place on even-num-bered years, this colourful celebration pays tribute to Brussels' long-established flower industry. The Grand Place is carpeted with millions of fresh flowers in patterns echoing historical scenes. The beautiful flower carpet meas-ures 2,000 sq m (21,000 sq ft).

AUTUMN

Fresh autumn days are the cue for many indoor events; innovative jazz is performed in the city's cafés and the French cultural centre in Le Botanique. Architecture is celebrated in the heritage weekend where the public can tour many private houses and personal art collections.

SEPTEMBER

The Birthday of Manneken Pis *(last weekend).* Brussels' celebrated mascot is clothed in a new suit by a chosen

The Grand Place, carpeted in millions of fresh flowers

AVERAGE MONTHLY TEMPERATURE

°C
30
24
18
12
6
-1

Jan Feb Mar Apr May Jun Jul Aug Sep Oct Nov Dec

°F
85
75
65
55
45
30

Temperature chart
This chart gives the average maximum and minimum temperatures for Brussels. Generally mild, Brussels' climate does produce chilly weather and cold winters from October to March. Spring sees milder temperatures and is followed by a warm summer.

dignitary from abroad.

Lucky Town Festival *(first weekend)*. Sixty concerts take place in over 30 of some of Brussels' best-known and atmospheric cafés.

Journées du Patrimoine/ Heritage Days *(second or third weekend)*. Private homes, listed buildings and art collections are opened for a rare public viewing to celebrate the city's architecture.

OCTOBER

Audi Jazz Festival *(early Oct–mid-Dec)*. All over Belgium informal jazz concerts bring autumnal cheer to country towns and the capital. Performers are mainly local, but some European stars fly in for performances in Brussels' Palais des Beaux-Arts. Ray Charles and Herbie Hancock have appeared in past years.

WINTER

Snow and rain typify Brussels' winter weather, and attractions move indoors. Art galleries launch world-class exhibitions and the Brussels Film Festival showcases new and established talent. As the festive season approaches, the ancient Lower Town is brightly lit and families gather for Christmas with traditional Belgian cuisine.

NOVEMBER

Nocturnes des Sablons *(last weekend)*. Shops and galleries stay open until

11pm around the Place du Grand Sablon. Horse-drawn carriages transport shoppers around the area, with mulled wine on offer in the festively decorated main square.

DECEMBER

Fête de Saint Nicolas *(6 Dec)*. The original Santa Claus, the patron saint of Christmas, is alleged to arrive in the city on this day. Children throughout the country are given their presents, sweetmeats and chocolate.

Reveillon/Fête de Noel *(24–25 Dec)*. In common with the rest of mainland Europe, Christmas is celebrated over a feast on the evening of 24 December. Gifts are given by adults on this day, and 25 December is traditionally for visiting extended family. The city's Christmas decorations provide a lively sight until 6 January.

JANUARY

Fête des Rois *(6 Jan)*. Epiphany is celebrated with almond cake, the *galette des rois*, and the search for the bean inside that declares its finder king for the night.

FEBRUARY

Antiques Fair *(middle fortnight)*. Brussels' crossroads location is useful here as international dealers

Christmas market in the Grand Place around the traditional Christmas Pine

gather in the historic Palais des Beaux-Arts *(see p60)*.

International Comic strip and Cartoon Festival *(middle fortnight)*. Artists and authors, both new and established, arrive for lectures and screenings in this city with its comic strip heritage.

PUBLIC HOLIDAYS

New Year's Day (1 Jan)
Easter Sunday (variable)
Easter Monday (variable)
Labour Day (1 May)
Ascension Day (variable)
Whit Sunday (variable)
Whit Monday (variable)
Belgian National Day (21 July)
Assumption Day (15 Aug)
All Saints' Day (1 Nov)
Armistice Day (11 Nov)
Christmas Day (25 Dec)

THE HISTORY OF BRUSSELS

As the cultural and civic heart of Belgium since the Middle Ages, Brussels has been the focus of much political upheaval over the centuries. But, from the battles of the 17th century to the warfare of the 20th century, it has always managed to re-create itself with vigour. Now, at the start of a new millennium, Belgium's capital is prospering as the political and economic centre of Europe.

When Julius Caesar set out to conquer the Gauls of northern Europe in 58 BC, he encountered a fierce tribe known as the Belgae (the origins of the 19th-century name "Belgium"). Roman victory led to the establishment of the region they called Gallia Belgica. The earliest mention of Brussels itself is as "Broucsella", or "settlement in the marshes" and dates from a 7th-century manuscript.

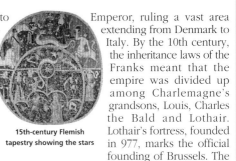

15th-century Flemish tapestry showing the stars

Following the collapse of the Roman Empire in the 5th century, a Germanic race known as the Franks came to rule the region and established the Merovingian dynasty of kings, based in their capital at Tournai. They were followed by the Carolingian dynasty, which produced one of the most important figures of the Middle Ages – Charlemagne (AD 768–814). His noted military expertise ensured that invaders such as the Northern Saxons and the Lombards of Italy were repelled. He was also credited with establishing Christianity as the major religion across western Europe. The pope rewarded him by crowning him Emperor of the West in AD 800; effectively he was the first Holy Roman Emperor, ruling a vast area extending from Denmark to Italy. By the 10th century, the inheritance laws of the Franks meant that the empire was divided up among Charlemagne's grandsons, Louis, Charles the Bald and Lothair. Lothair's fortress, founded in 977, marks the official founding of Brussels. The period had brought a measure of stability to the area's volatile feudal fiefdoms, leading to a trading boom in the new towns of the low countries.

INDUSTRIAL BEGINNINGS

At the start of the 12th century, commerce became the guiding force in western Europe and the centres of trade quickly grew into powerful cities. Rivers and canals were the key to the growth of the area's trading towns. Ghent, Ypres, Antwerp and Bruges became the focus of the cloth trade plied across the North Sea between France, Germany, Italy and England. Brussels, with its skilled craftsmen, became a trade centre, and buildings such as the Cathédrale Sts Michel et Gudule *(see pp70–71)*, started in 1225, demonstrated its stature.

TIMELINE

58–50 BC Gauls defeated by Julius Caesar and Roman occupation begins	**768** Charlemagne is born and goes on to rule most of Europe as the Holy Roman Emperor		**1106** Dukes of Louvain become the Dukes of Brabant

Charlemagne

600 AD	750	900	1050

695 First mention of Brussels as "Broucsella" in the Bishop of Cambrai's papers	**843** Emperor Otto II gives the region of Lower Lotharingia to Charlemagne's grandson, Lothair	**1000** Lotharingia now under the rule of the Holy Roman Emperor	**1005** Henry II, Count of Louvain, builds town walls around Brussels

◁ *Philip the Good*, **Duke of Burgundy (c.1500) by Rogier van der Weyden**

Nineteenth-century painting of the Battle of the Golden Spurs

THE CRAFTSMEN'S REBELLION

Over the next two hundred years Brussels became one of the foremost towns of the Duchy of Brabant. Trade here specialized in fine fabrics that were exported to lucrative markets in France, Italy and England. A handful of merchants became rich and exercised political power over the towns. However, conflict grew between the merchants, who wanted to maintain good relations with England, and their autocratic French rulers who relied upon tax revenue from the towns.

The 14th century witnessed a series of rebellions by the craftsmen of Bruges and Brussels against what they saw as the tyranny of the French lords. In May 1302, Flemish craftsmen, armed only with spears, defeated the French at the Battle of the Golden Spurs, named for the humiliating theft of the cavalry's spurs. Encouraged by this success, the Brussels craftsmen revolted against the aristocracy who controlled their trading economy in 1356. They were also angered by the Hundred Years' War between England and France, which began in 1337. The war threatened wool supplies from England which were crucial to their cloth-based economy. The subsequent depression marked the beginning of decades of conflict between the craftsmen and merchant classes. In 1356, Jeanne, Duchess of Louvain, gained control over Brussels, and instituted the workers' Charter of Liberties. Craftsmen were finally given some political powers in the city. Trade resumed, attracting new people to Brussels. As the population grew, new streets were built outside the city walls to accommodate them. Between 1357 and 1379 a second town wall was constructed around these new districts.

THE HOUSE OF BURGUNDY

The new town walls were also built in reply to the invasion of Brussels by the Count of Flanders. However, in 1369 Philip, Duke of Burgundy, married the daughter of the Count of Flanders, and when the count died in 1384 the Low Countries and eastern France came under the couple's Burgundian rule.

In the 1430s Brussels became the capital of Burgundy, a situation that was to change the city forever. Brussels

Richly detailed Brussels tapestries such as this *Allegory of Hope* (1525) were prized commodities

TIMELINE

St-Michel status

Medieval helmet

1225 Construction of Cathédrale Sts Michel et Gudule

1302 Battle of the Golden Spurs – Flemish defeat of French cavalry

1356 Craftsmen's leader Everard 't Serclaes expels Flemish from Brussels

1200	1250	1300	1350

1229 Brussels granted its first charter, and relations between England and Flanders break down

1338 Flemish towns become allied to England for the Hundred Years' War

1356 Duchess Jeanne of Louvain grants Charter of Liberties

Painting of the family of the Hapsburg King of Austria, Maximillian I and Mary of Burgundy

was now an administrative and cultural centre, famous for its grand architecture, in the form of mansions and churches, and its luxury crafts trade.

THE HAPSBURG DYNASTY

In 1477 Mary of Burgundy, the last heir to the duchy, married Maximillian of Austria. Mary died in 1482, leaving Maximillian and the Hapsburg dynasty rulers of the city at a time when Brussels was experiencing serious economic depression. In 1488 Brussels and the rest of Flanders rebelled against this new power which had reinstated relations with France. The Austrians held on to power largely because of the plague of 1490 which halved Brussels' population. Maximillian passed his rule of the Low Countries to his son, Philip the Handsome in 1494 the year after he became Holy Roman Emperor. When

Portrait of Charles V, Holy Roman Emperor

Maximillian died, his daughter, Regent Empress Margaret of Austria, moved the capital of Burgundy from Brussels to Mechelen, where she educated her nephew, the future emperor Charles V.

SPANISH RULE

In 1515, at the age of 15, Charles became Sovereign of Burgundy. The following year he inherited the Spanish throne and, in 1519, became the Holy Roman Emperor. As he was born in Ghent, and considered Flanders his real home, he restored Brussels as the capital of Burgundy. Dutch officials arrived to run the three government councils that were now based here.

For the first time the city had a court. Both aristocratic families and immigrants, eager to cash in on the city's expansion, were drawn to the heady mix of tolerance, intellectual sophistication and business. Brussels quickly emerged as the most powerful city in Flanders, overtaking its long-standing rivals Bruges and Antwerp.

However, the Reformation, begun in Germany by Martin Luther, was to usher in a period of religious conflict. When Charles V abdicated in 1555, he fractured the empire's unity by leaving the Holy Roman Empire to his brother Ferdinand and all other dominions to his devoutly Catholic son, Philip II of Spain. His persecution of the Protestant movement finally sparked the Revolt of the Netherlands led by the House of Orange. Brussels' Protestant rulers surrendered to Philip in 1585. His power ended when the English defeated the Spanish Armada in 1588, by which time 8,000 Protestants had been put to death.

	1419 Philip the Good succeeds as Count of Burgundy	**1506** Margaret of Austria moves the Burgundian capital from Brussels to Mechelen	**1515** Charles Hapsburg becomes Sovereign of Burgundy	**1555** Catholic Philip II succeeds Charles V as religious reformation comes to Brussels
1400	**1450**	**1500**		**1550**
	1430 Under Burgundian control, Brussels becomes the major administrative centre of the region	**1490** Plague decimates the city **1488** Civil war – Brussels joins Flanders against Maximillian of Austria	*Count Egmont*	**1566** Conseil des Troubles set up by Duke d'Alba. Prominent Counts Egmont and Hornes executed

The armies of Louis XIV, the Sun King, bombard Brussels' city walls

THE COUNTER-REFORMATION

From 1598 Archduchess Isabella and Archduke Albert were the Catholic rulers of the Spanish Netherlands, installing a Hapsburg governor in Brussels. They continued to persecute Protestants: all non-Catholics were barred from working. Thousands of skilled workers moved to the Netherlands. But new trades like lace-making, diamond-cutting and silk-weaving flourished. Isabella and Albert were great patrons of the arts, and supported Rubens in Antwerp *(see pp102–03)*.

Protestant prisoners paraded in Brussels during the Counter-Reformation under Albert and Isabella

INVASION OF THE SUN KING

The 17th century was a time of of religious and political struggle all over Europe. The Thirty Years War (1618–48) divided western Europe along Catholic and Protestant lines. After 1648, France's Sun King, Louis XIV, was determined to add Flanders to his territory.

By 1633 both Albert and Isabella were dead and Philip IV of Spain, passed control of the Spanish Netherlands to his weak brother, the Cardinal-Infant Ferdinand. Keen to pursue his ambitions, Louis XIV besieged Maastricht in the 1670s and took Luxembourg. Having failed to win the nearby enclave of Namur, the piqued Sun King moved his army to Brussels, whose defences were weaker.

On August 13, 1695, the French bombarded Brussels from a hill outside the city walls, destroying the Grand Place *(see pp42–3)* and much of its environs. The French withdrew, but their desire to rule the region was to cause conflict over subsequent decades.

A PHOENIX FROM THE ASHES

Despite the destruction incurred by the bombardment, Brussels was quick to recover. The guilds ensured that the Grand Place was rebuilt in a matter of years, with new guildhouses as a testament to the on-going success of the city's economic life and craftsmanship.

The building of the Willebroek canal during the 17th century gave Brussels access to the Rupel and Scheldt rivers, and thus to Antwerp and the North Sea. Large industries began to replace local market trading. Factories and mills grew up around the city's harbour, and Brussels became an export centre.

TIMELINE

1599 Artist Antony van Dyck born in Antwerp

1600 Antwerp becomes the centre of Flemish art

1621 Archduke Albert dies amid new bout of Protestant/Catholic fighting

1641 Van Dyck dies after glittering artistic career

Louis XIV of France in costume

| 1600 | 1625 | 1650 | 1675 |

1598 Isabella and Albert run strong Catholic, anti-Protestant regime

Manneken Pis

1619 Manneken Pis installed in Brussels

1633 Cardinal-Infant Ferdinand is new ruler

1640 Rubens dies after a 40-year career as painter of over 3,000 paintings

1670 Louis XIV beseiges Maastricht and Luxembourg; William of Orange goes on defensive

AUSTRIAN SUCCESSION

Subsequent decades were dogged by war as Austria and England sought to stave off French ambitions. When Philip of Anjou succeeded to the Spanish throne, it looked as if the combined threat of Spain and France would overwhelm the rest of Europe. Emperor Leopold I of Austria, together with England and many German states, declared war on France. The resulting 14-year War of the Spanish Succession ended with the Treaty of Utrecht in 1713, which ceded the Netherlands, including Brussels, to Austria.

Governor of Brussels, Duke Charles of Lorraine

The treaty did not end the conflict. Emperor Charles VI of Austria ruled after Leopold, but failed to produce a male heir. His death in 1731 sparked another 17 years of war – The War of the Austrian Succession over whether his daughter Maria Theresa should be allowed to inherit the crown. It was not until 1748, with the signing of the Treaty of Aix-la-Chapelle, that Maria Theresa gained control.

THE BOOM PERIOD

The endless fighting took its toll, and Brussels, along with the rest of Belgium, was impoverished. Despite the sophistication of the aristocratic elite, the majority of the population were still ruled by feudal laws: they could not change jobs or move home without permission; and only three per cent of the population was literate.

In the 1750s Empress Maria Theresa of Austria installed her brother, Charles of Lorraine, in Brussels. Under the influence of the Enlightenment, his court attracted European artists and intellectuals, and Brussels became the most glamorous city in Europe. Industry also boomed with the construction of new roads and waterways. Brussels was transformed as the Place Royale and Parc de Bruxelles were laid out.

THE WORKERS' REVOLT

While the aristocracy and new middle-classes flourished, Brussels' workers were suffering. As the city's population grew there were more workers than jobs: wages plummeted and factory conditions were harsh.

When Joseph II succeeded Maria Theresa in 1780, he enforced a series of reforms including freedom of religion. However, he also cancelled the 500-year-old Charter of Liberties.

Influenced by the ideas of the French Revolution of 1789, the Belgians now demanded reform. Their rebellion was to result in an independent state.

French prince Philip of Anjou became Philip V of Spain, sparking the War of the Spanish Succession

1700	1725		1750	1775
95 French ombardment Brussels	1713–14 Treaties of Utrecht and Rastatt mark beginning of Austrian period	*Ceramic Delft plate*	1760s Brussels is cultural and artistic centre of Europe	1788 Joseph II cancels Charter of Liberties which results in liberal opposition
1697 Willebroek Canal completed, links Brussels to the sea via Antwerp	1731 Beginning of the 17-year-long war against Austrian rule	1748 Treaty of Aix-la-Chapelle restores the Netherlands to Austrian rule	1753 New roads and canals constructed, which boosts industry in Brussels	1789 Belgian revolt for independence fired by French Revolution

The Fight for Independence

Belgium was again occupied by foreign powers between 1794 and 1830. First, by the French Republican armies, then, after Napoleon's defeat at Waterloo in 1815, by the Dutch. French radical reforms included the abolition of the guild system and fairer taxation laws. Although French rule was unpopular, their liberal ideas were to influence the Belgian drive for independence. William I of Orange was appointed King of the Netherlands (which included Belgium) after 1815. His autocratic style, together with a series of anti-Catholic measures, bred discontent, especially in Brussels and among the French-speaking Walloons in the south. The south was also angered when William refused to introduce tariffs to protect their trade – it was the last straw. The uprising of 1830 began in Brussels and Léopold I became king of the newly independent nation.

King William I of Orange
William's rule as King of the Netherlands after 1815 was unpopular.

A Cultural Revolution in Brussels
French ideas not only influenced the revolution, but also Belgian culture. Under Napoleon the city walls were demolished and replaced by tree-lined boulevards.

Liberals joined workers already protesting in the square outside.

The Battle of Waterloo
Napoleon's influence came to an end after the battle of Waterloo on 18 June, 1815. A Prussian army came to Wellington's aid, and by 5:30pm Napoleon faced his final defeat. This led to Dutch rule over Belgium.

Agricultural Workers
Harsh weather in the winter of 1829 caused hardship for both farmers and agricultural labourers, who also joined the protest.

The Revolution in Industry
Unemployment, low wages and factory closures during the early decades of the 19th century sparked unrest in 1830.

Le Théâtre de la Monnaie
A patriotic song, L'Amour Sacré de la Patrie *led the audience on the night of 25 August, 1830, to join demonstrators outside* (see pp48–9).

BELGIAN REVOLUTION

High unemployment, poor wages and a bad winter in 1829 provoked protests about living and working conditions. The revolution was ignited by a patriotic and radical opera at the Brussels' opera house, and the largely liberal audience rushed out into the street, raising the Brabant flag. Ten thousand troops were sent by William to quash the rebels, but the Belgian soldiers deserted and the Dutch were finally driven out of Belgium.

The initial list of demands asked for administrative independence from the Dutch, and for freedom of press.

This symbolic illustration of the revolution shows both liberals and workers ready to die for their country.

King of Belgium, Léopold I
The crowning of German prince, Léopold of Saxe-Coburg, in Brussels in 1831 finally established Belgium's independence.

TIMELINE

1790 Republic of United Belgian States formed. Temporary end of Austrian rule	**1799** Emperor Napoleon rules France *Wellington*	**1815** Battle of Waterloo. Napoleon defeated by army led by the Duke of Wellington	**1830** Rebellion begins at the Théâtre de la Monnaie in Brussels
1790	**1800**	**1810**	**1820**	**1830**

1794 Brussels loses its importance to The Hague	**1815** Belgium, allied with Holland under the United Kingdom of the Netherlands, is ruled by William I of Orange. Brussels becomes second capital	**1831** State of Belgium formed on 21 July. Treaty of London grants independence
1790 War between France and Austria		**1835** Continental railway built from Brussels to Mechelen

THE FLEMISH AND THE WALLOONS: THE BELGIAN COMPROMISE

Linguistically and culturally, Belgium is divided. In the north, the Flemish have their roots in the Netherlands and Germany. In the south are the Walloons, the French-speaking Belgians, culturally connected to France. The "Linguistic Divide" of 1962 officially sanctioned this situation, dividing Belgium into Flemish- and French-speaking zones. The exception is Brussels, an officially bilingual city since the formation of Bruxelles-Capitale in 1963, and a national region by 1989 when it came to comprise 19 outlying districts. Conflicts still erupt over the issue, but the majority of Belgians seem to be in favour of a united country.

Bilingual road signs

CONSOLIDATING THE NEW STATE

During its early days as an independent nation, Brussels was a haven for free-thinkers, including the libertarian poet Baudelaire, and a refuge for exiles, such as Karl Marx and Victor Hugo. Belgium's industries also continued to expand throughout the 19th century.

By 1870 there were no less than four main railway stations in Brussels able to export goods all over Europe. However, the population of Brussels had almost doubled, resulting in poor-quality housing and working conditions. Towards the end of the reign of Belgium's second monarch, Léopold II (r.1865–1909), industrial unrest led to new legislation which improved conditions, and all men over 25 gained the right to vote in 1893. But the king's principal concern was his colonialist policy in the Congo in Central Africa.

THE GERMAN OCCUPATIONS

Albert I succeeded Léopold II as Belgium's new king. He encouraged the nation's artists and architects, and was a keen supporter of Art Nouveau *(see pp18–19)*. All of this ended as the country entered its bleakest period.

Despite its neutral status, Belgium was invaded by the German army in the summer of 1914. All of the country, except for the northern De Panne region, was occupied by the Germans. Some of the bloodiest battles of World War I were staged on Belgian soil. Flanders was the scene of brutal trench warfare, including the introduction of poison gas at Ypres *(see p109)*. Today, Belgium contains several vast graveyards, which include the resting places of the tens of thousands of soldiers who died on the Western Front.

The Belgians conducted resistance from their stronghold in De Panne, cutting telephone wires and destroying train tracks. The Germans responded by confiscating property, deporting Belgians to German labour camps

King Léopold III visits a goldmine in the Congo in Africa

TIMELINE

1840	1870	1900	1925
1847 Opening of Europe's first shopping mall, the Galéries St Hubert	**1871** Under Léopold II, the River Senne is reclaimed, and new districts built to cope with the growing city	**1898** Flemish language given equal status to French in law	**1914–18** World War I. Germany occupies Belgium
The Belgian Congo	**1884** Léopold II is granted sovereignty over the Congo	**1910** World Fair in Brussels promotes Belgium's industrial boom. Art Nouveau flourishes	**1929–31** Great Depression and reduction in foreign trade
1839 Treaty of London grants neutrality to Belgium			

German troops raising the flag of the Third Reich at the Royal Castle at Laeken, near Brussels

INTERNATIONAL STATUS

Belgium's history in the latter half of the 20th century has been dominated by the ongoing language debate between the Flemish and the French-speaking Walloons. From 1970 to 1994 the constitution was redrawn, creating a federal state with three separate regions; the Flemish north, the Walloon south and bilingual Brussels. While this smoothed over conflicts, cultural divisions run deep. Today, all parliamentary speeches have to be delivered in both French and Flemish.

Like most of Europe, Belgium went from economic boom in the 1960s to recession and retrenchment in the 1970s and 1980s. Throughout these decades Brussels' stature at the heart of Europe was consolidated. In 1958, the city became the headquarters for the European Economic Community (EEC), later the European Union. In 1967 NATO also moved to Brussels.

THE EUROPEAN CAPITAL

Modern Brussels is a multilingual and cosmopolitan city at the forefront of Europe. This historically industrial city now prospers as a base for many large corporations such as ICI and Mitsubishi.

The European Parliament, Brussels

and murdering random hostages. Belgium remained under German occupation until the last day of the war, 11 November, 1918.

The 1919 Treaty of Versailles granted Belgium control of Eupen-Malmédy, the German-speaking area in the southeast. But by 1940 the country was again invaded by the Germans under Hitler. In May of that year, King Léopold III surrendered.

Despite national resistance to the Occupation, the King was interned at Laeken until 1944, after which he was moved to Germany until the end of the war. Rumours that Léopold had collaborated with the Nazis led to his abdication in 1951, in favour of his 20-year-old son, Baudouin.

Despite its flourishing status, the city has had its fair share of disasters, including the deaths of 38 Italian football supporters at the Heysel stadium in 1985. Also, two tragic paedophile murder cases in the 1990s led many Belgians to protest against the apparent failures of the police system. However, Brussels' future as a city of world importance seems certain as it lies at the political centre of the European Union.

1939–45 World War II. Germany again occupies Belgium	1951 Abdication of Léopold III; Baudouin I succeeds	1962 The Belgian Congo is granted independence		1993 King Baudouin I dies; Albert II succeeds	2002 The euro becomes legal tender

Baudouin I

European flag

1950		**1975**		**2000**		**2025**

1934 Albert I is killed in a climbing accident	1944 Benelux Unions with Holland and Luxembourg formed	1967 Brussels is new NATO HQ	1985 Heysel Stadium disaster	1989 Brussels is officially a bilingual city with 19 outlying districts	2001 Crown Prince Philippe and Princess Mathilde have a daughter, Elisabeth

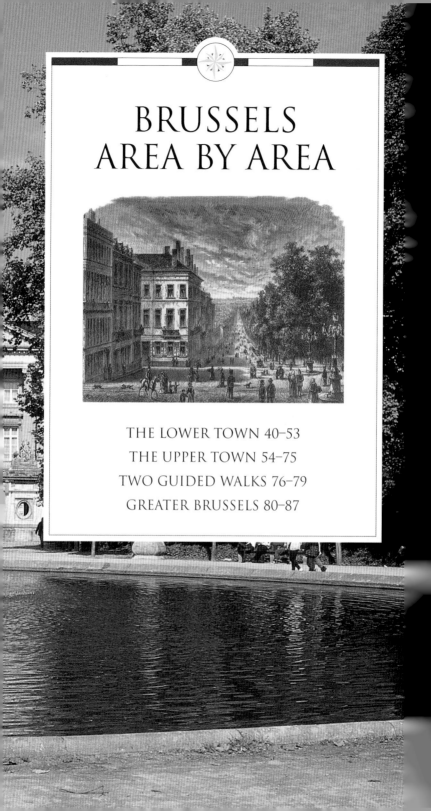

BRUSSELS
AREA BY AREA

THE LOWER TOWN

Maison du Cygne, Grand Place

Most visits to Brussels begin with a stroll around the Lower Town, the ancient heart of the city and home to its most famous area, the Grand Place (see pp42–3). The original settlement of the city was located here and most of the streets surrounding this market square date from the Middle Ages up to the 18th century. The architecture is an eclectic blend of Gothic, Baroque and Flemish Renaissance.

In and around the Place de Brouckère and the busy Boulevard Anspach are the more recent additions to the city's history. These appeared in the 19th century when the slums around the River Senne were cleared to make way for ornate constructions such as the financial centre, La Bourse, and Europe's first shopping arcade, Galeries St-Hubert. With its many restaurants and cafés, the Lower Town is also popular at night.

SIGHTS AT A GLANCE

Historic Buildings and Monuments
Hôtel de Ville pp44–45 **2**
Manneken Pis **3**
La Bourse **7**

Museums and Galleries
Musée du Costume et de la Dentelle **1**
Bruxella 1238 **8**
Centre Belge de la Bande Dessinée pp50–51 **14**
Maison de la Bellone **21**

Churches
Notre-Dame de la Chapelle **4**
Eglise St-Nicolas **9**
Eglise St-Jean-Baptiste **19**
Eglise Ste-Catherine **22**

Shopping
Galeries St-Hubert **10**
Rue Neuve **16**

Streets and Squares
Rue des Bouchers **11**
Place de Brouckère **18**

Theatres
Théâtre Marionnettes de Toone **12**
Théâtre Royal de la Monnaie **13**
Théâtre Flamand **20**

Cultural Centres
Le Botanique **15**

Historic Districts
Quartier Marolles **5**
Halles St-Géry **6**

Hotels
Hôtel Métropole **17**

KEY

🚉	Train station
🚏	Tram stop
Ⓜ	Metro station
🚌	Bus terminus
ℹ	Tourist information

THE GRAND PLACE

GETTING AROUND

The area is well served by trams which encircle the old town. However, the tiny streets are often pedestrianized, and usually the quickest and most enjoyable means of transport for short distances is on foot. Otherwise metro stations are well placed.

0 metres	500
0 yards	500

◁ Detail of the façade of the Hôtel de Ville in the Grand Place – centre of the Lower Town

The Grand Place

The geographical, historical and commercial heart of the city, the Grand Place is the first port of call for most visitors to Brussels. This bustling cobblestone square remains the civic centre, centuries after its creation, and offers the finest surviving example in one area of Belgium's ornate 17th-century architecture. Open-air markets took place on or near this site as early as the 11th century, but by the end of the 15th century Brussels' town hall, the Hôtel de Ville, was built, and city traders added individual guildhouses in a medley of styles. In 1695, however, two days of cannon fire by the French destroyed all but the town hall and two guild façades. Trade guilds were urged to rebuild their halls to styles approved by the Town Council, producing the harmonious unity of Flemish Renaissance buildings here today.

The morning flower market in bloom in the Grand Place

The Maison du Roi was first built in 1536 but redesigned in 1873. Once the residence of ruling Spanish monarchs, it is now home to the Musée de la Ville, which includes 16th-century paintings, tapestries, and the 650 tiny outfits of Manneken Pis.

① **NORTHEAST CORNER**

② **MAISON DU ROI**

The Hôtel de Ville occupies the entire southwest side of the square. Still a functioning civic building, Brussels' town hall is the architectural masterpiece of the Grand Place (see pp44–5).

Ornate stone carvings

The spire was built by Jan van Ruysbroeck in 1449 and stands 96 m (315 ft) high; it is slightly crooked.

Everard 't Serclaes was murdered defending Brussels in the 14th century; touching the bronze arm of his statue is said to bring luck.

⑤ **EVERARD 'T SERCLAES**

⑥ **HOTEL DE VILLE**

Le Pigeon was home to Victor Hugo, the exiled French novelist who chose the house as his Belgian residence in 1852. Some of the most complimentary comments about Brussels emerged later from his pen.

La Maison des Ducs de Brabant is a group of six guildhouses. Designed by the Controller of Public Works, Guillaume de Bruyn, the group is Neo-Classical with Flemish additions.

LOCATOR MAP
See Brussels Street Finder, map 2

Stone busts of the ducal line along the façade gave this group of houses their name.

③ LE PIGEON

④ LA MAISON DES DUCS DE BRABANT

Le Renard was built in the 1690s as the guild-house of the haber-dashers by the Flemish architects Marc de Vos and van Nerum. Façade details show St Nicolas, patron saint of mer-chants, and cherubs playing with haber-dashery ribbons.

Le Cornet displays Italianate Flemish style. This Boatmen's Guildhouse (1697) is most notable for its gable, which is constructed in the form of a 17th-century frigate's bow.

La Maison des Boulangers, also known as "Le Roi d'Esp-agne", was a showpiece built by the wealthy and powerful guild of bakers. The 1676 octag-onal copper dome is topped by a dancing golden figure.

Le Roi d'Espagne now houses the Grand Place's finest bar with a view of the bustling square and its splendours above ground level. *(see p162)*. The gilt bust over the entrance represents Saint Aubert, patron saint of bakers. There is a vast bust of Charles II of Spain on the third floor.

⑦ LE RENARD, LE CORNET AND LE ROI D'ESPAGNE

Musée du Costume et de la Dentelle ❶

Rue de la Violette 12, 1000 BRU.
Map 2 D3. **Tel** *(02) 213 4450.* Ⓜ
Bourse, Gare Centrale. ⏰ *10am–12:30pm, 1:30–5pm Mon, Tue, Thu, Fri; 2–5pm Sat, Sun.* ● *Wed, 1 Jan, 1 May, 1 & 25 Nov, 25 Dec.* ♿ &
📷 *on request, call (02) 279 4355.*

Found within two 17th-century gabled houses is the museum dedicated to one of Brussels' most successful exports, Belgian lace *(see pp20–21)*. The intricate skill employed by Belgian lace-makers has contributed a vital economic role in the city since the 12th century, and

A wedding dress at the Musée du Costume et de la Dentelle

the collection explains and displays the history of this delicate craft. On the ground floor costumes from the 18th to the 20th centuries are dis-

played on mannequins, demonstrating how lace has adorned fashions of every era. The second floor houses a collection of antique lace, carefully stored in drawers and demonstrating the various schools of lacemaking in France, Flanders and Italy.

Manneken Pis ❸

Rues de l'Etuve & du Chêne, 1000 BRU. **Map** 1C3. 🚌 *34, 48, 95, 96.* 🚊 *23, 52, 55, 56, 81.* Ⓜ *Bourse, Gare Centrale.*

An unlikely attraction, this tiny statue of a young boy barely 30 cm (1 ft) high relieving himself into a small pool is as much a part of Brussels as

Hôtel de Ville ❷

A detail of the delicately carved façade with stone statues

Stone gargoyle

The idea of having a town hall to reflect Brussels' growth as a major European trading centre had been under consideration since the end of the 13th century. It was not until 1401 that the first foundation stone was laid and the building was finally completed in 1459, emerging as the finest civic building in the country, a stature it still enjoys.

Jacques van Thienen was commissioned to design the left wing and belfry of the building, where he used ornate columns, sculptures, turrets and arcades. The tower and spire begun in 1449 by Jan van Ruysbroeck helped seal its reputation. In 1995, the 1455 statue of the city's patron saint, Michael, was restored and returned to its famous position on top of the tower in 1997, where it is used as a weather vane. Tours are available of the interior, which contains 15th-century tapestries and works of art.

137 statues adorn walls and many mullioned windows.

★ **Aldermen's Room**
Still in use today for the meetings of the aldermen and mayor of Brussels, this council chamber contains a series of 18th-century tapestries depicting the history of 6th-century King Clovis.

STAR SIGHTS

★ Conference Room
  Council Chamber

★ Aldermen's Room

the Trevi Fountain is part of Rome or Trafalgar Square's reclining lions are of London.

The original bronze statue by Jérôme Duquesnoy the Elder, was first placed on the site in 1619, the tongue-in-cheek design reflecting a genuine need for fresh drinking water in the area. Its popularity led, in 1770, to the addition of an ornate stone niche, giving more prominence to the small figure. Several attempts to steal the statue were made during the 18th century, notably by the French and then British armies in 1745, but it was the theft in 1817 by a former convict, Antoine Licas, which caused the most alarm – the robber smashed the bronze figure shortly after procuring it. A replica of the statue was cast the following year and returned to its revered site, and it is this copy that is seen today. In 1698 governor Maximilian-Emmanuel donated a suit of clothing with which to dress the statue. It was to be the beginning of a tradition that continues to this day. Visiting heads of state to Brussels donate miniature versions of their national costume for the boy, and now 650 outfits, including an Elvis suit, are housed in the Musée de la Ville (see p42).

(see p42)

THE LEGENDS OF MANNEKEN PIS

The inspiration for this famous statue remains unknown, but the mystery only lends itself to rumour and fable and increases the little boy's charm. One theory claims that in the 12th century the son of a duke was caught urinating against a tree in the midst of a battle and was thus commemorated in bronze as a symbol of the country's military courage.

The belfry was built by architect Jan van Ruysbroeck. A statue of St Michael tops the 96 m (315 ft) spire.

Aldermen's Room

The gabled roof, like much of the town hall, was fully restored in 1837, and cleaned in the 1990s.

VISITORS' CHECKLIST

Grand Place, 1000 BRU. **Map** 2 D3. **Tel** (02) 279 4365. 🚌 29, 34, 47, 48, 60, 63, 65, 66, 71, 95, 96. 🚊 23, 52, 55, 56, 81. Ⓜ Bourse, Gare Centrale. **Museum** ◻ 10am–5pm Tue–Sun. ⬤ pub hols, election days. 🎟 Apr–Sep: 3:15pm Tue & Wed, 10:45am & 12:15pm Sun; Oct–Mar: 3:15pm Tue & Wed.

★ **Conference Room Council Chamber**
The most splendid of all the public rooms, ancient tapestries and gilt mirrors line the walls above an inlaid floor.

Cabinets des Echevins

Ornamental stone balcony staircase

Wedding Room
A Neo-Gothic style dominates this civil marriage office, with its many ornate carved timbers, including ancient ebony and mahogany.

Notre-Dame de la Chapelle ❹

Place de la Chapelle 1, 1000 BRU. **Map**
1 C4. **Tel** (02) 512 0737. 🚌 27, 34,
95, 96. 🚋 91, 92, 93, 94. Ⓜ
Anneessens, Centrale. ⬤ 9am–7pm
daily; Mass 4pm Sat, 8pm Sun.

In 1134 King Godefroid I
decided to build a chapel
outside the city walls. It quickly
became a market church, serving the many craftsmen living
nearby. In 1210 its popularity
was such that it was made a
parish church, but it became
really famous in 1250, when a
royal donation of five pieces
of the True Cross turned the
church into a pilgrimage site.

Originally built in Romanesque style, the majority of the
church was destroyed by fire
in 1405. Rebuilding began in
1421 in a Gothic style typical
of 15th-century Brabant architecture, including gables decorated with finials and interior
capitals decorated with cab-
bage leaves at the base. The
Bishop of Cambrai consecrated
the new church in 1434.

One of the most striking
features of the exterior are the
monstrously lifelike gargoyles
which peer down on the community – a representation of
evil outside the sacred interior.
The Baroque belltower was
added after the 1695 bombardment by the French (see p32).
Another moving feature is the
carved stone memorial to the
16th-century Belgian artist
Pieter Brueghel the Elder
(see p16), who is buried here.

**The elegant interior of
Notre-Dame de la Chapelle**

Rue Haute in the Quartier Marolles, with old-style shops and cafés

Quartier Marolles ❺

Map 1 C5. 🚌 20, 27, 48. 🚋 91.
Ⓜ Louise, Porte de Hal.

Known colloquially as "Les
Marolles", this quarter of
Brussels is traditionally working
class. Situated between the
two city walls, the area was
home to weavers and
craftsmen. Street names of the
district, such as Rue des
Brodeurs (Embroiderers' St)
and Rue des Charpentiers
(Carpenters' St), reflect its
artisanal history.

Today the area is best known
for its fine daily flea market,
held in the **Place du Jeu de
Balle**. The flea market has
been held on this site since
1640. Between 7am and 2pm,
with the biggest and best markets on Thursday and Sunday,
almost anything from junk to
pre-war collector's items can
be found among the stalls.

Shopping of a different kind
is on offer on nearby Rue
Haute, an ancient Roman road.
A shopping district since the
19th century, it is still popular
with arty types with its specialist stores, interior and
antique shops. The street has
a long artistic history, too –
the elegant red-brick house at
No. 132 was home to Pieter
Brueghel the Elder and the
sculptor Auguste Rodin had a
studio at No. 224. No. 132
now houses the small **Maison
de Brueghel**, dedicated to the
16th-century painter.

At the southern end of Rue
Haute is Porte de Hal, the
stone gateway of the now-
demolished outer city walls.

Looming over the Marolles is
the imposing Palais de Justice
(see p69), which has hilltop
views of the area west of the
city, including the 1958 Atomium (see p87) and the Basilique
Sacré-Coeur (see p84).

🏛 **Maison de Brueghel**
Rue Haute 132, 1000 BRU.
Tel (02) 513 8940. ⬤ May–Sep:
Wed & Sun pm (groups with written
permission only). ⬤ Oct–Apr. 📷

**Busy restaurants and cafés
outside Halles St-Géry**

Halles St-Géry ❻

Place St-Géry, 1000 BRU. **Map** 1 C2.
🚌 47. 🚋 23, 52, 55, 56, 81.
Ⓜ Bourse.

In many ways, St-Géry can be
considered the birthplace of
the city. A chapel to Saint Géry
was built in the 6th century,
then in AD 977 a fortress took
over the site. A 16th-century
church followed and occu-
pied the location until the
18th century. In 1881 a

covered meat market was erected in Neo-Renaissance style. The glass and intricate ironwork was renovated in 1985, and the hall now serves as a cultural centre with an exhibition on local history.

La Bourse **7**

Palais de la Bourse, 1000 BRU. **Map** 1 C2. **Tel** (02) 509 1373. 🚌 47. 🚊 3, 52, 55, 56, 81. Ⓜ Bourse. ⚫ No longer open to the public.

Brussels' Stock Exchange, La Bourse, is one of the city's most impressive buildings, dominating the square of the same name. Designed in Palladian style by architect Léon Suys, it was constructed from 1867 to 1873. Among the building's most notable features are the façade's ornate carvings. The great French sculptor, Auguste Rodin, is thought to have crafted the groups representing Africa and Asia, as well as four caryatids inside. Beneath the colonnade, two beautifully detailed winged figures representing Good and Evil were carved by sculptor Jacques de Haen. Once the scene of frantic trading, La Bourse now houses the offices of Euronext, owners of the Belgian Stock Exchange, and all trading is computerized. The building is no longer open to the public.

Detail of a Rodin statue, La Bourse

Bruxella 1238 **8**

Rue de la Bourse, 1000 BRU. **Map** 1 C3. **Tel** (02) 279 4355. 🚌 34, 48, 95, 96. 🚊 3, 52, 55, 56, 81. Ⓜ Bourse, de Brouckère. ⚫ 1st Wed of month: 10:15am (English), 11:15am (French), 2pm (Dutch); by appt only at other times. 📷 🎫 obligatory, starts from Maison du Roi, Grand Place.

Once home to a church and 13th-century Franciscan convent, in the early 19th century this site became a Butter Market until the building of the Bourse started in 1867. In 1988 municipal roadworks

began alongside the Place de la Bourse. Medieval history must have been far from the minds of the city authorities but, in the course of working on the foundations for the Bourse, important relics were found, including 13th-century bones, pottery and the 1294 grave of Duke John I of Brabant. Visitors can see these and other pieces in a small museum built on the site.

Eglise St-Nicolas **9**

Rue au Beurre 1, 1000 BRU. **Map** 1 C2. **Tel** (02) 513 8022. 🚌 34, 48, 95, 96. 🚊 3, 52, 55, 56, 81. Ⓜ Bourse, de Brouckère. ⚫ 8am–6:30pm Mon–Fri, 9am–6pm Sat, 9am–7:30pm Sun & public hols.

At the end of the 12th century a market church was built on this site, but, like much of the Lower Town, it was damaged in the 1695 French Bombardment. A cannon ball lodged itself into an interior pillar and the belltower finally collapsed in 1714. Many restoration projects were planned but none came to fruition until 1956, when the west side the building was given a new, Gothic-style façade. Named after St Nicolas, the patron saint of merchants, the church contains choir stalls dating from 1381 which display detailed medallions telling St Nicolas' story. Another interesting feature is the chapel, constructed at an angle, reputedly to avoid the flow of an old stream. Inside the church, works of art by Bernard van Orley and Peter Paul Rubens are well worth seeing.

The 19th-century domed glass roof of Galeries St-Hubert

Galeries St-Hubert **10**

Rue des Bouchers, 1000 BRU. **Map** 2 D2. 🚌 29, 38, 60, 63, 65, 66, 71. Ⓜ Gare Centrale. ♿

Sixteen years after ascending the throne as the first king of Belgium, Léopold I inaugurated the opening of these grand arcades in 1847.

St-Hubert has the distinction of being the first shopping arcade in Europe, and one of the most elegant. Designed in Neo-Renaissance style by Jean-Pierre Cluysenaar, the vaulted glass roof covers its three sections, Galerie du Roi, Galerie de la Reine and Galerie des Princes, which house a range of luxury shops and cafés. The ornate interior and expensive goods on sale soon turned the galleries into a fashionable meeting place for 19th-century society, including resident literati – Victor Hugo and Alexandre Dumas attended lectures here. The arcades remain a popular venue, with shops, a cinema, theatre, cafés and restaurants.

Gothic-style façade of Eglise St-Nicolas

Pavement displays of restaurants along Rue des Bouchers

Rue des Bouchers ⓫

Map 2 D2. 🚋 29, 60, 63, 65, 66, 71. 🚊 3, 52, 55, 56, 81, 90. Ⓜ *de Brouckère, Gare Centrale, Bourse.*

Like many streets in this area of the city, Rue des Bouchers retains its medieval name, reminiscent of the time when this meandering, cobblestoned street was home to the butchers' trade. Aware of its historic importance and heeding the concerns of the public, the city council declared this area the Ilot Sacré (sacred islet) in 1960, forbidding any of the architectural façades to be altered or destroyed, and commanding those surviving to be restored. Hence Rue des Bouchers abounds with 17th-century stepped gables and decorated doorways.

Today, this pedestrianized thoroughfare is best known as the "belly of Brussels", a reference to its plethora of cafés and restaurants. Many cuisines are on offer here, including Chinese, Greek, Italian and Indian. But the most impressive sights during an evening stroll along the street are the lavish pavement displays of seafood, piled high on mounds of ice, all romantically lit by an amber glow from the streetlamps.

At the end of the street, at the Impasse de la Fidélité, is a recent acknowledgement of sexual equality. Erected in 1987, Jeanneke Pis is a coy, cheeky female version of her "brother", the more famous Manneken Pis *(see p45)*.

Théâtre Marionettes de Toone ⓬

Impasse Schuddeveldgang 6, off the Petite Rue des Bouchers, 1000 BRU. **Map** 2 D2. **Tel** *(02) 511 7137.* 🚋 29, 34, 48, 60, 63, 65, 66, 71, 95, 96. 🚊 3, 52, 55, 56, 81. Ⓜ *Bourse, Gare Centrale.* ◯ *bar: noon–midnight daily; theatre: performance times (8:30pm Wed–Sat).* ◯ *Mon, Tue, Sun, pub hols.* 🈯 🎫 *on request, for tour reservations* **Tel** *(02) 217 2753.* **Museum** ◯ *intervals.*

A popular pub by day, at night the top floor of this tavern is home to a puppet theatre. During the time of the Spanish Netherlands *(see p32),* all theatres were closed because of the satirical performances by actors aimed at their Latin rulers. This began a fashion for puppet shows, the vicious dialogue more easily forgiveable from inanimate dolls. In 1830, Antoine Toone opened his own theatre and it has been run by the

Harlequin puppet

Toone family ever since; the owner is the seventh generation, Toone VII. The classics are enacted by these wooden marionettes in the local Bruxellois dialect, and occasionally in French, English, German or Dutch.

Théâtre Royal de la Monnaie ⓭

Place de la Monnaie, 1000 BRU. **Map** 2 D2. **Tel** *(07) 023 3939.* 🚋 29, 60, 65, 66. 🚊 3, 52, 55, 56, 81. Ⓜ *de Brouckère, Bourse.* ◯ *performance times, Mon–Sat; box office: 11am–6pm Tue–Sat.* ◯ *Sun, public hols.* 🈯 🎫 *call to arrange, (02) 229 1372.* **www**.lamonnaie.be

This theatre was first built in 1817 on the site of a 15th-century mint (Hôtel des Monnaies) but, following a fire in 1855, only the front and pediment of the original Neo-Classical building remain. After the fire, the theatre was redesigned by the architect, Joseph Poelaert, also responsible for the imposing Palais de Justice *(see p69).*

The original theatre made its historical mark before its destruction, however, when on 25 August, 1830, a performance of *La Muette de Portici (The Mute Girl)* began a national rebellion. As the tenor began to sing the nationalist *Amour Sacré de la Patrie (Sacred love of the homeland),* his words incited an already discontented city, fired by the libertarianism of the revolutions occurring in France, into revolt. The audience ran into the street in a rampage that developed

The original Neo-Classical façade of Théâtre Royal de la Monnaie

The 19th-century glasshouse of Le Botanique in summer

Similar to London's Oxford Street, but now pedestrianized, this is the heart of commercial shopping. It houses well-known international chainstores and shopping malls, such as **City 2**, which has shops, cafés and the media store Fnac all under one roof. Inno department store was designed by Horta *(see p78)*, but after a fire in 1967 was entirely rebuilt.

To the east of Rue Neuve is Place des Martyrs, a peaceful square where a monument pays tribute to the 450 citizens killed during the 1830 uprising.

City 2
Rue Neuve 123, 1000 BRU.
Tel (02) 211 4060. ☐ 10am–7pm
Mon– Thu & Sat, 10am–8pm
Fri. ● Sun, public hols.

into the September Uprising *(see p34–5)*. The theatre today remains the centre of Belgian performing arts; major renovations took place during the 1980s. The auditorium was raised 4 m (13 ft) to accommodate the elaborate stage designs, but the luxurious Louis XIV-style decor was carefully retained and blended with the new additions. The central dome is decorated with an allegory of Belgian arts.

Centre Belge de la Bande Dessinée ⓴

See pp50–51.

Le Botanique ⓵

Rue Royale 236, 1210 BRU. **Map** 2 E1. *Tel* (02) 218 3732. ▦ 38, 58, 61. ▦ 92, 93, 94. Ⓜ Botanique. ☐ 10am–6pm daily. ♿

In 1797, the city of Brussels created a botanical garden in the grounds of the Palais de Lorraine as a source of reference for botany students. The garden closed in 1826, and new gardens were relocated in Meise, 13 km (9 miles) from Brussels.

A grand glass-and-iron rotunda was designed at the centre of the gardens by the French architect Gineste. This

iron glasshouse still stands, as does much of the 19th-century statuary by Constantin Meunier *(see p15)*, including depictions of the Four Seasons. The glasshouse is now home to the French Community Cultural Centre and offers plays, concerts and exhibitions.

Rue Neuve ⓶

Map 2 D2. ▦ 29, 60, 63, 65, 66, 71. ▦ 3, 52, 55, 56, 81, 90. Ⓜ Bourse, de Brouckère, Rogier.

Brussels shoppers have been flocking to the busy Rue Neuve since the 19th century for its reasonably priced goods and well-located stores.

Rue Neuve, the longest pedestrian shopping street in the city

Hôtel Métropole ⓷

Place de Brouckère 31, 1000 BRU.
Map 2 D2. *Tel* (02) 217 2300.
▦ 29, 60, 65, 66. ▦ 23, 52, 55, 56, 81. Ⓜ de Brouckère.
www.metropolehotel.be

The area lying between Place Rogier and Place de Brouckère is known as the hotel district of Brussels, and one of the oldest and grandest hotels in the area is the Métropole.

In 1891 the Wielemans Brewery bought the building and commissioned the architect Alban Chambon to redesign the interior, with money no object. The result was a fine Art Nouveau hotel which opened for business in 1895 and has since accommodated numerous acclaimed visitors, including actress Sarah Bernhardt. In 1911 the hotel was the location of the science conference Conseil Physique Solvay, attended by the great scientists Marie Curie and Albert Einstein.

The Hôtel Métropole continues to welcome guests from all walks of life, at surprisingly reasonable cost given its beauty, history and location. It is particularly popular for drinks in its café and heated pavement terrace, which are both open to non-residents to enjoy cocktails and cappuccinos in elegant surroundings.

Centre Belge de la Bande Dessinée

Affectionately known as *cébébédé*, the Museum of Comic Strip Art pays tribute to the Belgian passion for comic strips or *bandes dessinées* and to many world-famous comic strip artists from Belgium and abroad.

Arranged over three levels, the collection is housed in a Horta-designed Art Nouveau building. One of the most popular permanent exhibitions is a tour of the great comic strip heroes, from *Tintin* to *The Smurfs*, both of whose creators were Belgian. Other displays detail the stages of putting together a comic strip, from examples of initial ideas and pencil sketches through to final publication. The museum regularly holds major exhibitions featuring the work of famous cartoonists and studios, and also houses some 6,000 original plates, displayed in rotation, as well as a valuable archive of photographs and artifacts.

The famous Tintin rocket

Three Comic Figures
Tintin, Professor Calculus and Captain Haddock greet visitors on the 1st floor.

The Smurfs
These tiny blue characters first appeared in the Spirou journal in 1958. By the 1980s they had their own TV show and hit records.

A Suivre
Founded in 1978, A Suivre expanded the comic strip genre, and led to the new form of graphic novels: adult stories in cartoon form.

★ **Life-size Cartoon Sets**
A series of authentic comic scenes encourages children to enter the world of their favourite comic strip characters.

STAR SIGHTS

★ The Light Room

★ Life-size Cartoon Sets

VISITORS' CHECKLIST

20 rue des Sables, 1000 BRU.
Map 2 E2. **Tel** (02) 219 1980.
📟 38, 58, 61. 🚃 56, 81, 90.
Ⓜ Botanique, De Brouckère,
Rogier. ⬭ 10am–6pm Tue–Sun.
⬤ Mon, 1 Jan, 25 Dec. 💷 ♿
📷 🏪 🛈

★ **The Light Room**
*This airy space designed by
Victor Horta features stained
glass and wrought-ironwork.*

Comic Library
*The museum library
doubles as a study
centre for both art
students and enthu-
siasts of all ages. This
unique collection
includes a catalogue
of hundreds of old
comic strips, artists'
equipment, biogra-
phies, comic novels
and photographs.*

A HORTA-DESIGNED BUILDING

This beautiful building was constructed
between 1903 and 1906 to the design of
the Belgian Art-Nouveau architect Victor
Horta. Originally built as a fabric
warehouse, and known as the
Waucquez Building, it was one in a series of
department stores and warehouses in the city
designed by him. Saved from demolition by
the French Cultural Commission of Brussels,
in 1989 the building re-opened as a museum
dedicated to the comic strip, Belgium's so-
called Ninth Art *(see pp20–21)*. Carefully
restored, the building has many classic
features of Art Nouveau design, including
the use of curves on structural iron pillars.
In the impressive entrance hall is a display   **Cast-iron**
of Horta's architectural drawings for the   **pillar**
building, and on the right the Brasserie
Horta serves traditional Belgian dishes in a
charming glass and marble Art Nouveau setting.

**THE CHANGING FACE
OF HERGE'S TINTIN**
Perhaps the best-known Belgian
comic character, *Tintin* made his
debut in a children's paper in 1929.
He began life as a simple black line
drawing, featuring the famous quiff,
but no mouth. By 1930 Hergé began
to produce *Tintin* in book-form and
gave him both a mouth and a more
complex character suggested by a
greater range of facial expressions.
By the 1940s *Tintin* was appearing
in colour, alongside such new
characters as Captain Haddock, the
Thompsons and Professor Calculus.

Horta's drawing of the CBBD building

Nineteenth-century building in Place de Brouckère

Place de Brouckère ⓲

Map 2 D2. 🚌 *29, 60, 63, 65, 66, 71.* 🚋 *3, 52, 55, 56, 81, 90.* Ⓜ *de Brouckère, Bourse.*

In 1872 a design competition was held to encourage the construction of buildings of architectural interest in de Brouckère. Twenty winning applicants were selected and commissioned to give prominence to this Brussels junction. The Parisian contractor Jean-Baptiste Mosnier was responsible for taking the original plans through to completion.

The French influence of Mosnier and his workers is still evident on the square. Many of the buildings were erected in stone, common in France at the end of the 19th century, whereas brickwork was more usual in Brussels. Several original façades survive today, including the 1874 Hôtel Continental by Eugene Carpentier.

One of the great hotels of Brussels, the Hôtel Métropole *(see p49)* is situated on the south side of the square. The 1900–10 interior is splendidly gilded and can be seen either through the doorway or by pretending to be a guest. Café Métropole next door is, however, open to the public; here the lavishly ornate surroundings date from around 1890.

In the 20th century, architectural style was still at a premium in the district. In 1933 a Neo-Classical cinema was erected with an impressive Art Deco interior. During the 1960s, two imposing glass buildings blended the contemporary with the classical. Today, the varied historic architecture of Place de Brouckère enhances one of the city's busiest squares, despite recent additions of advertising hoardings.

Eglise St-Jean-Baptiste-au-Béguinage ⓳

Place du Béguinage, 1000 BRU. **Map** 1 C1. *Tel (02) 217 8742.* 🚌 *47.* Ⓜ *Ste-Cathérine.* ◯ *10am–5pm Tue–Sat, 10am–8pm Sun.* ◯ *Mon.* ♿

This stone-clad church was consecrated in 1676 around the long-standing and largest béguine community in the country, established in 1250. Fields and orchards around the site contained cottages and houses for up to 1,200 béguine women, members of a lay religious order who took up charitable work and enclosed living after widowhood or failed marriages. In medieval times the béguines ran a laundry, hospital and windmill for the people of the city. Still a popular place of worship, the church is also notable for its Flemish Baroque details from the 17th century, especially the onion-shaped turrets and ornamental walls. The nave is also Baroque, decorated with ornate winged cherubs, angels and scrolls. The confessionals are carved with allegorical figures and saints. A more unusual feature are the aisles, which have been widened to allow more light in. In the apse is a statue of St John the Baptist. The 1757 pulpit is a fine example of Baroque woodcarving, showing St Dominic and a heretic.

Théâtre Flamand ⓴

Rue de Laeken 146, 1000 BRU. **Map** 1 C1. *Tel (02) 210 1112.* 🚌 *47.* 🚋 *18.* Ⓜ *Rogier, Yser.* **www**.kvs.be

The former quay area of Brussels, on the banks of the old River Senne, still survives as a reminder that the city was once a thriving port. In 1882, architect Jean Baes was commissioned to enlarge one of the former waterfront warehouses and then turn it into a theatre but was asked to retain the original 1780 façade. Baes solved this problem ingeniously by placing the façade directly behind the frontage of

The ornate façade of Eglise St-Jean-Baptiste-au-Béguinage

the new building. In addition to this, the Théâtre Flamand has other interesting design features peculiar to the late 19th century. The four exterior metal terraces and a staircase leading to the ground were built for audience evacuation in the event of fire. The theatre has recently undergone major renovations, which have not only restored the fabric of the original building but have also improved the facilities.

The 19th-century interior staircase of Théâtre Flamand

Maison de la Bellone ㉑

Rue de Flandre 46, 1000 BRU.
Map 1 C2. *Tel (02) 513 3333.*
63. 🚋 *18.* Ⓜ *Ste-Catherine.* ◐
10am–6pm Tue–Fri (exhibition centre open noon–6pm). ● *Sat–Mon, Jul.*

This 17th-century aristocratic residence, now shielded under a glass roof and no longer visible from the street, was once the headquarters of the Ommegang procession *(see p25).* The original façade is notable for its decoration. There is a statue of Bellona (goddess of war), after whom the house is named, above the central arch, and the window ledges have medallions of Roman emperors.

Today the house, its exhibition centre and once-private theatre are open for dance and cinema shows, and temporary exhibitions of art and furniture.

Eglise Ste-Catherine ㉒

Place Ste-Catherine 50, 1000 BRU.
Map 1 C2. *Tel (02) 513 3481.*
🚌 *47.* 🚋 *3, 52, 55, 56, 81, 90.*
Ⓜ *Ste-Catherine, De Brouckère.* ◐
8am–5:30pm Mon–Sat, 10am–1:30pm Sun. ♿ *on request.*

Sadly, the only remnant of the first church here, built in the 15th century, is its Baroque tower, added in 1629. Inspired by the Eglise St-Eustache in Paris, the present church was redesigned in 1854–59 by Joseph Poelaert in a variety of styles. Notable features of the interior include a 14th-century statue of the Black Madonna and a portrait of St Catherine herself. A typically Flemish pulpit was installed at some stage; it may have come from the parish of Mechelen. Two impressive tombs were carved by Gilles-Lambert Godecharle. To the east of the church is the Tour Noire (Black Tower), a surviving remnant of the 12th-century stone city walls.

Although this area has been dedicated to the saint since the 13th century, the square of

Stonework on the Maison de la Bellone

Place Ste-Catherine was only laid in front of this large church after the basin once here was filled in. Paved in 1870, the square contrasts the peacefulness of the religious building with today's vigorous trade in good fish restaurants.

The central square was once the city's main fish market, and this is still the best place to indulge in a dish or two of Brussels' famous seafood, but prices are generally high. Flanking the square, Quai aux Briques and Quai au Bois à Brûler (Brick Quay and Timber Quay, named after their industrial past), contain lively parades of fish restaurants.

Eglise Ste-Catherine showing the spacious Victorian interior

THE UPPER TOWN

russels' Upper Town is separated from the lower part of the city by an escarpment that runs roughly north-south from the far end of Rue Royale to the Palais de Justice. Modern developments are now scattered across the whole city, and the difference between the two areas is less distinct than in the past; traditionally the Lower Town was mainly Flemish-speaking and a bustling centre for trade,

Peter Pan statue in Palais d'Egmont

while the Upper Town was home to French-speaking aristocrats and royalty. Today the Upper Town is known for its beautiful Gothic churches, modern architecture and fine museums. The late 18th-century elegance of the Parc de Bruxelles and Place Royale is complemented by "King of the Belgians" Leopold II's sweeping 19th-century boulevards that connect the Parc du Cinquantenaire to the centre.

SIGHTS AT A GLANCE

Historic Streets and Buildings
Hôtel Ravenstein **6**
Palais de Charles
  de Lorraine **8**
Palais d'Egmont **14**
Palais de Justice **15**
Palais Royal pp58–9 **2**
Place du Grand Sablon **11**
Place du Petit Sablon **13**
Place Royale **4**
Square Ambiorix **19**

Parks and Gardens
*Parc du Cinquantenaire
  pp74–5* **25**
Parc Léopold **24**

Museums and Galleries
BELvue Museum **1**
Institut Royal des Sciences
  Naturelles **23**
Musée Charlier **9**
Musée Instrumental **7**
Musée Wiertz **21**
*Musées Royaux des Beaux-
  Arts pp62–7* **10**

Churches and Cathedrals
*Cathédrale Sts Michel et Gudule
  pp70–71* **17**
Chapelle de la Madeleine **18**

Eglise St-Jacques-sur-
  Coudenberg **3**
Notre-Dame du Sablon **12**

Theatres and Concert Halls
Palais des Beaux-Arts **5**

Modern Architecture
Quartier Européen **20**
Parliament Quarter **22**

Shopping
Galérie Bortier **16**

0 metres	500
0 yards	500

KEY

⬛ Street-by-street map
   see pp 56–57

🚉 Train station

🚊 Tram stop

Ⓜ Metro station

🚌 Bus terminus

GETTING AROUND

The main metro stations for exploring the Upper Town are Parc and Porte de Namur in the west and Schuman and Maelbeek in the east. Most trams circle this area, so the best option is to take one of the many buses that run through the Upper Town.

◁ **Detail of a façade in a terrace of Art Nouveau houses in Square Ambiorix**

Street-by-Street: Quartier Royal

Fountain in park

The Quartier Royal has traditionally been home to Brussels' nobility and rulers. Chosen because the air was purer on the hill than it was in the Lower Town, the area once known as Coudenberg Hill was occupied by the 15th-century Coudenberg Palace, home to the Dukes of Brabant and Renaissance rulers. In 1731, the palace was destroyed in just six hours by a fire. Slowly rebuilt during the 18th and 19th centuries, four new palaces and much of the park were designed in Neo-Classical style chosen by Charles de Lorraine *(see p33)*. Today the Royal Quarter presents a peaceful elegance, with some of Europe's finest 18th-century buildings framing the tree-lined paths and fountains of Parc de Bruxelles.

Rue Royale runs for 2 km (1 mile) from the Quartier Royal to Jardin Botanique. In contrast to the 18th-century Neo-Classicism of its beginnings, along its route many fine examples of Victorian and Art Nouveau architecture stand out.

Eglise St-Jacques-sur-Coudenberg

One of Brussels' prettiest churches, St-Jacques' 18th-century façade was modelled exactly on a classical temple. The barrel-vaulted nave and half-domed apse are sprinkled with floral plasterwork and contain several fine Neo-Classical paintings ❸

★ Place Royale
In the centre of this attractive, symmetrical square is a statue of Godefroi of Bouillon, a Brabant soldier who fought the first Catholic Crusades and died in Palestine ❹

RUE ROYALE

PLACE ROYALE

KEY

--- Suggested route

STAR SIGHTS

★ Palais Royal

★ Parc de Bruxelles

★ Place Royale

Place des Palais divides Palais Royal and the park. In French, "Palais" refers to any large stately building, and does not have royal connotations.

| 0 metres | 100 |
| 0 yards | 100 |

★ Parc de Bruxelles

On the site of medieval hunting grounds once used by the dukes of Brabant, the park was redesigned in the 1770s with fountains, statues and tree-lined walks.

LOCATOR MAP
See Street Finder map 2

Palais de la Nation

Designed by French architect Barnabé Guimard, the Palais de la Nation was built in 1783 and restored in 1883 after a fire. Since 1831, it has been the home of both chambers of the Belgian Parliament.

★ Palais Royal

The largest of the palaces, the low-rise Palais Royal is the official home of the Belgian monarch and family. A flag flies to indicate when the king is in the country ❷

Palais des Académies

Built in 1823 as the residence of the Crown Prince, this has been the private premises of the Académie Royale de Belgique since 1876.

BELvue Museum ❶

Place des Palais 7, 1000 BRU. **Map** 2
E4. *Tel* (070) 220 492. ⛴ 20, 27, 34,
38, 54, 60, 71, 95, 96. 🚋 92, 93,
94. Ⓜ Trone, Parc. ⏱ 10am–6pm
Tue–Sun (5pm Oct–May). ● Mon, 1
Jan, Easter Sun, 1 May, 25 Dec. 🅰
♿ 🚻 🏛

The BELvue Museum houses
a wide collection of paintings,
documents and other royal
memorabilia charting the
history of the Belgian
monarchy from independence
in 1830 to the present day.
Since 1992 it has been housed
in the former Hôtel Bellevue,
an 18th-century Neo-Classical
building lying adjacent to
the Palais Royal, which was
annexed to the palace in 1902.
A permanent exhibition in
honour of the late, immensely
popular, King Baudouin
(r.1951–1993) was added in

**The Neo-Classical façade of the
BELvue Museum**

1998. As well as official
portraits, informal photographs
are on display which give a
fascinating insight into the
private lives of the Belgian
royal family. The collection
is displayed in chronological
order in a series of rooms
with a bust of the sovereign
to which it is devoted at the
entrance to each one.

Eglise St-Jacques-sur-Coudenberg ❸

Place Royale, 1000 BRU. **Map** 2 E4.
Tel (02) 511 7836. ⛴ 20, 27, 34, 38,
54, 60, 71, 95, 96. 🚋 92, 93, 94. Ⓜ
Trone, Parc. ⏱ 1–6pm Tue–Sat,
8:45am–5pm Sun.

The prettiest building in the
Place Royale, St-Jacques-sur-
Coudenberg is the latest in a
series of churches to have
occupied this site. There has
been a chapel here since the
12th century, when one was
built to serve the dukes of
Brabant. On construction of
the Coudenberg Palace in the
13th century, it became the
ducal chapel. The chapel
suffered over the years: it was
ransacked in 1579 during
conflict between Catholics
and Protestants, and was so
badly damaged in the fire
of 1731 that destroyed the

Palais Royal ❷

The Palais Royal is the most important of the palaces
around the Parc de Bruxelles. An official residence of the
Belgian monarchy, construction of the modern palace
began in the 1820s on the site of the old Coudenberg
Palace. Work continued under Léopold II (r.1865–1909),
when much of the exterior was completed. Throughout
the 20th century the palace underwent interior improvements and restoration of its older sections. It is open
only from July to September, but this is a
fine opportunity to tour Belgium's
lavish state reception rooms.

**The Field Marshal's
Room** contains a portrait
of the first Belgian king,
Léopold I, after Winter-
halter's 1843 original.

STAR SIGHTS

★ Throne Room

★ Small White Room

★ Throne Room
*One of Brussels' original state-
rooms, the huge throne room is
decorated in grand style, with
huge pilastered columns, 11
large candelabras and 28
wall-mounted chandeliers.*

The 19th-century cupola of Eglise St-Jacques-sur-Coudenberg

Coudenberg Palace that it was demolished soon after. The present church was built in the Neo-Classical style and was consecrated in 1787, although it served several years as a Temple of Reason and Law during the French Revolution, returning to the

Catholic Church in 1802. The cupola was completed in 1849. The interior is simple and elegant, with two large paintings by Jan Portaels on either side of the transept.

Place Royale ❹

Map 2 E4. 🚌 20, 27, 34, 38, 54, 60, 71, 95, 96. 🚊 92, 93, 94. Ⓜ Trone, Parc.

The influence of Charles de Lorraine is still keenly felt in the Place Royale. As Governor of Brussels from 1749 to 1780 he redeveloped the site once occupied by the Coudenberg Palace along Neo-Classical lines reminiscent of Vienna, a city he greatly admired.

When the area was being worked on, the ruins of the burnt-down palace were demolished and the entire site

was rebuilt as two squares. However, in 1995, excavation work uncovered ruins of the 15th-century Aula Magna, the Great Hall of the former palace. This was part of the extension of the palace started under the dukes of Brabant in the early 13th century and then developed under the rule of the dukes of Burgundy, in particular Philip the Good. It was in this room that the Hapsburg emperor Charles V abdicated in favour of his son, Philip II. The ruins can now be seen as part of the BELvue Museum.

Although criss-crossed by tramlines and traffic, the Place Royale maintains a feeling of dignity with its tall, elegant, cream buildings symmetrically set around a cobbled square. Visitors can tour the area on foot, admiring the exceptional Neo-Classical buildings.

The Long Gallery features exquisite late 19th-century ceiling paintings representing Dawn, Day and Dusk.

The Empire Room

★ Small White Room
Rows of 19th-century royal portraits dominate this gilt chamber with its large candle-lit chandeliers and late 18th-century rococo furnishings.

VISITORS' CHECKLIST

Place des Palais, 1000 BRU. **Map** 2 E4. **Tel** (02) 551 2020. 🚌 38, 60, 95, 96. 🚊 91, 92, 93, 94. Ⓜ Trone, Parc. ⬤ mid-Jul–mid-Sep: 10:30am–5pm Tue–Sun. ⬤ Mon, Oct–Jun. ♿ 📷

Hall of Mirrors
This large room is famous for its grandiose effect similar to the mirrored chamber at Versailles. The ceiling has recently been decorated in green beetle and wing designs by sculptor Jan Fabre.

The Victor Horta-designed façade of the Palais des Beaux-Arts

Palais des Beaux-Arts ❺

Rue Ravenstein 23, 1000 BRU. **Map** 2 E3. **Tel** (02) 507 8200, 511 3433. 20, 38, 71, 60, 95, 96. 92, 93, 94. Gare Centrale. 9am–6pm daily; for exhibitions 10am–6pm Tue–Sun. public hols. (02) 507 8468. www.bozar.be

The Palais des Beaux-Arts owes its existence to Henri Le Boeuf, a music-loving financier who gave his name to the main auditorium. In 1922 he commissioned the architect Victor Horta (see p78) to design a cultural centre which would house concert halls and exhibition areas open to all visitors and embracing the artistic fields of music, theatre, cinema and art. The construction took seven years as the building was on a slope but could not be so tall as to block the view of the town from the Palais Royal: Horta had to revise his plans six times. The centre was the first of its kind in Europe.

The complex has a fine reputation and has played a key role in the cultural life of Brussels for over 70 years. It is the focus for the city's music and dance, and is home to the Belgian National Orchestra.

The complex also houses the **Musée du Cinema**, set up in 1962, with its fine archive and exhibition of old cameras and lenses. It screens classic films.

🏛 Musée du Cinema
Rue Baron Horta 9, 1000 BRU. **Tel** (02) 507 8370. 5:30–10:30pm daily.

Hôtel Ravenstein ❻

Rue Ravenstein 3, 1000 BRU. **Map** 2 E3. 20, 38, 60, 71, 95, 96. 92, 93, 94. Gare Centrale, Parc. restaurant only.

Over the centuries the Hôtel Ravenstein has been the home of patrician families, soldiers and court officials, and, for the past 100 years, the Royal Society of Engineers. The building was designed at the end of the 15th century for Adolphe and Philip Cleves-Ravenstein; in 1515 it became the birthplace of Anne of Cleves. Consisting of two parts, joined by gardens and stables, it is the last remaining example of a Burgundian-style manor house. The Hôtel Ravenstein was acquired by the town in 1896 and used to store

The pretty open courtyard of the Hôtel Ravenstein

artworks. Sadly, it fell into disrepair and renovation took place in 1934. One half is now a Belgian restaurant, the other the Royal Society of Engineers' private HQ. However, the pretty, original inner courtyard can still be seen.

Musée Instrumental ❼

Rue Montagne de la Cour 2, 1000 BRU. **Map** 2 E4. **Tel** (02) 545 0130. 20, 38, 60, 71, 95, 96. 92, 93, 94. Gare Centrale, Parc. 9:30am–5pm Tue–Fri (to 8pm Thu), 10am–5pm Sat & Sun. 1 Jan, 1 May, 1 & 11 Nov, 25 Dec.

Once a department store, the building known as Old England is a striking showpiece of Art Nouveau architecture located by the Place Royale.

Architect Paul Saintenoy gave full rein to his imagination when he designed these shop premises for the Old England company in 1899. The façade is made entirely of glass and elaborate wrought iron. There is a domed gazebo on the roof, and a turret to one side. Surprisingly, it was only in the 1990s that a listed buildings policy was adopted in Brussels, which has secured treasures such as this. Old England is one of the buildings that has undergone extensive renovation work, having been used until recently as a temporary exhibition space. The building is now home to the Musée Instrumental, moved from the Sablon. Meanwhile, the Old England company is still flourishing, with its premises now at No. 419 in the fashionable Avenue Louise.

The collection of the Musée Instrumental began in the 19th century when the state bought 80 ancient and exotic instruments. It was doubled in 1876 when King Léopold II donated a gift of 97 Indian musical instruments presented to him

Old England, home to the Musée Instrumental

by a maharajah. A museum displaying all of these artifacts opened in 1877, and by 1924 the museum boasted 3,300 pieces and was recognized as a leader in its field. Today the collection contains more than 6,000 items and includes many fine examples of wind, string and keyboard instruments from medieval times to the present. Chief attractions include prototype instruments by Adolphe Sax, the Belgian inventor of the saxophone, mini violins favoured by street musicians and a violin maker's studio. In June 2000 the museum moved to its specially designed home in the newly renovated Old England building, where there is much more room in which to display this world-class collection.

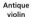

Antique violin

Palais de Charles de Lorraine ⑧

Place du Musée 1, 1000 BRU. **Map** 2 D4. **Tel** (02) 519 5311. 27, 34, 60, 65, 66, 71, 95, 96. 92, 93, 94. M Gare Centrale, Parc. ◯ 1–5pm Wed & Sat. Tue–Sun, Thu & Fri, last week in Aug, last week in Dec. for details **Tel** (02) 519 5786.

Hidden behind this Neo-Classical façade are the few

The state room with marble floor at the Palais de Charles de Lorraine

rooms that remain of the palace of Charles de Lorraine, Governor of Brussels during the mid-18th century. He was a keen patron of the arts, and the young Mozart is believed to have performed here. Few original features remain, as the palace was ransacked by marauding French troops in 1794. Extensive renovations were recently completed. The bas-reliefs at the top of the stairway, representing air, earth, fire and water, reflect Charles de Lorraine's interest in alchemy. Most spectacular of all the original features is the 28-point star set in the floor of the circular drawing room. Each of the points is made of a different Belgian marble, a much sought-after material used to construct St Peter's Basilica in Rome.

Musée Charlier ⑨

Avenue des Arts 16, 1210 BRU. **Map** 2 F2. **Tel** (02) 218 5382, 220 2690. 23, 63, 65, 66. M Madou, Arts-Loi. ◯ noon–5pm Tue–Fri. Sat–Mon, public hols. French & Dutch only.

This quiet museum was once the home of Henri van Cutsem, a wealthy collector and patron of the arts. In 1890 he asked the young architect Victor Horta to re-design his house as an exhibition space for his extensive collections. Van Cutsem died, and his friend, the sculptor Charlier, installed his own art collection in the house. Charlier commissioned Horta to build another museum, at Tournai in southern Belgium, to house van Cutsem's collection. On Charlier's death in 1925 the house and contents were left to the city as a museum.

The Musée Charlier opened in 1928. It contains paintings by a number of different artists, including portraits by Antoine Wiertz (see p72) and early landscapes by James Ensor. The collection also includes sculptures by Charlier, as well as glassware, porcelain, chinoiserie and silverware. Of special note are the tapestries, some from the Paris studios of Aubusson, on the staircases and the first floor, and the displays of Louis XV- and Louis XVI-style furniture on the first and second floors.

Musée Charlier, home to one of Belgium's finest individual collections of art and furnishings

Musées Royaux des Beaux-Arts: Musée d'art ancien ⑩

Hercules Sculpture

Jointly known as the Musées Royaux des Beaux-Arts, The Musée d'art ancien, Musée d'art moderne and Magritte Museum are Brussels' premier art museums. The museums' buildings, adjacent to the Place Royale, are home to exhibits from two eras, *ancien* (15th–18th century) and *moderne* (19th century–present day), including a large collection of works by Belgian surrealist René Magritte (1898–1967). Housed in a Neo-Classical building designed by Alphonse Balat between 1874 and 1880, the Musée d'art ancien is the largest of the museum's sections. The art collection dates back to the 18th century when it consisted of the few valuable works left behind by the French Republican army, which had stolen many of Brussels' treasures. This small collection grew and the present gallery opened in 1887. The Musée d'art ancien is best known for the finest collection of Flemish art in the world, and many Old Masters, including van Dyck and Rubens, are also well represented. Major changes taking place at the museum from 2009 mean that some areas may close and exhibitions may move.

Façade of Museum
Corinthian columns and busts of Flemish painters adorn the entrance.

★ **The Assumption of the Virgin** (*c.1610*)
Pieter Paul Rubens (1577–1640) was the leading exponent of Baroque art in Europe, combining Flemish precision with Italian flair. Here, Rubens suppresses background colours to emphasize the Virgin's blue robes.

Ground level

Entrance

Entrance to Musée d'art moderne

Lower level

Interior of the Main Hall
Founded by Napoleon in 1801 to relieve the packed Louvre in Paris, these are the oldest museums in Belgium. More than 2,500 works are exhibited in the museums' buildings.

STAR PAINTINGS

★ The Assumption of the Virgin by Rubens

★ The Annunciation by the Master of Flémalle

Upper level

VISITORS' CHECKLIST

Rue de la Régence 3, 1000 BRU.
Map 2 D4. **Tel** (02) 508 3211.
🚌 25, 95, 96. 🚋 91, 92, 93,
94. Ⓜ Gare Centrale, Parc. ⏱
10am–5pm Tue–Sun. ● Mon,
public hols. ♿ 📷 🏠 🛗 🍴
www.fine-arts-museum.be

The Census at Bethlehem *(1610)*
*Pieter Brueghel the Younger (c.1564–1638) produced
a version of this subject some 40 years after the original
by his father. Shown together, the two works illustrate
the development of Flemish painting in its peak period.*

**Madonna with Saint Anne
and a Franciscan Donor** *(1470)*
*Hugo van der Goes (c.1440–82) was
commissioned to paint this symbolic
work for the monk shown on the
right for his personal devotional use.*

★ **The Annunciation** *(c.1406–7)*
*The Master of Flémalle (c.1378–1444) sets the
holy scene of the Archangel Gabriel announc-
ing the impending birth of the Messiah in a
homely, contemporary setting, with daily objects
an apparent contrast to the momentous event.*

KEY

☐ 15th–16th century (blue route)

☐ 17th–18th century (brown route)

☐ Sculpture gallery (orange route)

☐ Temporary exhibitions

☐ Non-exhibition space

GALLERY GUIDE
*In the gallery different coloured signs are
used to lead the visitor through different
eras of art (see pp66–7). On the first floor,
in rooms 10 to 34, the blue route covers the
15th and 16th centuries. The brown route is
in rooms 50 to 62 and covers the 17th and
18th centuries. The sculpture gallery is
housed on the lower ground floor.*

Musées Royaux des Beaux-Arts: Musée d'art moderne

Opened in 1984, the Musée d'art moderne is situated in a unique setting: eight levels of the building are underground, but a lightwell allows many of the works to be seen by natural daylight filtering in from the Place du Musée. The collection of art is varied, and includes many well-known 20th-century artists from 1900 to the present day, though works by the Belgian Surrealists are the most popular. A new Magritte Museum will open in June 2009, adjacent to the Musées Royaux des Beaux-Arts, displaying over 170 paintings. Due to a revamp some exhibits may be relocated.

level 4

level 3

level 2

★ The Domain of Arnheim (1962)
The museum contains the world's largest collection of work by surrealist René Magritte (see p17). Here, an eagle-mountain rears over a small bird's nest. The inexplicable nature of the eerie composition draws its elements into question, but answers are made deliberately difficult.

Ground level (level 1)

Le Joueur Secret *(1927)*
This work was painted during Magritte's self-titled "Cavernous" period. During three prolific years, from 1927 to 1930, he painted roughly a canvas each day.

Level -1

To Musée d'art ancien

Level -2

STAR PAINTINGS

- ★ Woman in a Blue Dress by Rik Wouters

- ★ The Domain of Arnheim by René Magritte

GALLERY GUIDE
The yellow route is dedicated to the 19th century. The green route covers work from the first quarter of the 20th century and its various movements, such as Fauvism and Cubism. Level -5 contains the Surrealist collection and Level -6 includes the Jeune Peinture Belge and COBRA schools. Levels -7 and -8 exhibit works from the 1960s to the present day. A major revamp means that not all paintings may be on show. Many Magritte works will be relocated once the Magritte Museum opens in June 2009.

Composition *(1921)*
(detail shown)
Two stylized human figures form the centre of this work by Belgian painter Pierre-Louis Flouquet, combining Futurism and Cubism in a "plastic" style.

VISITORS' CHECKLIST

Place Royale 1, 1000 BRU. **Map** 2 D4. *Tel (02) 508 3211.* 20, 27, 34, 54, 60, 71, 95, 96. 91, 92, 93, 94. Gare Centrale, Parc. 10am–5pm Tue–Sun. Mon, public hols. **www**.fine-arts-museum.be

★ **Woman in a Blue Dress in front of a Mirror** *(1914)*
Rik Wouters was a Fauvist painter whose fascination with colour led him to innovative spatula painting techniques, as seen here.

Draped Woman on Steps *(1957–8)*
The prolific British artist Henry Moore is the world's most exhibited sculptor. This piece reveals his characteristic fluidity of line, together with tension in the waiting figure.

View of London *(1917)*
Heavily influenced by Monet's work, Emile Claus developed a variant of Impressionism with fellow artists called "Luminism". The Belgian Claus shows his Luminist interest in light effects through the damp fog of this London twilight scene.

level -4

level -3

level -6

level -5

level -8

level -7

KEY

19th century (yellow route)

20th century (green route)

Non-exhibition space

Exploring the Musées Royaux des Beaux-Arts

Six centuries of art, both Belgian and international, are displayed in the museums that make up the Musées Royaux des Beaux-Arts. The combination of the museums contains works from many artistic styles, from the religious paintings of the 15th-century Flemish Primitives to the graphic art of the 1960s and 1970s. The Musée d'art moderne also stages regular temporary exhibitions. The museums are very well set out, guiding the visitor easily through the full collection or, if time is short, directly to the art era of special interest. Each section is highly accessible, with both main museums divided into different coloured routes which relate to the art of each century, taking the visitor through galleries representing the varied schools of art by period.

Flemish still life, *Vase of Flowers* **(1704) by Rachel Ruysch**

THE BLUE ROUTE

This route leads visitors through a large display of works dating mostly from the 15th and 16th centuries. In the first few rooms are works by the renowned Flemish Primitive School *(see p16).* As is the case with painting of the Middle Ages, the pictures are chiefly religious in nature and depict a variety of biblical scenes and details from the lives of saints. A work of particular note is *The Annunciation* by the Master of Flémalle, which shows the Archangel Gabriel appearing to the Virgin Mary as she sits at her fireside in a typically Flemish parlour. Also on display are a number of pictures by Rogier van der Weyden, the most famous of all the Flemish Primitive artists and city painter to Brussels during the mid-15th century; of note is his version of the

Lamentation. The work of Bruges artist Hans Memling is mostly shown in his native city, but his *The Martyrdom of Saint Sebastian* is found here.

The most important works in this collection are the paintings by the Brueghels, father and son. Both were renowned for their scenes of peasant life, and on display are *The Bird Trap* (1565) by Pieter Brueghel the Elder, and *The Village Wedding* (1607) by his son, Pieter.

Also on view are beautiful tapestries and the Delporte Collection, which groups sculpture, paintings and *objets d'art* from around the world.

THE BROWN ROUTE

The second route wends its way through the works of the 17th and 18th centuries. The rooms are wider and taller here in order to house the larger canvases of that time.

A highlight of the route is the world-famous collection of works by Pieter Paul Rubens (1557–1640), which affords a fine overview of the artist's work. As well as key examples of his religious works, there are some excellent portraits, such as *Hélène Fourment,* a portrait of his young wife. Of special interest are the sketches and paintings made in preparation for Rubens' larger works, such as *Four Negro Heads,* a work made in preparation of the 1620 *Adoration of the Magi.*

Other works of note in this section are the paintings by Old Masters such as Van Dyck's *Portrait of a Genoese Lady with her Daughter* of the 1620s and Frans Hals' *Three Children with Goatcart,* as well as several paintings by representatives of later Flemish schools, including Jacob Jordaens and his depiction of myths, such as *Pan and Syrinx* (c.1645) and *Satyr and Peasant.* Baroque and Flemish art are all well represented on the tour, a journey through the best painting of the time.

Also on display are some small sculptures which were studies of larger works by Laurent Delvaux, a leading sculptor of the 18th century, particularly *Hercules and Erymanthian Boar,* a study for the sculpture by the staircase in the Palais de Charles de Lorraine *(see p61).*

Works of the Italian, Spanish and French schools of this era are also represented, notably a depiction by Claude Le Lorrain in 1672 of the classical poetic scene *Aeneas hunting the Stag on the Coast of Libya.*

Lamentation (c. 1420–50) by Rogier van der Weyden

THE YELLOW ROUTE

This section covers the 19th century and is closer to the contemporary collection both in position and period. It is an informed introduction to the cutting-edge displays nearby.

The works along the yellow route vary greatly in style and subject matter, from Romanticism, exemplified by David, and Neo-Classicism, to Realism and Symbolism. There are, as in the other sections, examples of work by artists from outside Belgium, including Pierre Bonnard's *Nude against the Light* (1907), Edouard Vuillard's *Two Schoolchildren* (1894) and Monet's *Sunset at Etretat* (1885), but once again most emphasis is on Belgian artists.

Social realist artist Constantin Meunier (1831–1905) is represented by many of his sculptures, including *Firedamp* (1888). Much of the work of James Ensor (1890–1949) remains in his native city Ostend, but many of his macabre works are displayed here, such as *Scandalized Masks* (1883) and *Two Skeletons Fighting over a Pickled Herring* (1891). This section also offers the chance to see pictures by artists who are less well known outside Belgium such as Henri Evenepoel (1872–99) whose lively Arab scene *Orange Market at Blidah* (1898) provides a contrast to the stark works of painters such as Ensor. The work of Impressionist Emile Claus is of value to followers of the movement. Of local interest is the landscape of Brussels by van Moer, painted in 1868,

The Orange Market at Blidah (1898) by Henri Evenepoel

which clearly shows the River Senne before it was covered for hygiene reasons. Moving from the passion of Romanticism to grim industrial realism and gentle Impressionism, this survey is definitive.

The underground Sculpture Gallery, with carvings and bronzes

THE ORANGE ROUTE

Anyone with an interest in sculpture should follow this route down to the lower ground level in the Musée d'art ancien. Here, 18th- and 19th-century stone, marble and bronze Belgian sculpture is displayed alongside an exhibition explaining various methods behind many of the works on show, from carving to casting and burnishing in the materials of past centuries. There is also access to a sculpture terrace from outside the entrance of the Musée d'art ancien.

THE GREEN ROUTE

The collection of art is wide and varied and includes works by well-known 18th-, 19th- and 20th-century painters from Belgium and around the world. There is no clearly defined route to follow within this section, nor are the exhibits strictly grouped by period or movement, so it is best to wander through the collection, stopping at areas of interest along the way.

There are a number of works by the leading Belgian artists of the 19th and 20th centuries, such as Fauvist painter Rik Wouters' (1882–1916) *The Flautist* (1914). International artists include Matisse, Paul Klee and Chagall. The work of the noted Surrealist, Paul Delvaux, is well represented with works such as *Evening Train* (1957) and *Pygmalion* (1939). The popular collection of Surrealist works by René Magritte (1898–1967) will be moved to the new Magritte Museum (located next to the Musées Royaux des Beaux Arts) on opening in June 2009. Belgian art of the 20th century tends to be severe and stark, but the postwar *Jeune Peinture Belge* school reintroduced colour in an abstract way and is represented in works such as Marc Mendelson's 1950s *Toccata et fugue*.

Sculpture highlights in this section include Ossip Zadkine's totem pole-like *Diana* (1937) and Henry Moore's *Draped Woman on Steps* (1957–8).

Death of Marat (1793) by Jacques-Louis David

Busy café scene at Place du Grand Sablon

Place du Grand Sablon

Map 2 D4. 🚌 *27, 34, 48, 95, 96.* 🚋 *92, 93, 94.* Ⓜ *Gare Centrale, Louise, Parc.*

Situated on the slope of the escarpment that divides Brussels in two, the Place du Grand Sablon is like a stepping stone between the upper and lower halves of the city. The name "sablon" derives from the French "*sable*" (sand) and the square is so-called because this old route down to the city centre once passed through an area of sandy marshes.

Today the picture is very different. The square, more of a triangle in shape, stretches from a 1751 fountain by Jacques Berge at its base uphill to the Gothic church of Notre-Dame du Sablon. The fountain was a gift of the Englishman Lord Bruce, out of gratitude for the hospitality shown to him in Brussels. The square is surrounded by elegant town houses, some with Art Nouveau façades. This is a chic, wealthy and busy part of Brussels, an area of up-market antiques dealers, fashionable restaurants and trendy bars, which really come into their own in warm weather when people stay drinking outside until the early hours of the morning: a good place in which to soak up the

atmosphere. Wittamer, at No. 12, is a justifiably well-known *patisserie* and chocolate shop, which also has its own tea room on the first floor.

Every weekend the area near the church plays host to a lively and thriving, if rather expensive, antiques market.

Notre-Dame du Sablon

Place du Grand Sablon, 1000 BRU. **Map** 2 D4. **Tel** (02) 511 5741. 🚋 *92, 93, 94.* Ⓜ *Gare Centrale, Louise, Parc.* ⏰ *9am–6:30pm Mon–Fri, 10am–7pm Sat & Sun.* ♿ ✏ *on request.*

Along with the Cathédrale Sts Michel et Gudule (*see p70–71*), this lovely church is one of the finest remaining examples of Brabant Gothic architecture in Belgium.

A church was first erected here when the guild of crossbowmen was granted permission to build a chapel to Our Lady on this sandy hill. Legend has it that a young girl in Antwerp had a vision of the Virgin Mary who instructed her to take her statue to Brussels. The girl carried the statue of the Virgin to Brussels down the Senne river by boat and gave it to the crossbowmen's chapel, which rapidly became a place of pilgrimage. Work to enlarge the church began around 1400 but, due to lack of funds, was not completed until 1550. All

Notre-Dame du Sablon window

that remains today are two carvings depicting the young girl in a boat, since the statue was destroyed in 1565.

The interior of the church is simple but beautifully proportioned, with inter-connecting side chapels and an impressive pulpit dating from 1697. Of particular interest, however, are the 11 magnificent stained-glass windows, 14 m (45 ft) high, which dominate the inside of the church. As the church is lit from the inside, they shine out at night like welcoming beacons. Also worth a visit is the chapel of the Tour et Taxis family, whose mansion once stood near the Place du Petit Sablon. In 1517 the family had tapestries commissioned to commemorate the legend that led to the chapel becoming a place of pilgrimage. Some now hang in the Musées Royaux d'art et d'histoire in Parc du Cinquantenaire (*see p75*), but others were stolen by the French Revolutionary army in the 1790s.

The magnificent interior of the church of Notre-Dame du Sablon

Place du Petit Sablon

Map 2 D4. 🚌 *20, 27, 34, 48, 95, 96.* 🚋 *92, 93, 94.* Ⓜ *Gare Centrale, Louise, Parc.*

These pretty, formal gardens were laid out in 1890 and are a charming spot to stop for a rest. On top of the railings that enclose the gardens are 48 bronze statuettes by Art Nouveau artist Paul Hankar, each one representing a differ-

One of the lavish fountains in the gardens of Petit Sablon

ent medieval guild of the city. At the back of the gardens is a fountain built to commemorate Counts Egmont and Hornes, the martyrs who led a Dutch uprising against the tyrannical rule of the Spanish under Philip II, and were beheaded in the Grand Place in 1568 (*see p31*). On either side of the fountain are 12 further statues of 15th- and 16th-century figures, including Bernard van Orley, whose stained-glass windows grace the city's cathedral, and the Flemish mapmaker Gerhard Mercator, whose 16th-century projection of the world forms the basis of most modern maps.

Statue of Peter Pan in Palais d'Egmont gardens

has twice been rebuilt, in 1750 and again in 1891, following a fire. Today it belongs to the Belgian Foreign Ministry. It was here that Great Britain, Denmark and Ireland signed as members of the EEC in 1972.

Though the palace itself is closed to the public, the gardens, whose entrances are on the Rue du Grand Cerf and the Boulevard de Waterloo, are open. There is a statue of Peter Pan, a copy of one found in Kensington Gardens, in London. Many of the gardens' buildings are now run down, but the ancient orangery has been restored and houses a restaurant.

Palais d'Egmont ⓮

Rue aux Laines, 1000 BRU.
Map 2 E4. 🚌 27, 34, 95, 96. 🚊 91, 92, 93, 94. Ⓜ Louise, Parc. ♿

The Palais d'Egmont (also known as the Palais d'Arenberg) was originally built in the mid-16th century for Françoise of Luxembourg, mother of the 16th-century leader of the city's rebels, Count Egmont. This palace

Palais de Justice ⓯

Place Poelaert 1, 1000 BRU. **Map** 1 C5. **Tel** (02) 508 6578. 🚌 34. 🚊 91, 92, 93, 94. Ⓜ Louise. ⬜ 8am–5pm Mon–Fri. ● Sat & Sun, Jul, public hols. ♿ 📷 on request.

The Palais de Justice rules the Brussels skyline and can be seen from almost any vantage point in the city. Of all the ambitious projects of King Leopold II, this was perhaps the grandest. It occupies an area larger than St Peter's Basilica in Rome, and was one of the world's most impressive 19th-century buildings. It was built between 1866 and 1883 by architect Joseph Poelaert who looked for inspiration in classical temples, but sadly died mid-construction in 1879. The Palais de Justice is still home to the city's law courts.

Detail of a cornice at the Palais de Justice

Galérie Bortier ⑯

Rue de la Madeleine 55, 1000 BRU.
Map 2 D3. 🚌 20, 38. 🚊 92, 93,
94. Ⓜ Gare Centrale. ◗ 9am–6pm
Mon–Sat. ◗ Sun, public hols. ♿

Galérie Bortier is the only
shopping arcade in the city
dedicated solely to book and
map shops, and it has become
the haunt of students, enthus-
iasts and researchers looking
for secondhand French books
and antiquarian finds.

The land on which the
gallery stands was originally
owned by a Monsieur Bortier,
whose idea it was to have a
covered arcade lined with
shops on either side. He put
160,000 francs of his own
money into the project, quite
a considerable sum in the
1840s. The 65-m (210-ft) long
Galérie Bortier was built in
1848 and was designed by
Jean-Pierre Cluysenaar, the
architect of the Galéries St-
Hubert nearby *(see p47)*. The
Galérie Bortier opened along
with the then-adjacent Marché
de la Madeleine, but the latter
was unfortunately destroyed
by developers in 1958.

A complete restoration of
Galérie Bortier was ordered by
the Ville de Bruxelles in 1974.
The new architects kept strictly
to Cluysenaar's plans and
installed a replacement glass
and wrought-iron roof made
to the original 19th-century
Parisian style. The Rue de la
Madeleine itself also offers
plenty of browsing material
for bibliophiles and art lovers.

**Crammed interior of a bookshop
at the Galérie Bortier**

Cathédrale Sts Michel et Gudule ⑰

The Cathédrale Sts Michel et Gudule is the national
church of Belgium, although it was only granted
cathedral status in 1962. It is the finest surviving example
of Brabant Gothic architecture. There has been a church
on the site of the cathedral since at least the 11th
century. Work began on the Gothic cathedral in 1225
under Henry I, Duke of Brabant, and continued over a
period of 300 years. It was finally completed with the
construction of two front towers at the beginning of
the 16th century under Charles V. The cathedral is
made of a sandy limestone, brought from local
quarries. The interior is very bare;
this is due to Protestant iconoclast
ransacking in 1579–80 and thefts
by French revolutionists in
1783. It was fully restored and
cleaned in the 1990s and
now reveals its splendour.

The twin towers rise above
the city. Unusually, they were
designed as a pair in the
1400s; Brabant architecture
typically has only one.

★ **Last Judgement Window**
At the front of the cathedral,
facing the altar, is a magnificent
stained-glass window of 1528
depicting Christ awaiting saved
souls. Its vivid reds, blues and
yellows place it in the 16th-century
style. The Renaissance panes are
surrounded by later Baroque
garlands of flowers.

STAR SIGHTS

★ Last Judgement
    Window

★ Baroque Pulpit

Romanesque remains of
the first church here, dating
from 1047, were discovered
during renovation work.
They can be seen and
toured in the crypt.

Chapelle de la Madeleine ⑱

Rue de la Madeleine, 1000 BRU.
Map 2 D3 . **Tel** *(02) 511 2845.*
🚌 *20, 38.* 🚊 *92, 93, 94.* Ⓜ *Gare Centrale.* ⭕ *7am–7pm Mon– Sat; 7am–noon, 5pm–8pm Sun.* ♿

This little church once stood on the site now occupied by the Gare Centrale, but it was moved, stone by stone, further down the hill to make way for the construction of the Art Deco-style station and its car park during the early 1950s.

The 17th-century façade of the church has been restored. The original 15th-century interior has been replaced by a plain, modest decor, with simple stone pillars and modern stained-glass windows. Off the regular tourist track, the chapel is used by people as a quiet place for worship. The Baroque chapel which was once attached has now gone.

A view of the Chapelle de la Madeleine with restored brickwork

The transept windows represent the rulers of Belgium in 1537/38. Jan Haeck made the designs after Bernard van Orley's sketches.

The Lectern

Sainte Gudule
This 7th-century saint is very dear to the people of Brussels. Her relics were scattered to the winds by ransacking Protestants in 1579, but this only served to reinforce her cult.

The Statue of St Michael is the cathedral's symbol of its links with the city. While the gilded plaster statue is not itself historically exceptional, its long heritage is; the patron saint of Brussels, the Archangel St Michael is shown killing the dragon, symbolic of his protection of the city.

Sainte Gudule

★ Baroque Pulpit
The flamboyantly carved pulpit in the central aisle is the work of an Antwerp-born sculptor, Henri-François Verbruggen. Designed in 1699, it was finally installed in 1776.

The Art Nouveau façade of No. 11
Square Ambiorix

Square Ambiorix ⑲

Map 3 B2. 🚌 54, 63. Ⓜ Schuman.

Close to the EU district, but
totally different in style and
spirit, lies the beautiful Square
Ambiorix. Together with the
Avenue Palmerston and the
Square Marie-Louise below
that, this marshland was
transformed in the 1870s into
one of the loveliest residential
parts of Brussels, with a large
central area of gardens, ponds
and fountains.

The elegant houses, some
Art Nouveau, some older, have
made this one of the truly
sought-after suburbs in the
city. The most spectacular Art
Nouveau example is at No. 11.
Known as the Maison St Cyr
after the
painter

The Justus Lipsius, the pink granite EU Council building

whose home it once was, this
wonderfully ornate house, with
its curved wrought-iron balus-
trades and balconies, is a fine
architectural feat considering
that the man who designed it,
Gustave Strauven, was only
22 years old when it was built
at the turn of the 20th century.

Quartier Européen ⑳

Map 3 B3. 🚌 20, 21, 22, 27, 34,
38, 54, 68, 80, 95, 96. Ⓜ
Maelbeek, Schuman.

The area at the top of the
Rue de la Loi and around the
Schuman roundabout is
where the main buildings
of the European Union's
administration are found.

The most recognizable of
all the EU seats is the tricorn-
shaped Berlaymont building,
which has now reopened
following the removal of large
quantities of asbestos
discovered in its structure.
This is the headquarters of
the European Commission,
whose workers are, in effect,
civil servants of the EU. The
Council of Ministers, which
comprises representatives of
member-states' governments,
now meets in the sprawling
pink granite block across the
road from the Berlaymont.
This building is known
as Justus Lipsius, after a
Flemish philosopher.

Further down the road from
the Justus Lipsius building is
the Résidence Palace, a luxury
1920s housing complex that
boasts a theatre, a pool and
a roof garden as well as
several floors of private flats.
It now houses the
International

Press Centre. Only the theatre
is open to the public, but
EU officials have access to the
Art Deco pool.

This whole area is naturally
full of life and bustle during
the day, but much quieter
in the evenings and can feel
almost deserted at weekends.
What is pleasant at any
time, though, is the proximity
of a number of the city's
wonderful green spaces,
which include Parc du
Cinquantenaire (*see pp 74–5*),
Parc Léopold and the
verdant Square Ambiorix.

Paintings and sculpture on show
in the Musée Wiertz gallery

Musée Wiertz ㉑

Rue Vautier 62, 1000 BRU. **Map** 3
A4. **Tel** *(02) 648 1718.* 🚌 *21, 22,
27, 34, 38, 54, 59, 60, 80, 95, 96.*
Ⓜ *Maelbeek, Schuman, Trone.*
◯ *10am–noon, 1–5pm Tue–Sun.*
⬤ *Mon, weekends Jul–Aug,
public hols.*

Musée Wiertz houses some
160 works, including oil
paintings, drawings and sculptures, that form the main body
of Antoine Wiertz's (1806–65)
artistic output. The collection
fills the studio built for Wiertz
by the Belgian state, where
he lived and worked from 1850
until his death in 1865, when
the studio became a museum.

The huge main room con-
tains Wiertz's largest paintings,
many depicting biblical and
Homeric scenes, some in the
style of Rubens. Also on
display are sculptures and his
death mask. The last of the
six rooms contains his more
gruesome efforts, one entitled
Madness, Hunger and Crime.

A tall European parliament building rising up behind the trees of Parc Léopold in the Parliament Quarter

Parliament Quarter ㉒

Map 3 A4. 🚌 21, 22, 27, 34, 38, 54, 60, 80, 95, 96. Ⓜ Maelbeek, Schuman.

The vast, modern, steel-and-glass complex, situated just behind Quartier Léopold train station, is one of three homes of the European Parliament, the elected body of the EU. Its permanent seat is in Strasbourg, France, where the plenary sessions are held once a month. The administrative centre is in Luxembourg and the committee meetings are held in Brussels.

This gleaming state-of-the-art building has many admirers, not least the parliamentary workers and MEPs themselves. But it also has its critics: the huge domed structure housing the hemicycle that seats the 700-plus MEPs has been dubbed the *"caprice des dieux"* ("whim of the gods"), which refers both to the shape of the building which is similar to a French cheese of the same name, and to its lofty aspirations. Many people also regret that, to make room for the new complex, a large part of Quartier Léopold has been lost. Though there are still plenty of restaurants and bars, a lot of the charm has gone. When the MEPs are absent, the building is often used for meetings of European Union committees.

Institut Royal des Sciences Naturelles ㉓

Rue Vautier 29, 1000 BRU. **Map** 3 A4. **Tel** (02) 627 4238. 🚌 20, 21, 22, 34, 38, 54, 59, 60, 80, 95, 96. Ⓜ Maelbeek, Schuman, Trône. ◯ 9:30am–4:45pm Tue–Fri, 10am–6pm Sat & Sun. ⬤ Mon, 1 Jan, 1 May, 24, 25 & 31 Dec. 🅿🎫♿🖥🖨 **www**.sciencesnaturelles.be

The Institut Royal des Sciences Naturelles is best known for its fine collection of iguanadon skeletons dating back 250 million years. The museum also contains interactive and educational displays covering all eras of natural history.

Parc Léopold ㉔

Rue Belliard. **Map** 3 B4. 🚌 20, 27, 59, 80. Ⓜ Maelbeek, Schuman.

Parc Léopold occupies part of the grounds of an old estate and a walk around its lake follows the old path of the Maelbeek river which was covered over in the 19th-century for reasons of hygiene.

At the end of the 19th century, scientist and industrialist Ernest Solvay put forward the idea of a science park development. Solvay was given the Parc Léopold, the site of a zoo since 1847, and set up five university centres here. Leading figures including Marie Curie and Albert Einstein met here to discuss new scientific issues. The park is still home to many scientific institutes, as well as a haven of peace in the heart of this busy political area.

Whale skeleton inside the Institut Royal des Sciences Naturelles

Parc du Cinquantenaire ㉕

Musée de l'Armée gun

The finest of Leopold II's grand projects, the Parc and Palais du Cinquantenaire were built for the Golden Jubilee celebrations of Belgian independence in 1880. The park was laid out on unused town marshes. The palace, at its entrance, was to comprise a triumphal arch and two large exhibition areas, but by the time of the 1880 Art and Industry Expo, only the two side exhibition areas had been completed. Further funds were eventually found, and work continued for 50 years. Before being converted into museums, the large halls on either side of the central archway were used to hold trade fairs, the last of which was in 1935. They have also been used for horse races and to store homing pigeons. During World War II, the grounds of the park were used to grow vegetables to feed the Brussels people.

★ Musée de l'Armée
Opened in 1923, the museum covers all aspects of Belgium's military history, and exhibits over 200 years of militaria. Historic aircraft are on display in the hall next door.

View of Park with Arch
Based on the Arc de Triomphe in Paris, the arch was not completed in time for the 50th Anniversary celebrations but was finished in 1905.

The Grand Mosque was built in Arabic style as a folly in 1880. It became a mosque in 1978.

Tree-lined Avenue
In part formal garden, part forested walks, many of the plantations of elms and plane trees date from 1880.

Pavillon Horta

STAR SIGHTS

★ Musées Royaux d'Art et d'Histoire

★ Musée de l'Armée

Underpass

0 metres	100
0 yards	100

The Central Archway

Conceived as a gateway into the city, the arch is crowned by the symbolic bronze sculpture Brabant Raising the National Flag.

VISITORS' CHECKLIST

Ave de Tervuren, 1040 BRU. **Map** 3 C3. 🚌 21, 22, 27, 28, 36, 61, 80. 🚋 81, 82. **M** Schuman, Mérode. 🚻 🅿 **Autoworld:** (02) 736 4165. ⏰ 10am–5pm (Apr–Sep: to 6pm). ⬤ 1 Jan, 25 Dec. 🎫 🚻 🅿 **Grand Mosque:** (02) 735 2173. ⏰ 9am–4pm Mon–Thu. Please dress with respect.

Autoworld

Housed in the south wing of the Cinquantenaire Palace, Autoworld is one of the best collections of automobiles in the world. There are some 300 cars, including an 1886 motor, and a 1924 Model-T Ford that still runs.

The park is popular with Brussels' Eurocrats and families at lunchtimes and weekends.

★ Musées Royaux d'Art et d'Histoire

Belgian architect Bordiau's plans for the two exhibition halls, later permanent showcases, were partly modelled on London's Victorian museums. The use of iron and glass in their construction was inspired by the Crystal Palace.

Musées Royaux d'Art et d'Histoire

Parc du Cinquantenaire 10. **Tel** *(02) 741 7211.* ⏰ *9:30am–5pm Tue–Sun (from 10am Sat, Sun and public hols).* ⬤ *1 Jan, 1 May, 1 & 11 Nov, 25 Dec.* 🎫

Also known as the Musée du Cinquantenaire, this excellent museum has occupied its present site since the early 1900s, but the history of the collections goes back as far as the 15th century. Sections on ancient civilizations include Egypt and Greece, and also Persia and the Near East. Other displays feature Byzantine and Islam, China and the Indian Subcontinent, and the Pre-Columbian civilizations of the Americas. There are decorative arts from all ages, with glassware, silverware and porcelain as well as a fine collection of lace and tapestries. Religious sculptures and stained glass are displayed around a courtyard in the style of church cloisters.

The aircraft display at the Musée Royal de l'Armée

Musée Royal de l'Armée et d'Histoire Militaire

Parc du Cinquantenaire 3. **Tel** *(02) 737 7811.* ⏰ *9am–noon, 1–4:45pm Tue–Sun.* ⬤ *Mon, 1 Jan, 1 May, 1 Nov, 25 Dec.*

Together with the section on aviation, displays cover the Belgian Army and its history from the late 1700s to today, including weapons, uniforms, decorations and paintings. There is a section covering the 1830 struggle for independence (see p34–5). Two new sections show both World Wars, including the activities of the Resistance.

A 90-Minute Walk Around the Heart of Brussels

It is impossible to tire of the Grand Place, and there is no better place to start a walk that traces the history of the city. The route leads first to the island site where Brussels originated, and follows the watery landscape of the old, walled city before the river and canals disappeared. The walk then passes the opera house where Belgian independence was born *(see p48)*, leads to the cathedral, and then to the grand Galeries Royales de Saint-Hubert. Finally, it meanders through the Îlot Sacré, the web of medieval streets around the Grand Place.

The Grand Place, Brussels' theatrical centrepiece

Grand Place and Place St Géry

You could start with a quick wander around the Grand Place, to savour its magnificent gilded architecture *(see pp42–3)*. The fact that this was once the medieval trading centre is recorded in the names of the streets all around it: Rue des Harengs (herrings), Rue Chair et Pain (meat and bread), and so on. Leave the square on the Rue au Beurre (butter), an appropriate address of the Biscuiterie Dandoy ① at No. 31, famous for its traditional,

TIPS FOR WALKERS

Starting point: *Grand Place*
Length: *3.25 km (2 miles)*
Getting there: *The nearest Metro stop is Bourse; numerous buses also go to the Bourse, and to De Brouckère/Place de la Monnaie a short walk away.*
Stopping off points: *This area is packed with places to eat and drink. The area around Place Ste-Catherine is famous for its fish restaurants. Among the many attractive yet average establishments in the Îlot Sacré, Aux Armes de Bruxelles stands out.*

buttery biscuits. On the opposite side of the road is the atmospheric Église St-Nicholas *(see p47)* ②, while ahead lies the Neo-Classical façade of the Stock Exchange, La Bourse ③. Go left; facing the Bourse on Rue Henri Maus is Falstaff ④, one of the few genuine Art Nouveau cafés in Brussels, dating from 1903. Ahead lies the Boulevard Anspach ⑤; this was once the route of Brussels' river, the Senne, which was canalized and covered over in around 1870. This area was all marshland when Brussels was settled in the 7th century: "Broucsella" meant "settlement in the marshes". The Halles St-Géry *(see p46)*– the old meat market on Place St-Géry ⑥ – is now the hub of a trendy new area of the city; this square was an island until the mid-19th century, and the site of one of Brussels' earliest chapels. The River Senne still runs beneath here; in the courtyard of renovated

apartments at No.23 Place St-Géry ⑦ some of the river can still be seen. Leave the square by the Rue Pont de la Carpe (carp bridge) and turn left at Rue Dansaert. ⑧

Place Ste-Catherine

The Rue du Vieux Marché aux Grains (old grain market) opens up into the Place Ste-Catherine ⑨, with the Eglise Ste-Catherine *(see p53)* ⑩ in its midst. Walk to the right of the church; at the far end, on the right, you

[Map with labels:]
⑬
Ste-Cathérine St-Katelijne Ⓜ
QUAI AUX BRIQUES BAKSTEENKAAI
⑫
R D LAEKEN
PLACE STE-CATHERINE ⑩
⑪
RUE DE BISSCHO
De Br
⑨
RUE ANTOINE DANSAERT STR ⑧
RUE DE LA VIERGE NOIRE ZWARTE LIEVEVROUWSTR
RUE DES HALLES HALLENSTR.
RUE DU MARCHE AUX KIEKEN MARKT
ANSPACHLAAN
Bourse Beurs Ⓜ
⑤
ANSPACH
⑥
⑦
BOULEVARD
④
③ R DU MIDI ZUIDSTR

Ruined, J. DANDOY
31 J. DANDOY
DANDOY biscottes-spéculaus pains à la grecque
MAISON J.DANDOY

Traditional Belgian butter biscuits at Biscuiterie Dandoy ①

will see the Tour Noire (Black Tower) ⑪. This is a rare remnant of the first ring of city walls built to protect Brussels in the 12th century. Loop round the eastern end of the Eglise Ste-Catherine to the broad, open space lined by the Quai au Bois à Brûler (firewood quay) and Quai aux Briques (brick quay) ⑫. The area between them – filled with pools and fountains – was once a canal; it was covered over in 1870, and the fish market was relocated here. This tradition is maintained by the numerous fish restaurants in these streets. The Rue du Peuplier leads to the Eglise St-Jean-Baptiste-au-Béguinage *(see p52)* ⑬; this beautiful Baroque church once stood at the heart of a *béguinage (see p53)* that occupied much of northwest Brussels in medieval times.

Place des Martyrs and La Monnaie

Via the Rue de Laeken, Rue des Hirondelles, and Boulevard Émile Jacqumain, you can reach the Place de Brouckère *(see p52)*. On the opposite side is the Hôtel Métropole *(see p49)* ⑭, one of the city's grandest hotels. From the Boulevard Adolphe Max, turn right to walk through the Passage du Nord ⑮, a shopping arcade built in 1882. At the end lies Rue Neuve *(see p49)* ⑯, one of Brussels' main shopping streets. From here the Rue St-Michel leads to the Place des Martyrs ⑰. In the middle of this quiet square is a marble statue of "Belga", under which is a mausoleum for the 450 "martyrs" killed in the 1830 Revolution that secured Belgium its independence. The building on the north of the square, decked with Flemish flags, is the seat of the Flemish government ⑱. Retrace your steps, then continue to the Place de la Monnaie ⑲. Named after the mint that once stood here, it is now the site of the fine Neo-Classical opera house, the Théâtre Royal de la Monnaie *(see p48)* ⑳.

The Îlot Sacré

By walking some 200 m (220 yd) along the Rue de l'Écuyer, you come to the

The entrance to the Hôtel Métropole, one of Brussels' oldest Art Nouveau hotels ⑭

Marionettes de Toone puppet ㉔

northern entrance of the Galeries St-Hubert *(see p47)* ㉑, a magnificent shopping arcade built in 1847. Walk through the arcade to the point, halfway along, where it is intersected by the pedestrianized Rue des Bouchers ㉒, the "butchers street" lined with colourful restaurants. You are now in the Îlot Sacré, a term that dates back to 1960 when this area was decreed a "sacred island" to be protected from development. Take the second left, the Petite Rue des Bouchers ㉓; halfway down, on the left-hand side, is an alley called the Impasse

Galeries St-Hubert, continental Europe's oldest shopping arcade ㉑

Schuddeveld, at the end of which is the Théâtre Marionettes de Toone *(see p48)* ㉔, the famous and historic puppet theatre. By continuing along the Petite Rue des Bouchers and the Rue Chair et Pain, you will return to the Grand Place.

KOOLSTR.

R AUX CHOUX

BLVD ADOLPHE MAX LAAN

RUE ST MICHEL ST MICHIELSTRAAT

⑱

⑮

⑰

⑯

PLACE DES MARTYRS MARTELAARS PLEIN

⑭
DE KERE IN

UE DU FOSSE

RUE NEUVE NIEUW STR

RUE D'ARGENT ZILVERSTR

AUX LOUPS WOLVENGRACHT

⑲

PLACE DE LA MONNAIE

⑳

RUE DE L'ECUYER SCHILDKNAAPSSTR

RUE D'ARENBERG ARENBERGSTR

⑭

㉒

㉓

R D BOUCHERS BEENHOUWER STRAAT

RUE DE LA MONTAGNE BERGSTRAAT

R D MARCHE
ND
ICE
OTE
RKT
AUX HERBES GRAS-MARKT

0 metres 100

0 yards 100

KEY

• • • Walk Route

Ⓜ Metro station

A 90-Minute Walk in the Sablons and Coudenberg

Brussels was historically divided into an Upper and Lower Town. The Upper Town, on the Coudenberg ("Cold Hill"), was the royal quarter, the site of a palace destroyed by fire in 1731. This walk climbs gently from the Grand Place in the Lower Town, past remnants of the old city walls and the working-class Marolles district, before entering the chic area of Sablon. On the Coudenberg, the route passes the elegant 18th-century palace of Charles of Lorraine before descending to Brussels' cathedral and returning to the Grand Place.

Cafés and restaurants in the Grand Place, or Grote Markt

Manneken Pis and the Marolles

Leave the Grand Place via the Rue Charles Buls, named after a Burgomaster of the 1890s who did much to preserve the historic face of Brussels. At the first crossroad is the Hôtel Amigo ①, on the site of a prison named the Amigo by the 16th-century rulers of the Spanish Netherlands. Opposite, on the wall of Rue des Brasseurs 1, is a plaque ② marking the hotel where, in 1873, the French poet Paul Verlaine shot fellow poet Arthur Rimbaud at the end of their affair. The next street, the Rue de la Violette, contains the lace museum, the Musée

du Costume et de la Dentelle (see p44) ③. Continue along Rue de l'Étuve ④, Athe site of a public bathhouse in the Middle Ages. At the corner with the Rue du Chêne is the famous statue of the Manneken Pis (see pp44–5) ⑤. Take the Rue du Chêne, then the Rue de Villers to reach the Tour de Villers ⑥, the remains of a tower and section of the 12th-century city walls. Across Boulevard de l'Empereur is the church of Notre-Dame de la Chapelle (see p46) ⑦, with its black bell tower. Rue Blaes and Rue Haute lead off to the south into the Quartier Marolles (see p46). If you

walk along Rue Haute to the north, you reach the Tour d'Angle (or Tour d'Anneessens) ⑧, another remnant of the old city walls.

The Sablon

Walk up the picturesque Rue de Rollebeek ⑨. At the top, take a look down Rue Joseph Stevens to where the Maison du Peuple ⑩ once stood on the Place E. Vandervelde. Built for the Société Coopérative, it was one of Victor Horta's great Art Nouveau masterpieces, but it was demolished in 1965. The sloping triangular space nearby is the Place du Grand Sablon (see p68) ⑪.

Musee du Costume et de la Dentelle ③

High-quality patisseries at renowned chocolatiers Wittamer ⑬

The Musées Royaux de Beaux-Arts ⑱

The fountain of Minerva ⑫, in the middle of the square, was erected in 1751 with funds from Thomas Bruce, an exiled friend of King James II of England. The Sablon still retains an upmarket air, and it is home to Wittamer ⑬, one of Brussels' most celebrated chocolate makers (shop and small café at No.12; café at No.6).

At Rue des Sablons 11 is a branch of Le Pain Quotidien ⑭, famed for its bread and pastries. At the upper end of the Place du Grand Sablon is the beautiful Notre-Dame du Sablon (see p68) ⑮. On the Rue de la Régence, look right for a view of the Palais de Justice (see p69) ⑯. Directly opposite you is the Place du Petit Sablon (see pp68–9) ⑰, a pretty garden with statues of medieval guildsmen.

Place Royale and cathedral
Heading north along the Rue de la Régence, you reach the Musées Royaux des Beaux-Arts (see pp62–7) ⑱, the city's most important art gallery. Beyond lies the Place Royale (see p59) on the top of the Coudenberg, the site of royal palaces since medieval times. The present royal palace is just around the corner (see pp57–9), and is directly connected to the Eglise St-Jacques-sur-

Coudenberg (see pp58–9) ⑲. On the opposite side of the square is the Musée Instrumental (see pp60–1) ⑳. Leave the Place Royale by the cobbled Rue du Musée, which leads to the Palais de Charles de Lorraine (see p61) ㉑. The Protestant Chapelle Royale ㉒, to the right, was where King Léopold I worshipped, as did Charlotte Brontë when she taught at a local school in the 1840s. At the top of Rue Ravenstein is the 15th-century Hôtel Ravenstein (see p60) ㉓, birthplace of Anne of Cleves. You can see the spire of the Hôtel de Ville (in the Grand Place) over the gardens on the Mont des Arts to the northeast. The modern building to the left of the gardens is the Bibliothèque Royale Albert I ㉔, the national library. Walk through the gardens to the equestrian statue of Albert I (reigned 1909–34) ㉕, the "Soldier King" revered for leading Belgian troops in World War I. The arch at the lower end of the street called Mont des Arts has a carillon clock ㉖ on the side facing up the hill that includes figures from Belgian history that move on the hour. From here, a walk of 400 m (437 yd) leads to the Cathédrale Sts Michel et Gudule (see pp70–1) ㉗. On the route back to the Grand Place, stop in the Place Agora to admire Burgomaster Charles Buls and his dog, portrayed in a charming bronze statue ㉘.

The modern carillion clock on the arch in the Mont des Arts ㉖

KEY

• • • Walk Route

Ⓜ Metro station

0 metres   100

0 yards   100

GREATER BRUSSELS

Detail from annexe of Chinese Pavilion, Laeken

Past the heart-shaped ring-road of Brussels city centre lie 19 suburbs *(communes)* which form the Bruxelles-Capitale region. While many are residential, a handful are definitely worth the short ride to sample outlying treasures of Brussels' fascinating history. For fans of early 20th-century architecture, the suburb of St-Gilles offers numerous original examples of striking Art Nouveau buildings including Musée Horta. In Koekelberg and visible from the Upper Town is the huge Sacré-Coeur basilica, started in 1904. To the north, Heysel offers attractions whose modernity contrasts with the historical city centre. The 1958 Atomium, now restored, stands next to the Bruparck theme park. To the east, the Central Africa Museum reflects Belgium's colonial past in the Congo, and the tram museum takes a journey through Brussels' urban past. Peace and tranquillity can be found close to the metropolis, in the orderly landscape of Royal Laeken and the lush green spaces of the Bois de la Cambre and the Fôret de Soignes.

SIGHTS AT A GLANCE

Churches and Cathedrals
Basilique Nationale du
  Sacré-Coeur **8**

Historic Monuments, Buildings and Districts
Anderlecht **7**
Avenue Louise **2**
Ixelles **4**
St-Gilles **3**
Uccle **6**

Parks and Gardens
Bruparck **13**
Domaine de Laeken
  see pp86–7 **11**
Fôret de Soignes **5**

Museums and Exhibition Areas
The Atomium **12**
Musée Horta see p82 **1**
Musée du Tram **9**

Musée Royal de
  l'Afrique Centrale **10**

KEY

▢	Central Brussels
▢	Greater Brussels
✈	Airport
▬	Major Road
▬	Minor Road

◁ **The Atomium towering over Mini-Europe in the Bruparck**

Musée Horta ❶

Art Nouveau candelabra

Architect Victor Horta (1861–1947) is considered by many to be the father of Art Nouveau, and his impact on Brussels architecture is unrivalled by any other designer of his time. A museum dedicated to his unique style is today housed in his restored family home, which he designed from 1898 to 1901. His skill lay not only in his grand, overall vision but in his equal talent as an interior designer, blending themes and materials into each detail. The airy interior of the building displays trademarks of the architect's style – iron, glass and curves – in every detail, while retaining a functional approach.

VISITORS' CHECKLIST

Rue Américaine 25, 1060 BRU. *Tel* (02) 543 0490. ▣ 54. ▤ 81, 82, 91, 92. Ⓜ Albert, Louise. ⏱ 2–5:30pm Tue–Sun. ● Mon, public hols. 🖼 **www**.hortamuseum.be

★ Central Staircase
Decorated with curved wrought iron, the stairs are enhanced further by mirrors and glass, bringing natural light into the house.

The bedroom features Art Nouveau furniture, including a wardrobe inlaid with pale and dark wood.

★ Dining Room
White enamel tiles line the walls, rising to an ornate ceiling, decorated with the scrolled metalwork used in other rooms.

Madame Horta's sitting-room features blue-and-cream wool rugs woven to Horta's design, and a marble fireplace.

Front Entrance

STAR FEATURES

★ Central Staircase

★ Dining Room

Living Room
The detail of Horta's work can be best seen here, from sculpted bannister ends to finely wrought door handles that echo larger forms.

Exclusive boutique in the chic Avenue Louise

Avenue Louise ❷

Map 2 D5. 🚌 *34, 54.* 🚊 *81, 82, 93, 94.* Ⓜ *Louise.*

Most visitors to Brussels travelling by car will come across this busy thoroughfare, its various underpasses constructed in the 1950s and 1960s to link up the city centre with its suburbs. In fact, the avenue was constructed in 1864 to join the centre with the suburb of Ixelles. However, the north end of the avenue retains a fine chic atmosphere; by the Porte de Namur, fans of designer labels can indulge themselves in Gucci and Versace, as well as investigating the less expensive but no less chic boutiques.

The avenue also has its architectural treasures. The **Hôtel Solvay** at No. 224 was built by Victor Horta in 1894 for the industrialist Solvay family. Its ornate doorway, columns and balconies are a fine example of Art Nouveau style *(see pp18–19)*. The house is still a private home. At No. 346, **Hôtel Max Hallet** is one of Horta's masterpieces, built in 1903. Continuing south leads to the peaceful atmosphere of Ixelles and its parkland.

St-Gilles ❸

🚌 *20, 48.* 🚊 *23, 55, 81, 82, 90.* Ⓜ *Porte de Hal, Parvis St-Gilles.*

Named after the patron saint of this district's main church, St-Gilles is traditionally one of Brussels' poorer areas. However, amid the low-quality functional housing are architectural survivors which make the suburb well worth a visit. Art Nouveau and *sgraffiti* gems *(see p19)* can be found in streets such as Avenue Jean Volders and Rue Vanderschrick. The **Hôtel Hannon** (1902), now a photography gallery, remains one of the city's most spectacular Art Nouveau structures. Restored in 1985, it has a stained-glass window and ornate statuary that take this architectural style to its peak *(see p18)*.

Art Nouveau details can be seen in the nearby streets, particularly in Rue Felix Delhasse and in the nearby Rue Africaine.

One of the most striking features of St-Gilles is the **Porte de Hal**. Brussels' second set of town walls, built in the 14th century, originally included seven gateways, of which Porte de Hal is the only survivor *(see p14)*. Used as a prison from the 16th to 18th centuries, it was restored in 1870. Today it houses a small small museum of folk art, including a collection of 19th-century toys.

Art Nouveau detail on façade in Rue Africaine

🚇 Hôtel Hannon
Ave de la Jonction 1, BRU 1060. **Tel** *(02) 538 4220.* Ⓜ *Albert.*

🏛 Porte de Hal
Blvds du Midi & de Waterloo, BRU 1000. **Tel** *(02) 534 1518.* 🚌 *20, 48.* 🚊 *3, 55, 90.* Ⓜ *Porte de Hal.*
🕐 *10am–4:45pm Tue–Sun.* 📷 ♿

Ixelles ❹

🚌 *54, 71, 95, 96.* 🚊 *23, 81, 82, 90, 93, 94.* Ⓜ *Porte de Namur.*

Although one of Brussels' largest suburbs and a busy transport junction, the heart of Ixelles remains a peaceful oasis of lakes and woodland.

The idyllic **Abbaye de la Cambre** was founded in 1201, achieving fame and a degree of fortune in 1242, when Saint Boniface chose the site for his retirement. The abbey then endured a troubled history in the wars of religion during the 16th and 17th centuries. It finally closed as an operational abbey in 1796 and now houses a school of architecture. The abbey's pretty Gothic church can be toured and its grassy grounds and courtyards offer a peaceful walk.

South of the abbey, the Bois de la Cambre remains one of the city's most popular public parks. Created in 1860, it achieved popularity almost immediately when royalty promenaded its main route. Lakes, bridges and lush grass make it a favoured picnic site.

The **Musée Communal d'Ixelles** nearby has a fine collection of posters by 19th- and 20th-century greats, such as Toulouse Lautrec and Magritte, as well as sculptures by Rodin. The former home of one of Belgium's finest sculptors is now **Musée Constantin Meunier**, with 170 sculptures and 120 paintings by the artist, and his studio preserved in its turn-of-the-century style.

🚇 Abbaye de la Cambre
Ave de Général de Gaulle, BRU 1050. **Tel** *(02) 648 1121.* 🕐 *7:15am–noon, 3–6pm daily.* 🔒 *public hols.*

🏛 Musée Communal d'Ixelles
Rue J Van Volsem 71, BRU 1050. **Tel** *(02) 515 6421.* 🕐 *1–6:30pm Tue–Fri, 10am–5pm Sat–Sun.* 🔒 *Mon, public hols.* ♿

🏛 Musée Constantin Meunier
Rue de l'Abbaye 59, BRU 1050. **Tel** *(02) 648 4449.* 🕐 *10am–noon, 1–5pm Tue–Sun.* 🔒 *Mon, public hols.*

The Forêt de Soignes, once a royal hunting ground and now a park

Forêt de Soignes **⑤**

🚌 *71, 72.* 🚋 *23, 90.* Ⓜ *Demey, Hermann Debroux.* 🔲 *for members only* **Tel** *(02) 215 1740.*

The large forested area to the southeast of Brussels' city centre has a long history: thought to have had prehistoric beginnings, it was also here that the Gallic citizens suffered their defeat by the Romans (*see p29*). However, the forest really gained renown in the 12th century when wild boar roamed the landscape, and local dukes enjoyed hunting trips in the woodland.

The density of the landscape has provided tranquillity over the ages. In the 14th and 15th centuries it became a favoured location for monasteries and abbeys. Few have survived, but Abbaye de Rouge-Cloître is a rare example from this era.

In a former 18th-century priory is the **Groenendaal Arboretum**, in which more than 400 forest plants are housed, many of which are extinct elsewhere. The most common sight, however, is the locals enjoying a stroll.

🏞 **Groenendaal Arboretum**
Duboislaan 14, 1560 BRU.
Tel *(02) 657 2203.*
🕗 *8:30am–5pm, Mon–Fri.*

Uccle **⑥**

🚌 *49, 50, 60.* 🚋 *18, 23, 52, 90.*

Uccle is a smart residential district, nestling in its tree-lined avenues. Not immediately a tourist destination, it is worthwhile taking a trip to the **Musée David et Alice van Buuren**. The 1920s residence of this Dutch couple is now a small museum, displaying their eclectic acquisitions. Amid the Dutch Delftware and French Lalique lamps are great finds, such as original sketches by Van Gogh. Visitors will also enjoy the modern landscaped gardens at the rear.

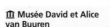

Mirò-style drawings, Anderlecht

🏛 **Musée David et Alice van Buuren**
Ave Léo Errera 41, 1180 BRU. **Tel** *(02) 343 4851.* 🕗 *2–5:30pm Wed–Mon.* ⚫ *Tue, 25 Dec, 1 Jan.* 📷

Anderlecht **⑦**

🚌 *46, 49, 63, 89.* 🚋 *56, 82.* Ⓜ *Bizet, Clemenceau, St-Guidon.*

Considered to be Brussels' first genuine suburb (archaeological digs have uncovered remnants of Roman housing), Anderlecht is now best known as an industrial area, for its meat market, and its successful football club of the same name. Despite this, the Modernist Spanish painter Joan Mirò added a unique artistic contribution inspiring bright cartoon-like murals on Rue Porcelaine.

Although only a few pockets of the suburb are now residential, during the 15th century this was a popular place of abode and some houses remain from that era. **Maison d'Erasme**, built in 1468, is now named after the great scholar and religious reformer, Erasmus (1466–1536), who lived here for five months in 1521. The house was restored in the 1930s. Now a museum dedicated to the most respected thinker of his generation, it displays a collection of 16th-century furniture and portraits of the great humanist by Holbein and van der Weyden.

Nearby is the huge edifice of **Eglise Sts-Pierre-et-Guidon**. This 14th-century Gothic church, completed with the addition of a tower in 1517, is notable for its sheer size and exterior gables, typical of Brabant architecture. The life of St Guidon, patron saint of peasants, is depicted on interior wall murals.

Illustrating a more recent history, the **Musée Gueuze** is al family brewery that has opened its doors to the public to witness the production of classic Belgian beers.

Maison Erasme in Anderlecht, with its courtyard and fountain

The Basilique Nationale du Sacré-Coeur rising over the city

🏛 **Maison d'Érasme**
Rue du Chapitre 31, 1070 BRU.
Tel (02) 521 1383. ⬜ 10am–5pm
Tue–Sun. ● Mon, 1 Jan, 31 Dec. ♿

🔒 **Eglise Sts-Pierre-et-Guidon**
Place de la Vaillance, 1070 BRU.
⬜ 2–5pm Mon–Fri. ● Sat & Sun.

🏛 **Musée Gueuze**
Rue Gheude 56, 1070 BRU. **Tel** (02)
521 4928. ⬜ 8:30am–5pm Mon–
Fri, 10am–5pm Sat. ● Sun, public
hols. ♿ including 1 free beer.

Basilique Nationale du Sacré-Coeur ❽

Parvis de la Basilique 1, Koekelberg,
1083 BRU. **Tel** (02) 425 8822.
Ⓜ Simonis. 🚌 49, 87. ⬜ 19.
⬜ 9am–6pm daily. Dome: 10am–
5pm May–Oct. ♿ for dome. 📷 by
appointment.

Although a small and popular suburb among Brussels' residents, there is little for the visitor to see in Koekelberg other than the striking Basilique Nationale du Sacré-Coeur, but this does make the journey worthwhile for those interested in Art Deco.

King Léopold II was keen to build a church in the city which could accommodate vast congregations to reflect the burgeoning population of early 20th-century Brussels. He commissioned the church in 1904, although the building was not finished until 1970. Originally designed by Pierre Langerock, the final construction, which uses sandstone and terracotta, was the less expensive adaptation by Albert van Huffel. Very much a 20th-century church, in contrast to the many medieval religious buildings in the city centre, it is dedicated to those who died for Belgium, in particular the thousands of Belgian soldiers who were never to return from the two world wars, killed in battles fought on their own terrain.

The most dominating feature of the church is the vast green copper dome, rising 90 m (295 ft) above ground. For those who do not manage to visit the church itself, it is this central dome that is visible from many points in the city, including the Palais de Justice.

Musée du Tram ❾

Ave de Tervuren 364b, BRU 1150. **Tel**
(02) 515 3108. 🚋 39, 44. ⬜ Apr–
Sep: 1:30pm–7pm Sat & Sun, pub hols.
Group tours possible. Every Sun and
pub hol, the museum organizes a tour
to Heysel (9:45am). ● Oct–Mar. ♿

This museum traces the history of public transport in Belgium, with marvellous displays of heritage machinery. Horse-drawn trams are available to transport visitors round the site, which features fully-working early versions of the electric tram, buses and plenty of interactive exhibits.

Musée Royal de l'Afrique Centrale ❿

Leuvensesteenweg 13, Tervuren
3080. **Tel** (02) 769 5211. 🚌 44.
⬜ 10am–5pm Tue–Fri, 10am–6pm
Sat & Sun. ● Mon, public hols. ♿
www.africamuseum.be

In the 19th century, the colony of the Belgian Congo was Belgium's only territorial possession. It was handed back to self-government in 1960 and eventually renamed Zaire (now the Democratic Republic of Congo). This museum, opened in 1899, is a collection gleaned from over 100 years of colonial rule. Galleries show ceremonial African dress and masks, and displays on colonial life.

Dugout canoes, pagan idols, weapons and stuffed wildlife, feature heavily. There is a horrifying collection of conserved giant African insects, much beloved by children. A revamp is planned by 2010, so exhibits are liable to move.

The Musée Royal de l'Afrique Centrale façade in Tervuren

Domaine de Laeken ⑪

In the 11th century Laeken became popular among pilgrims after reported sightings of the Virgin Mary. Since the 19th century, however, it has been firmly etched in the minds of all Belgians as the residence of the nation's monarchy. A walk around the sedate and peaceful area reveals impressive buildings constructed in honour of the royal location, not least the sovereign's official residence and its beautifully landscaped parkland. More surprising is the sudden Oriental influence. The great builder, King Léopold II, wanted to create an architectural world tour; the Chinese and Japanese towers are the only two buildings that came to fruition, but show the scope of one monarch's vision.

★ **Pavillon Chinois**
Architect Alexandre Marcel designed this elaborate building (built 1901–09) that houses Oriental porcelain.

Tour Japonais

Parc Royal

Villa Belvedere was once the residence of the Royal Family, and is now home to the king and queen.

Monument Léopold stands as the focus of the park complex and layout. It honours Léopold I, first king of the Belgians. Built in Neo-Gothic style, it has a filigree cast-iron canopy and tracery around the base.

Place de la Dynastie is part of the attractive park that was once the Royal Family's private hunting ground.

Château Royal
The Belgian royal residence, in the heart of the 160-ha (395-acre) estate, was heavily restored in 1890, with a façade by architect Poelaert covering the 18th-century original.

★ **Serres Royales**
These late 19th-century glasshouses are home to exotic trees, palms and camellias. Open to the public annually in April, they are the King's private property.

VISITORS' CHECKLIST

Laeken, 1020 BRU. 🚌 *53, 84, 89.* 🚊 *19, 23, 81, 94.* Ⓜ *Heysel.* **Château Royal** *Ave du Parc Royal.* 🚫 *to public.* **Serres Royales** *Ave de Prince Royal.* **Tel** *(02) 551 2020.* ⬜ *mid-Apr–mid-May (phone for details).* 🎟 *evenings only.* **Pavillon Chinois** *Ave J van Praet 44.* **Tel** *(02) 268 1608.* ⬜ *10am– 5pm Tue–Sun.* 🎟 **Tour Japonais** *Avenue J van Praet 44.* **Tel** *(02) 268 1608.* ⬜ *10am–5pm Tue–Sun.* 🎟 **Eglise Notre Dame de Laeken** *Paris Notre Dame.* **Tel** *(02) 479 2362.* ⬜ *2–5pm Tue–Sun.*

Domaine Royale de Laeken is the royal estate, adjacent to the Parc de Laeken in the city district of Laeken; the woodland features old magnolias and blooming hawthorns.

The Atomium rising 100 m (325 ft) over the Bruparck at dusk

The Atomium ⑫

Boulevard du Centenaire, 1020 BRU. **Tel** *(02) 475 4777.* 🚌 *84, 89.* 🚊 *23, 81.* Ⓜ *Heysel.* ⬜ *10am–6pm daily.* 🎟 🍴 www.atomium.be

Built for the 1958 World Fair *(see p37),* the Atomium is probably the most identifiable symbol of Brussels. As the world moved into a new age of science and space travel at the end of the 1950s, so the design by André Waterkeyn reflected this with a structure of an iron atom, magnified 165 billion times. Each of the nine spheres that make up the "atom" are 18 m (60 ft) in diameter, and linked by escalators. They include exhibition rooms and a smart restaurant at the top of the structure.

Bruparck ⑬

Boulevard du Centenaire, 1020 BRU. **Tel** *(02) 474 8377.* 🚌 *84, 89.* 🚊 *23, 81.* Ⓜ *Heysel.* **Mini-Europe & Océade Tel** *(02) 474 1313 (Mini-Europe); (02) 478 4320 (Océade).* ⬜ *Apr–Sep: 9:30am–6pm daily (Jul–Aug: to 8pm); Oct–mid-Jan: 10am–6pm daily.* ⬛ *end Jan–Mar.* 🎟 **Kinepolis Tel** *(02) 474 2600.* ⬜ *performances.* 🎟 *for films.* 🍴 www.minieurope.be

Although nowhere near as large or as grand as many of the world's theme parks, Bruparck's sights and facilities are a popular family destination.

The first and favourite port of call for most visitors is Mini-

Europe, where more than 300 miniature reconstructions take you around the landscapes of the European Union. Built at a scale of 1:25, the collection displays buildings of social or cultural importance, such as the Acropolis in Athens, the Brandenburg Gate of Berlin and the Houses of Parliament from London. Even at this scale the detail is such that it can be second only to visiting the sights themselves.

For film fans, Kinepolis cannot be beaten. Large auditoriums show a range of popular films from different countries on 29 screens. The IMAX cinema features surround sound and a semi-circular 600 sq m (6,456 sq ft) widescreen.

If warmth and relaxation are what you are looking for, Océade is a tropically heated water park, complete with giant slides, wave machines, bars, cafés and even realistic re-created sandy beaches.

London's Houses of Parliament in small scale at Mini-Europe

STAR SIGHTS

★ Serres Royales

★ Pavillon Chinois

0 metres 250

0 yards 250

BEYOND
BRUSSELS

BEYOND BRUSSELS

*B**russels is at the heart not only of Belgium, but also of Europe. The city marks the divide between the Flemish north and the French-speaking Walloon south. Its central position makes Brussels an ideal base for visitors: within easy reach are the ancient Flemish towns of Antwerp, Ghent and Bruges, each with their exquisite medieval architecture, superb museums and excellent restaurants.*

Although Belgium is a small country, it has one of the highest population densities in Europe. An incredibly efficient road and rail network also means that large numbers of people move around the country every day, with around half the population employed in industry, particularly in textiles, metallurgy and chemicals. Despite this, parts of Belgium are still farmed. Stretching south from the defences of the North Sea is the plain of Flanders, a low-lying area which, like the Netherlands, has reclaimed land or *polders*, whose fertile soil is intensively cultivated with wheat and sugar beet. Bordering the Netherlands is the Kempenland, a sparsely populated area of peat moors, which in the 19th century was mined for coal.

There are small farms here today which cultivate mainly oats, rye and potatoes. Northeast Belgium also contains the large port of Antwerp, a major centre of European industry, with its ship-building yards and car factories. The towns of Leuven, Lier and Mechelen are noted for their medieval town centres. Ghent has an elegant grandeur and Bruges has superb medieval buildings and excellent museums.

Brussels itself is surrounded by both Flemish and Walloon Brabant, a fertile region famous for its wheat and beet farms and pasture for cows. Just a few kilometres south of the capital is Waterloo, the most visited battlefield in the world, where Napoleon was defeated by Wellington in 1815.

Visitors sail under the Blinde Ezelstraat Bridge on a tour of Bruges

◁ The Brabo Fountain in Antwerp's Grote Markt

Exploring Beyond Brussels

Belgium occupies one of the most densely populated parts of Europe, with a concentration of towns and villages across the flat landscapes of the Flemish plain. Along the North Sea coast there are fewer settlements, set among fertile farmland. To the north and west of Brussels are the three easy-to-reach towns of Antwerp, Ghent and Bruges which, with their ancient buildings and vibrant cultural life, are attractive destinations. East of Brussels is the charming university town of Leuven, and to the south of the city is the site of Napoleon's defeat at the hands of the British army at Waterloo.

Bronze statue of Silvius Brabo in Antwerp's Grote Markt

SEE ALSO

- *Where to Stay* pp132–43
- *Where to Eat* pp144–67

KEY

══	Motorway
━	Major road
┅	Minor road
┅	Main railway
━	Minor railway
▨	International border
═	Province border

View over Bruges from the Belfort

GETTING AROUND

In Belgium distances are short, with a wide choice of routes – even the tiniest village is easily reached. Brussels sits at the hub of several major highways such as the A10 and the A1 (which link the capital to the country's principal towns). The fully integrated public transport system has frequent train services and a comprehensive bus network.

The imposing walls of Ghent's Het Gravensteen

Antwerp ❶

Antwerp is Belgium's second city and the largest city in Flanders, and it has one of Europe's busiest ports (its docks situated well to the north of the centre). Beginning as a settlement on the banks of the River Scheldt in the 2nd century, Antwerp became part of the Duchy of Brabant in 1106, and its main port. Within 200 years it was a thriving hub of the European cloth industry. But its golden age came during the era of Spanish rule (see p31), when it was illuminated by the artistic genius of its most famous son, Pieter Paul Rubens (1577–1640). Today, mirroring this vigorous mercantile and cultural past, Antwerp is undergoing a spirited regeneration, seen in its widespread programme of rebuilding and renovation, and in its reputation as a key European source of cutting-edge fashion design.

Carvings above the cathedral door depicting the Last Judgement

Visitors touring Antwerp on an historic horse-drawn bus

Getting Around

The best way to get around Antwerp is by using the public transport system. The excellent bus and tram network is focused on Centraal Station, where most visitors arrive. Fast and frequent trams and buses travel from here to the centre. Most of the city's main sights are within walking distance of the Grote Markt.

🚩 Grote Markt

Grote Markt. **Tel** (03) 232 0103 (tourist office). ♿
Antwerp's central square, or Grote Markt, is flanked by the ornately gabled Stadhuis (town hall), which was completed in 1564 by the architect and sculptor Cornelis Floris. The square's north side has a series of guildhouses, each of which is decorated with gilded figures. The tallest of these is the House of the Cross-bowmen at number seven, on top of which is a statue of St George and the dragon. The central Brabo fountain is one of Antwerp's noted landmarks.

KEY

🟫 Street-by-Street pp96–7

0 metres   400
0 yards   400

Key to Symbols see back flap

Fresco paintings of the dukes of Brabant in the Stadhuis, Grote Markt

Onze Lieve Vrouwe Kathedraal

Groenplaats 21 or Handschoenmarkt. **Tel** (03) 213 9951. ◯ 10am–5pm Mon–Fri, 10am–3pm Sat, 1–4pm Sun.

The building of Antwerp's Onze Lieve Vrouwe Kathedraal (Cathedral of Our Lady) took almost two centuries, from 1352 to 1521. This magnificent structure has a graceful tiered spire that rises 123 m (404 ft) above the winding streets of the medieval city centre. Inside, the impression of light and space owes much to its seven-aisled nave and vaulted ceiling. The collection of paintings and sculpture includes three works by Rubens, of which two are trip-tychs – the *Raising of the Cross* (1610) and the *Descent from the Cross* (1612).

SIGHTS AT A GLANCE

Etnografisch Museum

Suikerrui 19. **Tel** (03) 220 86 00. ◯ 10am–5pm Tue–Sun, Easter Monday. ● Mon, 1 & 2 Jan, 1 May, Ascension, 1 & 2 Nov, 25 & 26 Dec. ◯ http://museum.antwerpen.be/etnografisch_museum

The huge range of ethnographic artifacts in this delightful and intriguing museum includes Brazilian headdresses, Indian sculpture, pre-Columbian American pottery, Japanese paintings, New Guinea drums, a Maori war canoe, and numerous pieces from the Belgian Congo. Begun in 1864 and now comprising 33,000 objects, it serves as a reminder that – through trade and empire – Antwerp has historic links that spanned the world.

Vleeshuis

Vleeshouwersstraat 38–40. **Tel** (03) 233 6404. ◯ 10am–5pm Tue–Sun, Easter Mon. ● Mon, 1 & 2 Jan, 1 May, Ascension, 1 & 2 Nov, 25 & 26 Dec.

There has been a Vleeshuis (Meat Hall) on this site since 1250, but the existing hall was completed in 1504 to a design by architect Herman de Waghemakere. The structure features slender towers with five hexagonal turrets and rising gables, all built in alternate strips of stone and brick – giving the building a streaky bacon-like appearance.

The fine Gothic interior has been renovated to create a museum called "City Sounds", presenting 500 years of Antwerp's musical life.

Museum Aan De Stroom (MAS)

Hanzestedenplaats. **Tel** (03) 206 0940 (for enquiries until 2010). ● until 2010.

Located in the old docks area just north of the historical centre is Antwerp's most innovative project, the Museum Aan De Stroom (MAS), meaning Museum on the River. Due to open in 2010, the museum on the

VISITORS' CHECKLIST

500,000. ✕ 6 km (3 miles) E of the city. ◻ Centraal, Pelikaanstraat. ◻ Franklin Rooseveltplaats. ◻ Steenplein. ◻ Grote Markt 15, (03) 232 0103.

waterfront will combine the best of the collections from the former Maritime and Folklore Museums along with some of the Vleeshuis's collection. A broad range of objects will be on display, covering everything from paintings and silverware to wood carvings, archaeological finds, folk art, maritime artifacts and model ships. These pieces span the prehistoric era through to the present day. The museum will also feature a cultural events space.

Imposing exterior of Antwerp's Sint Pauluskerk

Sint Pauluskerk

St-Paulusstraat 22 or Veemarkt 14. **Tel** (03) 232 3267. ◯ May–Sep: 2–5pm daily. ◯ 3pm Sun & pub hols.

Completed in the early 17th century, this splendid church is distinguished by its combination of both Gothic and Baroque features. The exterior dates from about 1517, and has an added elaborate Baroque gateway. The interior is noted for its intricately carved wooden choir stalls. St Paulus also possesses a series of paintings illustrating the Fifteen Mysteries of the Rosary, one of which, *The Scourging of the Pillar*, is an exquisite canvas by Rubens. There are also paintings by van Dyck and Jordaens.

Street-by-Street: Around Grote Markt

Fanning out from the east bank of the River Scheldt, Antwerp was and is one of the leading trading cities of northern Europe. Today, the city's industries lie away from its medieval core whose narrow streets and fine buildings cluster around the cathedral and the Grote Markt. Packed with evidence of Antwerp's rich history, this is a delightful area to wander in. Most sites of interest are within easy walking distance of the Grote Markt whose surrounding streets house museums, shops and exuberant cafés and bars.

Gilt statue on guildhouse

To Koninklijk Museum voor Schone kunsten

The Vleeshuis
Occupied by the Butcher's Guild for three centuries, this beautiful 1504 building has striking layers of brick and stone that look like alternating strips of fat and lean meat.

The Ethnografisch Museum has artifacts from around the world.

Stadhuis
Flanking Antwerp's spectacular central square is the elegant 16th-century Stadhuis (town hall), designed by Cornelis Floris (1514–75).

KEY

– – – Suggested route

STAR SIGHTS

★ Grote Markt

★ Kathedraal

The Brabo Fountain
This statue, in the centre of the Grote Markt, depicts the fearless soldier, Silvius Brabo. Said to be the nephew of Julius Caesar, Brabo is shown throwing the hand of the mythical giant, Antigonius, into the River Scheldt.

Sint Pauluskerk

This imposing church was built in 1517, but has a magnificent Baroque gate and spire dating from the late 17th century. Inside, there is a noted collection of paintings, including one especially fine work by Rubens.

To Central Station

★ Grote Markt

Antwerp's golden age of trade in the 16th century is reflected in the square's cosmopolitan 1564 town hall, built by architects from all over Europe.

ZIRKSTRAAT

VERSMIDSTRAAT

★ Onze Lieve Vrouwe Kathedraal

The largest Gothic cathedral in Belgium, this building occupies a 1-ha (2.5-acre) site in Antwerp's centre. Work began on this elegant church in 1352 and took almost two centuries to complete.

To Rubenshuis

Groenplaats

The Groenplaats or Green Square is a pleasant open space with trees and flower beds. Lined with cafés, bars and restaurants, the square is a popular spot with both locals and visitors for a peaceful stroll or meal.

| 0 metres | 50 |
| 0 yards | 50 |

Exploring Antwerp

Antwerp stretches out from its centre into its sprawling suburbs to a distance of some 7 km (4.3 miles). Badly damaged in both World Wars, the city has a broad mixture of architecture, ranging from the medieval to the ultra-modern. The old city centre is concentrated around the cathedral, Onze Lieve Vrouwe Kathedraal, and the Grote Markt (see pp96–97). The area around the Centraal Station is the centre of the international diamond trade. The Zuid (South) district is an area of drained docks; recently rejuvenated, this is a now a vibrant part of town, and the old dockland architecture of the Waalse Kaai and Vlaamse Kaai has become home to clubs, bars and museums. The area around the old, water-filled docks to the north of the city centre is now also undergoing rapid redevelopment. To the east of the cathedral – beyond Antwerp's pioneering 1930s skyscraper, the Boerentoren – lies the Meir, Antwerp's premier shopping street.

Late 16th-century printing press in the Museum Plantin-Moretus

Dress exhibits displayed at the Modemuseum

🏛 Modemuseum (MoMu)

Nationalestraat 28. **Tel** (03) 470 27 70. ⬜ 10am–6pm Tue–Sun; 10am–9pm first Thu of every month. ● Mon. 📷 **www**.momu.be
Following the rise to celebrity of the influential fashion designers called the Antwerp Six in the 1980s, the city has entered the stratosphere of international of haute-couture, and maintains a glowing reputation for nurturing new talent. This fashion museum provides the historical context to Antwerp's rise to glory. Fashion items and accessories are shown in innovative ways in changing exhibitions, to serve as both an instructive resource and a fount of inspiration.

🏛 Museum Plantin-Moretus

Vrijdagmarkt 22–23. **Tel** (03) 221 1450. ⬜ 10am–5pm Tue–Sun, Easter Mon. ● Mon, 1 & 2 Jan, 1 May, Ascension, 1 & 2 Nov, 25 & 26 Dec. 📷 free last Wed of month. **www**.museumplantinmoretus.be
This fascinating museum occupies a large 16th-century house that belonged to the printer Christopher Plantin, who moved here in 1576. The house is built around a court-yard, and its ancient rooms and narrow corridors resemble the types of interiors painted by Flemish and Dutch masters. The museum is devoted to the early years of printing, when Plantin and others began to produce books that bore no resemblance to earlier, illuminated medieval manuscripts.

Antwerp was a centre for printing in the 15th and 16th centuries, and Plantin was its most successful printer. Today, his workshop displays several historic printing presses, as well as woodcuts and copper plates. Plantin's library is also on show. One of the gems here is an edition of the Gutenberg Bible – the first book to be printed using moveable type, a new technique invented by Johannes Gutenberg in 1455.

⛪ Sint-Carolus Borromeuskerk

Hendrik Conscienceplein. **Tel** (03) 231 3751. ⬜ 10am–12:30pm and 2–5pm Mon–Sat.
This Jesuit church is celebrated for its elegant Baroque façade, which forms one flank of a charming 17th-century square. Rubens played a part in the design of both the exterior and interior when the church was built in 1615–21, and supplied 39 ceiling paintings, but sadly these were lost in a fire in 1718. The surviving parts of the interior indicate how lavish it once was – a triumphant showpiece of the Counter-Reformation.

The Baroque interior of Sint-Carolus Borromeuskerk

⊞ Rockoxhuis

Keizerstraat 12. *Tel* (03) 201 9250.
◷ 10am–5pm Tue–Sun. ● Mon, 1
& 2 Jan, Ascension, 1 & 2 Nov, 25 &
26 Dec. ☒ www.rockoxhuis.be

Nicholaas Rockox (1560–1640)
was mayor of Antwerp, a
humanist, philanthropist, and
a friend and patron of
Rubens. These attributes are
reflected in his beautifully
renovated home – a series of
rooms set around a formal
courtyard garden. They
contain a fine collection of
contemporary furniture and
miscellaneous artifacts, all
interesting and well-chosen.
The paintings and
drawings include
work by Rubens,
Jordaens and Van
Dyck, as well as
work by Frans
Snyders (1579–1657),
who lived next
door, was much
admired by Rubens,
and painted flowers
and fruit in
Rubens' work.

**Detail from
Fishmarket Antwerp,
by Frans Snyders, at
the Rockoxhuis**

🔒 Sint Jacobskerk

Lange Nieuwstraat 73–75,
Eikenstraat. *Tel* (03) 225 0414.
◷ Apr–Oct: 2–5pm Mon–Sat;
Nov–Mar: 9am–noon, Mon–Sat. ☒
Noted as Rubens' burial place
– his tomb is in his family's
chapel behind the high altar –
this sandstone church was
built from 1491 to 1656. Sint
Jacobskerk's rich interior
contains the tombs of several
other notable Antwerp
families, as well as a
collection of 17th-century art,
including sculptures by
Hendrik Verbruggen, and
paintings by van Dyck, Otto
Venius (Rubens' first master)
and Jacob Jordaens.

⊞ Rubenshuis

See pp102–3.

🏛 Museum Mayer van de Bergh

Lange Gasthuisstraat 19.
Tel (03) 232 4237. ◷
10am–5pm Tues–Sun, Easter
Mon. ● Mon, 1 & 2 Jan, 1
May, Ascension, 1 & 2 Nov,
25 & 26 Dec. ☒ http://
museum.antwerpen.be/
mayervandenbergh

Fritz Mayer van den
Bergh (1858–91) was
the scion of a wealthy trading
family, but instead of
following in his father's
footsteps, he chose to
devote himself to
collecting art and curios.
After his death aged just
33, his mother
created this
museum to display
his collections.
Among the many
treasures are
tapestries, furniture,
ivories, stained glass,
medieval and
Renaissance sculpture
and a number of excellent
paintings, including *Dulle
Griet* (Mad Meg), a powerful
image of a chaotic world by
Pieter Brueghel the Elder.

🏛 Koninklijk Museum voor Schone Kunsten

See pp100–101.

🏛 MuHKA (Museum voor Hedendaagse Kunst Antwerpen)

Leuvenstraat 32. *Tel* (03) 260 9999.
◷ 10am–5pm Tue–Sun. ● Mon, 1
Jan, 1 May, Ascension, 25 Dec. ☒
▯▯ ▯ www.muhka.be

This museum is what you
might expect from a city famed
for its sense of style and

A room at the Museum Mayer van de Bergh

design. A huge, sculptural
building that was once a
1920s dockside grain silo
and warehouse has been
transformed into a series of
unusual spaces to display art
from the front line of
international contemporary art
(1970–present). This includes
work by many of the artists
who have helped to place
Belgium at the forefront of
the art scene in recent years,
such as Panamarenko, Luc
Tuymans, Jan Fabre and
Wim Delvoye.

🏛 FotoMuseum

Waalse Kaai 47. *Tel* (03) 242 9300
◷ 10am–6pm Tue–Sun.
● Mon, 25 & 26 Dec, 1 & 2 Jan
☒ ▯
www.fotomuseum.be

Antwerp's excellent museum
of photography, displaying a
wide range of historical
artifacts and images, has
recently undergone a complete
makeover, and has embraced
the moving image as well by
incorporating the Antwerp
Film Museum (which offers
scheduled film viewings). In
addition to its extensive
permanent collection, the
museum mounts regular
exhibitions of photography.

🏛 Diamond Museum

Koningin Astridplein 19–23.
Tel (03) 202 4890. ◷ 10am–5:30pm
Mon, Tue, Thu–Sun. ● Wed, 25 &
26 Dec, Jan. ☒ ▯

This museum is dedicated to
the world of diamonds and
includes treasure chambers as
well as multimedia exhibits
highlighting the processes used
to extract and cut the precious
stone. On weekdays (except
Wednesdays), you can watch a
diamond-cutter at work in one
of the museum's workshops.

A stained-glass window in Sint Jacobskerk

Koninklijk Museum voor Schone Kunsten

Antwerp's largest and most impressive fine art collection is exhibited in the Museum voor Schone Kunsten, which occupies a massive late 19th-century Neo-Classical building. The permanent collection contains both ancient and modern works. The earlier collection on the upper floor begins with medieval Flemish painting and continues through the 19th century, with the "Antwerp Trio" of Rubens, van Dyck and Jordaens well represented. At ground level, modern exhibits include the work of Belgian artists Magritte, Ensor and Delvaux, as well as a major collection of work by Rik Wouters. Tissot and van Gogh are among the foreign artists on show. The museum will close for renovation for two years from January 2010. Some works will be relocated to other Antwerp museums.

First Floor

Main Entrance

Façade of Gallery
Building began on this imposing structure in 1884. The Neo-Classical façade with its vast pillars has carved women charioteers atop each side. It was opened in 1890.

★ **Woman Ironing** *(1912)*
This peaceful domestic scene by Rik Wouters employs the muted colours of Impressionism. This was a productive period for Wouters who painted 60 canvases in 1912.

Madame Récamier *(1967)*
René Magritte's macabre version of the original painting by David is a classic Surrealist work.

Pink Bows *(1936)*
Paul Delvaux's dream-like style clearly shows the influence of Sigmund Freud's psychoanalytic theories on Surrealist painting.

★ Saint Barbara *(1437)*
Jan van Eyck's painting of Saint Barbara in several tones of grey shows the saint sitting in front of a huge Gothic cathedral tower still under construction, while a prayer book lies open on her lap.

VISITORS' CHECKLIST

Leopold de Waelplaats 1–9. **Tel** (03) 238 7809. 🚌 1, 23, 290. 🚊 4, 8, 12, 24. ◯ 10am–5pm Tue–Sun. ⬤ 1, 2 Jan, 1 May, Ascension, 25 Dec. 🖼 🚻 🛍 📷 🎦

GALLERY GUIDE
The gallery is divided into two floors. Flemish Old Masters and 19th-century painters are housed on the first floor, while the ground floor focuses on James Ensor and the 20th century. Each room is lettered and visitors may view exhibits chronologically, starting in the entrance hall.

★ Adoration of the Magi *(1624)*
One of Rubens' masterpieces, this painting displays a remarkable freedom of composition.

As the Old Sang, the Young Play Pipes *(1638)*
Jacob Jordaens' (1593–1678) joyous celebration of life in this painting of a family enjoying a musical evening contrasts with his religious paintings.

Ground Floor

STAR PAINTINGS

★ Saint Barbara
by Jan van Eyck

★ Adoration of
the Magi by Pieter
Paul Rubens

★ Woman Ironing
by Rik Wouters

KEY

▢ 15th-century paintings	▢ 19th-century paintings
▢ 16th-century paintings	▢ 19th-century salon
▢ 16th–18th-century sketches	▢ 20th-century paintings
▢ 17th-century paintings	▢ Temporary exhibitions
▢ 19th-century sculpture	▢ Museum history
	▣ Non-exhibition space

Rubenshuis

Statue of Neptune

Rubenshuis, on Wapper Square, was Pieter Paul Rubens' home and studio for the last 29 years of his life, from 1611 to 1640. The city bought the premises just before World War II, but by then the house was little more than a ruin, and what can be seen today is the result of careful restoration. It is divided into two sections. To the left of the entrance are the narrow rooms of the artist's living quarters, equipped with period furniture. Behind this part of the house is the kunstkamer, or art gallery, where Rubens exhibited both his own and other artists' work, and entertained his friends and wealthy patrons, such as the Archduke Albert and the Infanta Isabella. To the right of the entrance lies the main studio, a spacious salon where Rubens worked on – and showed – his works. A signposted route guides visitors through the house.

Façade of Rubenshuis
The older Flemish part of the house sits next to the later house, whose elegant early Baroque façade was designed by Rubens.

Formal Gardens
The small garden is laid out formally and its charming pavilion dates from Rubens' time. He was influenced by such architects of the Italian Renaissance as Vitruvius when he built the Italian Baroque addition to his house in the 1620s.

★ Rubens' Studio
It is estimated that Rubens produced some 2,500 paintings in this large, high-ceilinged room. In the Renaissance manner, Rubens designed the work which was usually completed by a team of other artists employed in his studio.

STAR SIGHTS

★ Kunstkamer

★ Rubens' Studio

Bedroom

The Rubens family lived in the Flemish section of the house, with its small rooms and narrow passages. The portrait by the bed is said to be of Rubens' second wife, Helena Fourment.

The Familia Kamer, or family sitting room, is cosy and has a pretty tiled floor. It overlooks Wapper Square.

VISITORS' CHECKLIST

Wapper 9–11. **Tel** (03) 201 1555. ▦ 9. ▦ 7, 8, 11, 12. ◯ 10am–5pm Tue–Sun, Easter Mon, Whit Mon. ● 1 & 2 Jan, 1 & 2 Nov, 25 & 26 Dec, Ascension Day. ▨

Dining Room

Intricately fashioned leather panels line the walls of this room, which also displays a noted work by Frans Snyders.

★ Kunstkamer

This art gallery contains a series of painted sketches by Rubens. At the far end is a semi-circular dome, modelled on Rome's Pantheon, displaying a number of marble busts.

Chequered mosaic tiled floor

Baroque Portico

One of the few remaining original features, this portico was designed by Rubens, and links the older house with the Baroque section. It is adorned with a frieze showing scenes from Greek mythology.

A 90-Minute Walk Across Antwerp

Antwerp handles 80 per cent of the world's entire trade in rough diamonds, yet this business is carried out in a distinctly unglamorous quarter in the east of the city; even the railway station is more elegant. This walk starts in the diamond district and heads west to the Meir, Antwerp's main shopping thoroughfare, before visiting the haunts of Rubens and his contemporaries at the Rubenshuis, Sint Jacobskerk and the Rockoxhuis. It then passes through medieval Antwerp to the reach the broad sweep of the River Scheldt.

Diamond District and the Meir

Centraal Station ① is a palatial Neo-Classical building completed in 1905 that is worth visiting in its own right. It looks out over Koningin Astridplein, named after the hugely popular Queen Astrid (wife of Leopold III and mother of the present King Albert II) who died tragically in a car accident, aged 29, in 1935. On the far side of the square is the Hotel Astrid Park Plaza ②, a bold example of post-modern architecture. For a good overview of Antwerp's connection with diamonds, go to the Diamond Museum *(see p99)* ③, at Koningin Astridplein 19–23. To simply look at the diamond shops and get a flavour of this distinctively Jewish neighbourhood, walk down Pelikaanstraat ④ and Vestingstraat ⑤. By continuing alwong De Keyserlei and Leysstraat you enter the Meir ⑥, a broad, pedestri-anized high street packed with large shops.

The bar area in the impressive Hotel Astrid ②

The Protvincial Diamond Museum ③

Rubenshuis and Rockoxhuis

Turn left off the Meir into the broad street called the Wapper ⑦. On the left-hand side of the street is the Rubenshuis *(see pp102–03)* ⑧, the impressive mansion that Rubens bought as his home and studio in 1610. At the end of the Wapper, at Hopland 2, is the Grand Café Horta ⑨, a dynamic café-restaurant built in 2000 around structural remnants salvaged from Victor Horta's classic Art Nouveau building, the Maison du Peuple, in Brussels *(see p78)*. Returning to the Meir,

One of the rooms inside the Rockoxhuis ⑫

look left – the tallest building is the KBC Tower ⑩. Complete with Art Deco detailing, it was Europe's highest skyscraper when topped out in 1931. By walking up Lange Clarenstraat, you can reach the Sint Jacobskerk *(see p99)* ⑪ on Lange Nieuwestraat. This richly decorated church is famous as the burial place of Rubens. St-Jacobsstraat and Keizerstraat lead to the Rockoxhuis *(see p99)* ⑫, which offers an insight into how the homes of the rich looked in the time of Rubens. Wijngaardstraat will bring you to the little square called Hendrik Conscienceplein ⑬, named after the Flemish author who wrote the novel *The Lion of Flanders* (1838), a stirring tale about the Battle of the Golden Spurs of 1302; the book was a landmark in the resurgence of Flemish national pride. Overlooking the square is the fine Baroque façade of the Sint Carolus-Borromeuskerk (see p98) ⑭.

The Cathedral and the Scheldt
Continue along Wijngaardstraat to reach Lijnwaadmarkt (Linen Market) ⑮. The street names here recall the specialist markets that once clustered around the cathedral. Note how buildings have been constructed right up against the cathedral walls, such as the restaurant Het Vermoeide Model ("The Artist's Sleepy Model") ⑯. The bar on the corner on the other side of the street called Het Elfde Gebod ⑰, at Torfbrug 10, is packed with religious

The Grote Markt and its elegant 16th-century Stadhuis (town hall) ⑲

statuary and the walls adorned with paintings of saints – the name means "The Eleventh Commandment". Continue to the Handschoenmarkt (Glove Market) from where there is a magnificent view of Onze Lieve Vrouwe Kathedraal (see p95) ⑱. There is a well in the square decorated

KEY

··· Walk route

Ⓜ Metro station

TIPS FOR WALKERS

Starting point: Centraal Station
Length: 3.2 km (2 miles)
Getting there: Centraal Station is served by bus and tram routes from all over the city.
Stopping-off points: There are plenty of welcoming refreshment stops along the way. For a touch of class, try the Grand Café Horta (No. 9 on this walk). The walk also passes other noted watering holes, such as Het Vermoeide Model (No. 16), Het Elfde Gebod (No. 17), De Vagant (No. 20), and De Groote Witte Arend (No. 21). Or save yourself for the spectacular Zuiderterras (No. 23) overlooking the River Scheldt.

with metalwork foliage and a figure; this is said to have been forged by the painter Quentin Metsys in around 1495. The figure depicts the Roman soldier Silvius Brabo, throwing the hand of the evil giant Antigonius into the River Scheldt – the folkloric origin of the name Antwerp (handwerpen means "hand-throw"). Now go to the Grote Markt

(see p94) ⑲, Antwerp's spectacular main square, where you will see the more famous version of Brabo, by the noted Antwerp sculptor Jef Lambeaux, and the town hall. Head down the Oude Koornmarkt (Old Cornmarket) and Pelgrimsstraat. On the corner with Reyndersstraat is the pub called De Vagant ⑳, which specializes in jenever gin. De Groote Witte Arend (The Great White Eagle) ㉑, at Reyndersstraat 18, is an old and celebrated tavern with a courtyard. On Vrijdagmarkt (Friday Market) you will find the Museum Plantin-Moretus (see p98) ㉒, a museum of early printing, set in the 16th-century house of the printer who gave us the typeface called Plantin. From here walk down Steenhouwersvest to the square St-Jansvliet, with the River Scheldt beyond. For the most part, Antwerp turns its back on its wide and windy river, but not the café-restaurant Zuiderterras ㉓ – an award-winning modern building with fine views across the water.

Boats moored on the busy dockside of the River Scheldt

The Centenary Clock on Lier's Zimmertoren or watchtower

Lier ❷

🏠 *30,000.* 🚉 🚌 **ℹ** *Grote Markt 57, (03) 800 0313.* **www**.*lier.be*

Lier is an attractive small town, just 20 km (12 miles) southeast of Antwerp. The Grote Markt is a spacious cobbled square framed by handsome historic buildings. The Stadhuis (town hall) was built in 1740, and its elegant dimensions contrast strongly with the square, turreted 14th-century Belfort (belfry) adjoining. Nearby is the **Stedelijk Museum Wuyts**, with its collection of paintings by Flemish masters including Jan Steen, Brueghel and Rubens. East of here the church of St Gummaruserk, with its soaring stone pillars and vaulted roof, evokes medieval times, and the carved altarpiece is notable for the intricate detail of its biblical scenes. The stained-glass windows are among the finest in Belgium and were a gift from Emperor Maximillian I in 1516.

One of Lier's highlights is the **Zimmertoren**, a 14th-century watchtower that now houses the clocks of Lodewijk Zimmer (1888–1970). This Lier merchant wanted to share his knowledge of timepieces.

🏛 **Stedelijk Museum Wuyts**
Florent van Cauwenberg Straat 14. **Tel** *(03) 800 0396.* ◯ *10am–midday 1–5pm Tue–Sun.* ⬤ *Mon, public hols.* 🈂

🎫 **Zimmertoren**
Zimmerplein 18. **Tel** *(03) 800 0395.* ◯ *Tue–Sun.* 🈂

Mechelen ❸

🏃 *75,000.* 🚉 🚌 **ℹ** *Hallestraat 2, Grote Markt, (015) 29 7655.*

The seat of the Catholic Archbishop of Belgium, Mechelen was the administrative capital of the country under the Burgundian prince, Charles the Bold, in 1473. Today, it is an appealing town whose expansive main square is flanked by pleasant cafés and bars. To the west of the square is the main attraction, **St Romboutskathedraal**, a huge cathedral that took some 300 years to complete. The building might never have been finished but for a deal with the Vatican: the cathedral was allowed to sell special indulgences (which absolved the purchaser of their sins) to raise funds, on condition that the pope received a percentage. Completed in 1546, the cathedral's tower has Belgium's finest carillon, a set of 49 bells, whose peals ring out at weekends and on public holidays. The church also contains *The Crucifixion* by Antony van Dyck (1599–1641).

Less well-known in Mechelen are three 16th-century houses by the River Dilje. They are not open to visitors, but their exteriors are delightful. The "House of the Little Devils" is adorned with carved demons.

Mechelen is famous for its local beers, and visitors should try the Gouden Carolus, a dark brew, which is said to have been the favourite tipple of the Emperor Charles V.

🏛 **St Romboutskathedraal**
St Romboutskerkhof. **Tel** *(015) 29 7655.* 📷 *obligatory for tower.* ◯ *Apr–Oct: 1:30–5:30pm daily; Nov–Mar: 1:30–4:30pm daily. Tours depart Tourist Office.*

Mechelen's main square, the Grote Markt, on market day

Dendermonde ❹

🏃 *40,000.* 🚉 🚌 **ℹ** *Stadhuis, Grote Markt, (052) 21 3956.*

A quiet, industrial town, Dendermonde is about 20 km (12 miles) southeast of Ghent. Its strategic position, at the confluence of the Scheldt and Dender rivers, has attracted the attention of a string of invaders

Vleeshuis façade on the Grote Markt in Dendermonde

Wood panelled walls and paintings in the hall at Gaasbeek Castle

for its beers, especially lambic and gueuze. Lambic is one of the most popular types of beer in Belgium *(see pp150–51)*.

⚜ **Gaasbeek**
Kasteelstraat 40. **Tel** (02) 531 0130.
◐ Apr–Nov: 10am–6pm Tue–Sun.
● Dec–Mar. (Park open all year.) 🅿️

Halle ➏

🏠 30,000. 🚉 🚌 🛈 Stadhuis, Grote Markt, (02) 363 2211.
www.halle.be

Located on the outskirts of Brussels, in the province of Brabant, Halle is a peaceful little town. It has been a major religious centre since the 13th century because of the cult of the Black Virgin, an effigy in the Onze Lieve Vrouwebasiliek, the town's main church. The holy statue's blackness is due to its stained colour, which is said to have occurred through contact with gunpowder during the religious wars of the 17th century.

The virgin has long been one of Belgium's most venerated icons and each year, on Whit Sunday, the statue is paraded through the town.

over the centuries, including the Germans who shelled Dendermonde in 1914. But the town is perhaps best-known as the site of the Steed Bayard, a carnival held every ten years at the end of August.

Today, the town's spacious main square is framed by the quaint turrets and towers of the the Vleeshuis or Meat Hall. The Town Hall is an elegant 14th-century building which was extensively restored in 1920. Dendermonde also possesses two exquisite early religious paintings by Anthony van Dyck which are on display in the Onze Lieve Vrouwekerk (Church of Our Lady).

Pajottenland ➎

🏠 111,700. 🛈 Toerisme Pajottenland en Zennevalaaei, (02) 356 4259.
www.visitflanders.com

The Pajottenland forms part of the Brabant province to the southwest of Brussels, and is bordered in the west by the Dender River. The gentle rolling hills of the landscape contain many farms, some of which date back to the 17th century. The village of Onze Lieve Vrouw Lombeek, just 12 km (7 miles) west of Brussels, is named after its church, an outstanding example of 14th-century Gothic architecture.

Just a short distance south of the village lies the area's main attraction, the castle and grounds of **Gaasbeek**. The

castle was remodelled in the 19th century, but actually dates from the 13th century, and boasts a moat and a thick curtain wall, strengthened by huge semi-circular towers. The castle's interior holds an excellent collection of fine and applied arts. Among the treasures are rich tapestries, 15th-century alabaster reliefs from England, silverware and a delightful ivory and copper hunting horn which belonged to the Protestant martyr Count Egmont in the 16th century. The Pajottenland is also known

THE STEED BAYARD

Dendermonde's famous carnival of the Steed Bayard occurs every ten years at the end of August. The focus of the festival is a horse, the Steed Bayard itself, represented in the carnival by a giant model. It takes 34 bearers to carry the horse which weighs 700 kg (1,540 lb) and is 5.8 m (19 ft) high. A procession of locals dressed in medieval costume re-enact the Steed Bayard legend – a complex tale of chivalry and treachery, family loyalty and betrayal. The four Aymon brothers (who were said to be the nephews of Emperor Charlemagne) ride the horse, and it is their behaviour towards the animal which serves to demonstrate their moral worth.

Waterloo ❼

Death mask of Napoleon

The Battle of Waterloo was fought on 18 June, 1815. It pitted Napoleon and his French army against the Duke of Wellington, who was in command of troops mostly drawn from Britain, Germany and the Netherlands. The two armies met outside the insignificant hamlet of Waterloo, to the south of Brussels. The result was decisive. The battle began at 11:30am and just nine hours later the French were in full retreat. Napoleon abdicated and was subsequently exiled to the island of St Helena, where he died in mysterious circumstances six years later.

Despite its importance, the battlefield has not been conserved, and part of it has been dug up for a highway. However, enough remains to give a general sense of the battle. The best place to start a visit here is at the Musée Wellington, some 3 km (2 miles) from the battlefield.

earthen mound built on the spot where one of Wellington's Dutch generals, the Prince of Orange, was wounded during the battle. Steps lead to the top, which is guarded by a huge cast-iron lion, and from here there is a great view over the battlefield. The French army

The Butte de Lion viewed from the Waterloo battlefield

🏛 Musée Wellington

Chaussée de Bruxelles 147. **Tel** *(02) 357 2860.* ◯ *Apr–Sep: 9:30am–6:30pm daily; Oct–Mar: 10am–5pm daily.* ● *1 Jan, 25 Dec.* 🖼
www.museewellington.com
The Waterloo inn where the Duke of Wellington spent the night before the battle has been turned into a museum, its rooms packed with curios alongside plans and models of the actual battle. One of the more quirky exhibits is the artificial leg of Lord Uxbridge, one of Wellington's commanders. His leg was blown off during the battle and buried in Waterloo. After his death, the leg was sent to join the rest of him in England and, as recompense, his relatives sent his artificial one back to Waterloo.

🔓 Eglise St-Joseph

Chaussée de Bruxelles.
Tel *(02) 354 0011.*
Across the road from the Musée Wellington is the tiny church of St-Joseph, which was originally built as a royal chapel at the end of the 17th century. Its dainty, elegant cupola predates the battle, after which it was extended, with the newer portions containing dozens of memorial plaques and flagstones dedicated to those British soldiers who died at Waterloo. Several of these plaques were paid for by voluntary contributions from ordinary soldiers in honour of their officers.

🏰 Butte du Lion

315 Route du Lion, Ring Ouest exit 25, 3km (2 miles) S of Waterloo. **Tel** *(02) 385 1912.* ◯ *daily.* 🖼
Dating from 1826, the Butte du Lion is a 45-m (148-ft) high

WATERLOO TOWN CENTRE

Musée Wellington ①
Eglise St-Joseph ②
Butte du Lion ③
Panorama de la Bataille ④
Musée de Cire ⑤
Napolean's Last Headquarters ⑥

Brussels

Waterloo

Mont-St-Jean

Braine l'Alleud

Plancenoit

Charleroi

0 kilometres 0
0 miles 0

KEY

🚉   Train station
═   Motorway
▬   Major road
═   Minor road
—   Railway

approached from the south and fought up the slope across farmland that became increasingly marshy as the day went on, while their opponents had the drier ridge at the foot of the mound. A plan of the battle is displayed at the top.

🎪 Panorama de la Bataille

252–254 Route du Lion, Braine-L'Alleud. N5, 3 km (2 miles) S of Waterloo. *Tel (02) 385 1912.* ◯ 10am–5pm daily. 🗟

This is perhaps the most fascinating of the several attractions beneath the Butte de Lion. This circular painting of the battle by artist Louis Demoulin was erected in 1912. It is 110 m (360 ft) long and stretches right round a circular, purpose-built gallery. This is one of the few late 19th-century panoramic, circular paintings that remain intact.

🏛 Musée de Cire

315 Route du Lion, N5, 3 km (2 miles) S of Waterloo. *Tel (02) 384 6740.* ◯ Apr–Oct: daily; Nov–Mar: pub hols, Sat & Sun. 🗟

The Musée de Cire is a wax museum where pride of place goes to the models of soldiers dressed in the military regalia of 1815. It seems strange today that the various armies dressed their men in such vivid colours, which made them easy targets. Indeed, many commanders paid for the uniforms of their men themselves.

🏛 Napoleon's Last Headquarters

66 Chaussée de Bruxelles, Vieux-Genappe, N5, 7 km (4.5 miles) S of Waterloo. *Tel (02) 384 2424.* ◯ Apr–Oct: 10am–6:30pm; Nov–Mar: 1–5pm. ● 1 Jan, 25 Dec. 🗟

Napoleon spent the eve of the battle in a farmhouse, Le Caillou. This is now a museum that is often referred to as the Caillou Museum, containing a number of artifacts from Napoleon's army, a bronze death mask of the Emperor, and his army-issue bed. A building in the garden contains the bones of some of the soldiers from the battle.

Leuven ❽

See pp110–11.

The summer drawing room in the 18th-century Chateau d'Attre, near Ath

Ath ❾

🏠 11,700. 🚃 🚌 ⓘ *Rue de Pintamont 18, (068) 26 5170.*

This quiet town is known for its festival – the Ducasse – which occurs every year on the fourth weekend in August. It features the "Parade of the Giants", a procession of gaily decorated giant figures representing characters from local folklore and the Bible.

A few kilometres northeast is one of the most popular attractions in the region, the **Château d'Attre**. This handsome 18th-century palace was built in 1752 by the Count of Gomegnies, chamberlain to the Hapsburg Emperor Joseph II.

♣ Château d'Attre

Attre. Tel (068) 45 4460. 🚃 *to Attre.* ◯ *Jul–Aug: Thu–Tue; Apr–Jun & Sep–Oct: Sat & Sun.* ● *Nov–Mar.*

Ieper ❿

🏠 35,000. 🚃 🚌 ⓘ *34 Market Square, (057) 23 9220.*

Ieper is the Flemish name of the town familiar to British soldiers as Ypres. During World War I, this town was used as a supply depot for the British army. The Germans shelled Ieper to pieces, but after the war the town was rebuilt to its earlier design, complete with a replica of its 13th-century Lakenhalle (cloth hall). Part of its interior has been turned into the "In Flander's Fields" Museum, a thoughtfully laid-out series of displays that attempt to conjure the full horrors of World War I.

There is also the Menin Gate memorial, inscribed with the names of over 50,000 British and Commonwealth troops who died in the area but have no known resting place.

THE YPRES SALIENT

The Ypres Salient was the name given to a bulge in the line of trenches that both the German and British armies felt was a good place to break through each others' lines. This led to large concentrations of men and four major battles including Passchendaele in July 1917, in which hundreds of thousands of men died. Today, visitors can choose to view the site with its vast cemeteries and monuments by car or guided tour.

View of the battlefield at Passchendaele Ridge in 1917

Leuven 8

Font Sapienza

Within easy striking distance of Brussels, the historic Flemish town of Leuven traces its origins to a fortified camp constructed here by Julius Caesar. In medieval times, the town became an important centre of the cloth trade, but it was as a seat of learning that it achieved international prominence. In 1425, Pope Martin V and Count John of Brabant founded Leuven's university, and by the mid-1500s it was one of Europe's most prestigious academic institutions, the home of such famous scholars as Erasmus and Mercator. Even today, the university exercises a dominant influence over the town, and its students give Leuven a vibrant atmosphere. The bars and cafés flanking the Oude Markt, a large square in the centre of town, are especially popular. Adjoining the square is the Grote Markt, a triangular open space which boasts two fine medieval buildings, the Stadhuis and St Pieterskerk.

Huge buttresses supporting the tower of St Pieterskerk

Lively café society in the Oude Markt

Oude Markt

This handsome, cobblestoned square is flanked by a tasteful ensemble of high-gabled brick buildings. Some of these date from the 18th century; others are comparatively new. At ground level these buildings house the largest concentration of bars and cafés in town, and as such attract the town's university students in their droves.

Stadhuis

Grote Markt. **Tel** (016) 28 2317. daily. obligatory. At 3pm daily (Apr–Sep: also at 11am Mon–Fri).
Built between 1439 and 1463 from the profits of the cloth trade, Leuven's town hall, the Stadhuis, was designed to demonstrate the wealth of the city's merchants. This distinctive, tall building is renowned for its lavishly carved and decorated façade. A line of narrow windows rise up over three floors beneath a steeply pitched roof adorned with dormer windows and

pencil-thin turrets. It is, however, in the fine quality of its stonework that the building excels, with delicately carved tracery and detailed medieval figures beneath 300 niche bases. There are grotesques of every description as well as representations of folktales and biblical stories, all carved in exuberant late-Gothic style. Within the niche alcoves is a series of 19th-century statues depicting local dignitaries and politicians. Guided tours of the interior are available, and include three lavishly decorated reception rooms.

Stone carvings of medieval figures decorate the Stadhuis façade

St Pieterskerk and Museum voor Religieuze Kunst

Grote Markt. **Tel** (016) 29 5133. Mar–Oct: daily, Nov–Feb: Tue–Sun. to museum.
Across the square from the Stadhuis rises St Pieterskerk, a massive church built over a period of two hundred years from the 1420s. The nave and aisles were completed first, but when the twin towers of the western façade were finally added in 1507, the foundations proved inadequate and they soon began to sink. With money in short supply, it was decided to remove the top sections of the towers – hence the truncated versions of today.

Inside the church, the sweeping lines of the nave are intercepted by an impressive 1499 rood screen and a Baroque wooden pulpit, depicting the conversion of Saint Norbert. Norbert was a wealthy but irreligious German noble, who was hit by lightning while riding. He was unhurt but his horse died under him, and this led to his devoting himself to the church.

The church also houses the Religious Art Museum which has three exquisite paintings by Dirk Bouts (1415–75). Born in the Netherlands, Bouts spent most of his working life in Leuven, where he became the town's official artist. In his *Last Supper* (1468), displayed here, Bouts painted Judas's face in shadow, emphasizing the mystery of Holy Communion rather than the betrayal.

🚻 Fochplein

Adjacent to the Grote Markt is the Fochplein, a narrow triangular square containing some of Leuven's most popular shops, selling everything from fashion to food. In the middle is the Font Sapienza, a modern fountain that shows a student pouring water through his empty head – a pithy view of the town's student population.

🏛 Museum Vander Kelen-Mertens

Savoyestraat 6. **Tel** (016) 22 6906.
⬤ closed until Sep 2009. 📷

The Museum Vander Kelen-Mertens has fair claim to be Leuven's most enjoyable museum, with its well-presented collection arranged over two floors. Once the home of the Vander Kelen-Mertens family, the rooms are furnished in a variety of historical styles, ranging from a Renaissance salon to a rococo dining room.

Much of the art on display is by the early Flemish masters, including the work of Quentin Metsys (1466–1550), who was born in Leuven and is noted for introducing Italian style to north European art. The collection also includes a beautiful *Holy Trinity* by Rogier

van der Weyden (1400–1464). The museum has expanded to house the existing collection as well as a contemporary one. It is currently closed for renovation, re-opening in September 2009.

🔒 St Michielskerk

Naamsestraat.
◯ Jun–Sep: Wed, Sat & Sun.

One of Leuven's most impressive churches, St Michielskerk was built for the Jesuits in the middle of the 17th century. The church was badly damaged during World War II, but has since been carefully restored. Its graceful façade with its flowing lines is an excellent illustration of the Baroque style. The interior is regularly open to visitors for three afternoons during the summer months. The stunning 1660 carved woodwork around the altar and choir are well worth seeing.

🔒 Groot Begijnhof

Schapenstraat. ◯ daily, for street access only.

Founded around 1230, the Groot Begijnhof was once one of the largest béguinages in Belgium, home to several hundred béguines (see p53).

VISITORS' CHECKLIST

🏙 85,000. 🚉 Bondgenoten-
laan. 🚏 Grote Markt 9.
🛈 Grote Markt 9, 3000 Leuven,
(016) 20 3020.

The complex of 72 charming red-brick cottages (dating mostly from the 17th century) is set around the grassy squares and cobbled streets near the River Dilje. Leuven university bought the complex in 1961 and converted the cottages into student accommodation.

The red-brick houses of Leuven's Groot Begijnhof

LEUVEN TOWN CENTRE

0 metres   300
0 yards   300

Key to Symbols see back flap

Street-by-Street: Ghent ⓫

Bell on display in the Belfort

As a tourist destination, the Flemish city of Ghent has long been over-shadowed by its neighbour, Bruges. In part this reflects their divergent histories. The success of the cloth trade during the Middle Ages was followed by a period of stagnation for Bruges, while Ghent became a major industrial centre in the 18th and 19th centuries. The resulting pollution coated the city's antique buildings in layers of grime from its many factories. In the 1980s Ghent initiated a restoration programme. The city's medieval buildings were cleaned, industrial sites were tidied up and the canals were cleared. Today, it is the intricately carved stonework of its churches and antique buildings, as well as the city's excellent museums and stern, forbidding castle that give the centre its character.

★ **Het Gravensteen**
Ghent's centre is dominated by the thick stone walls and imposing gatehouse of its ancient Castle of the Counts.

★ **Design Museum Ghent**
This elegant 19th-century dining room is just one of many charming period rooms in the decorative arts museum. The collection is housed in an 18th-century mansion and covers art and design from the 1600s to the present.

Graslei
One of Ghent's most picturesque streets, the Graslei overlooks the River Leie on the site of the city's medieval harbour. It is lined with perfectly preserved guildhouses; some date from the 12th century.

To Ghent
St-Pieters

Korenmarkt
This busy square was once the corn market; the commercial centre of the city since the Middle Ages. Today, it is lined with popular cafés.

STAR SIGHTS

★ St Baafskathedraal

★ Het Gravensteen

★ Design Museum Ghent

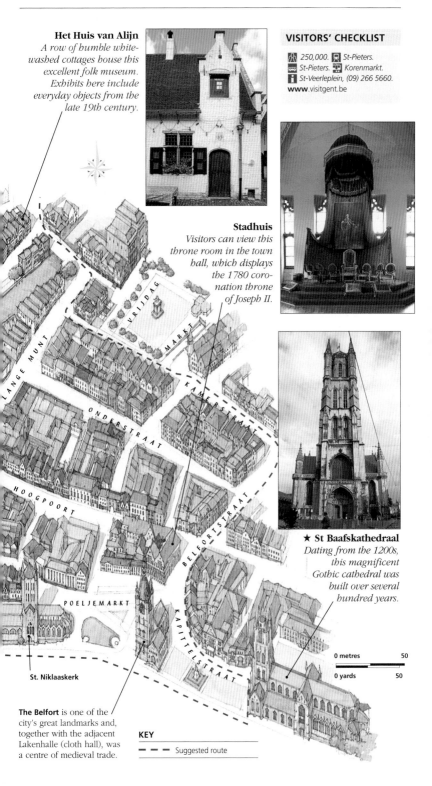

Het Huis van Alijn
A row of humble white-washed cottages house this excellent folk museum. Exhibits here include everyday objects from the late 19th century.

VISITORS' CHECKLIST

250,000. St-Pieters.
St-Pieters. Korenmarkt.
St-Veerleplein, (09) 266 5660.
www.visitgent.be

Stadhuis
Visitors can view this throne room in the town hall, which displays the 1780 coronation throne of Joseph II.

★ **St Baafskathedraal**
Dating from the 1200s, this magnificent Gothic cathedral was built over several hundred years.

St. Niklaaskerk

POELJEMARKT

HOOGPOORT

LANGE MUNT

ONDERSTRAAT

VRIJDAG MARKT

KAMERSTRAAT

BELFORTSTRAAT

KAPITTELSTRAAT

0 metres 50
0 yards 50

The Belfort is one of the city's great landmarks and, together with the adjacent Lakenhalle (cloth hall), was a centre of medieval trade.

KEY

– – – Suggested route

Exploring Ghent

Charles V's coat of arms

The heart of Ghent's historic centre was originally built during the 13th and 14th centuries when the city prospered as a result of the cloth trade. Ghent was founded in the 9th century when Baldwin Iron-Arm, the first Count of Flanders, built a castle to protect two abbeys from Viking raids. Despite many religious and dynastic conflicts, Ghent continued to flourish throughout the 16th and early 17th centuries. After 1648, the Dutch sealed the Scheldt estuary near Antwerp, closing vital canal links, which led to a decline in the fortunes of both cities. The 19th-century boom in cotton spinning reinvigorated Ghent and led to the building of wide boulevards in the south of the city. Today, textiles still feature in Ghent's industry, while its university lends a youthful vibrancy to city life.

Tiled flooring forms a maze in the Pacification Hall in Ghent's Stadhuis

Getting around

Ghent is a large city with an excellent bus and tram system. The main rail station, Ghent St-Pieters, adjoins the bus station from where several trams travel to the centre every few minutes. However, many of Ghent's main sights are within walking distance of each other. Canal boat trips are also available.

St Baafskathedraal

Sint Baafsplein. **Map** F2. *Tel (09) 225 1626.* ◯ *daily.* **Adoration of the Mystic Lamb** ◯ *daily.* 📷

Built in several stages, St Baafskathedraal (St Bavo's Cathedral) has features representing every phase of Gothic style, from the early chancel through to the later cavernous nave, which is supported by slender columns and is the cathedral's architectural highlight. In a small side chapel is one of Europe's most remarkable paintings, Jan van Eyck's polyptych *Adoration of the Mystic Lamb* (1432). St Bavo (or Bavon) was Ghent's own 7th-century saint, who abandoned the life of a wealthy degenerate to become a missionary in France and Flanders and then a hermit. He was buried in about AD653.

Stadhuis

Botermarkt 1. **Map** F2. *Tel (09) 266 5111.* 📷 📷 May–Oct: 3pm Mon–Thu. Tours depart 2.30pm from the Tourist Office.

The Stadhuis façade displays two different architectural styles. Overlooking Hoogstraat, the older half dates from the early 16th century, its tracery in the elaborate Flamboyant Gothic style. The plainer, newer part, which flanks the

THE ADORATION OF THE MYSTIC LAMB

The 12 panels of the painting, with the main image at the centre

In a side-chapel of Sint Baafskathedraal, in the centre of Ghent, is one of the greatest cultural treasures of Northern Europe. *The Adoration of the Mystic Lamb* is a monumental, multi-panelled painting by the first of the great early Flemish artists, Jan van Eyck, and his lesser-known brother, Hubrecht.

Completed in 1432, it is not only exquisitely painted; it is also an expression of the deepest beliefs of Christianity – that human salvation lies in the sacrifice of Christ, the Lamb of God. What you see today is almost entirely original; only the lower left panel is a modern copy, following its theft in 1934. This is a remarkable achievement, given the painting's history. It was rescued from Protestant church-wreckers in 1566 and from fire in 1822; parts of it were removed by French soldiers in 1794, and other parts were sold in 1816. Audioguides to the painting (included in the price of the entry ticket) explain the significance of the 12 panels.

Botermarkt, is a characteristic example of post-Reformation architecture. The statues in the niches on the façade were added in the 1890s. Among this group of figures it is possible to spot the original architect, Rombout Keldermans, who is shown studying his plans.

The building is still the city's administrative centre. Guided tours pass through a series of rooms, the most fascinating of which is the Pacification Hall. This was once the Court of Justice and the site of the signing of the Pacification of Ghent (a treaty between Catholics and Protestants against Hapsburg rule) in 1576.

⛫ Belfort
Emile Braunplein. **Map** F2. **Tel** (09) 233 3954. ⬜ Open daily 10am–6pm 15 Mar–15 Nov. 📷 ✦ May–Oct.
Ghent's belfry, a prominent landmark rising 91 m (299 ft) to the gilded-copper dragon on the tip of its spire, is situated between the cathedral and the town hall. A lift to its parapet at 65 m (213 ft) offers magnificent views over the city. Originally built in 1380, the Belfort was restored in the 19th and 20th centuries. Its bells today include a 54-bell carillon, which plays tunes to accompany the clock chimes every 15 minutes, and for keyboard concerts every Friday and Sunday at noon. Below the Belfort is the *Lakenhalle* (Cloth Hall), a fine Flemish-Gothic building from 1425 where the city's cloth-trade was carried out (guided tours only, on request). The building also incorporates a small prison.

⛪ St Niklaaskerk
Sint-Veerleplein. **Map** E2. ⬜ daily.
This merchants' church, built in the 13th–15th centuries, was dedicated to their patron saint, St Nicholas, Bishop of Myra (and Santa Claus). The church is a fine example of the distinctive and austere style called Scheldt Gothic. The interior was once packed full of guild shrines and chapels, until Protestant church-wreckers destroyed them in 1566; today it is remarkable for its pure architectural forms, with

soaring columns brightly lit by high windows. The space is punctuated by a massive and extravagantly Baroque altar screen, a clarion call to the Counter-Reformation; unusually for such latter-day alterations, it harmonizes with the rest of the church to exhilarating effect.

🏛 Graslei and Korenlei
Map E2.
These are two embankments that face each other across the Tusschen Brugghen, once Ghent's main medieval harbour. The Graslei, on the eastern side, possesses a fine set of guildhouses. Among them, at No. 14, the sandstone façade of the Guildhouse of the Free Boatmen is decorated with finely detailed nautical scenes, while the Corn Measurers' guildhouse next door is adorned by bunches of fruit and cartouches. The earliest building here is the 12th-century *Spijker* (Staple House) at No. 10. This simple Romanesque structure stored the city's grain supply for hundreds of years until a fire destroyed its interior. The gabled buildings of the Korenlei, facing the Graslei across the water, date from later centuries, but gracefully complement the Graslei. The views from the St Michielsbrug, the bridge at the southern end, are among the most beautiful in Ghent.

Views of Graslei and 16th-century guildhouses along the River Leie

🏛 Design Museum Ghent
Jan Breydelstraat 5. **Map** E1. **Tel** (09) 267 9999. ⬜ 10am–6pm Tue–Sun. ● 1 Jan, 24, 25 & 31 Dec. 📷 http://design.museum.gent.be
This decorative arts museum has a large collection contained within an elegant 18th-century town-house. The displays are arranged in two sections, beginning at the front with a series of lavishly furnished period rooms that feature textiles, furniture and artifacts from the 17th to the 19th centuries. At the back, an extension completed in 1992 focuses on modern design from Art Nouveau to contemporary works, and includes furniture by Victor Horta (*see p82*), Marcel Breuer and Ludwig Mies van der Rohe.

Sofa at Design Museum

Gothic turrets of Sint-Niklaaskerk seen from St Michael's Bridge

🏛 Groot Vleeshuis

Groentenmarkt 7. **Map** E1. **Tel** (09) 267 86 10. ◯ 10am–6pm, Tue–Sun. ⬤ Mon ▢ ⚹

The "Great Meat Hall" was built in 1407–19, and its long, low interior space still reflects its basic, original purpose as a covered butchers' market, complete with ancient beams and wonky flooring. Into this space a large, modern glass box has been ingeniously inserted to serves as a centre to promote East Flemish food: on the one side, a small restaurant serves interesting and good-value Flemish dishes; on the other is a delicatessen.

The original covered butchers' market of the Groot Vleeshuis

🏛 Dulle Griet. **Map** F1.

Groot Kanonplein (off Vrijdagmarkt). This giant cannon, sitting on the embankment of the River Leie, is famous in the folklore of Ghent. Cast in about 1450, 5 m (16 ft 5 in) long and weighing 16 tonnes, it could

The Dulle Griet cannon

fire stone cannonballs the size of a beachball; it was brought to Ghent in 1578, during an era of Calvinist government in defiance of Spain. The name Dulle Griet means "Mad Meg", a legendary medieval character who embodied mad, violent frenzy and disorder. It was recently repainted its original red, reflecting its other nickname "Groten Rooden Duyvele" (Great Red Devil).

⚓ Het Gravensteen. **Map** E1.

Sint-Veerleplein. **Tel** (09) 225 9306. ◯ 9am–6pm daily (to 5pm Oct–Mar). ⬤ 1 Jan, 24, 25 & 26 Dec. 📷

Once the seat of the counts of Flanders, the imposing stone walls of Het Gravensteen (or the Castle of the Counts) eloquently recall the unsettled and violent context of Ghent's early medieval past. Parts of the castle date back to the late 1100s, but most are later additions. Up to the 14th century the castle was Ghent's main military stronghold, and from then until the late 1700s it was used as the city's jail. Later, it became a cotton mill.

From the gatehouse, a long and heavily fortified tunnel leads up to the courtyard, which is overseen by two large buildings, the count's medieval residence and the earlier keep. Arrows guide visitors round the interior of both buildings, and in the upper rooms there is a spine-chilling collection of medieval torture instruments.

🏛 Het Huis van Alijn. **Map** E1.

Kraanlei 65. **Tel** (09) 269 23 50. ◯ 11am–5pm Tue–Sat, 11am–4pm Sun. ⬤ Mon, 1 Jan, 25 Dec. 📷 ▢ www.huisvanalijn.be (Dutch only) This is one of Belgium's best folk museums, graphically evoking daily life in the past through a huge collection of fascinating artefacts – dolls and other toys, games, clothes, furniture, kitchenware, funerary mementoes, as well as complete shops and craftsmen's workshops. There

Het Gravensteen, a classic medieval castle complete with turrets and torture instruments

is also a puppet theatre, which presents plays (in Dutch) throughout the year. The museum is set out in a sequence of rooms in a pretty group of whitewashed almshouses, "The House of Alijn", surrounding a grassy courtyard. Although mainly 16th-century, the almshouses were originally founded in 1363 as a children's hospital – not out of philanthropy, but as an act of penance by the Rijm family for the murder of two members of the rival Alijn family.

🏛 The Patershol. **Map** E1.

North of the Kraanlei are the quaint little lanes and low brick houses of the Patershol, a district that developed in the 17th century to house the city's weavers. This once down-at-heel area underwent extensive refurbishment in the 1980s and

The Patershol's 17th-century buildings which now house shops and cafés

is now one of the trendiest parts of town, with upmarket restaurants, cafés and shops.

🎭 Vlaamse Opera. Map E3.
Schouwburgstraat 3. *Tel (070) 22 02 02.* ☐ *for performances; guided tours one Saturday each month.* 🎫 www.vlaamseopera.be

This classic opera house was built in 1837–40; it has been recently restored to reclaim its reputation as one of the most spectacular theatres in Europe, with an auditorium and adjoining salons encrusted with gilding, chandeliers, mural paintings and sculptural decorations. The resident company is the much-respected Vlaamse Opera (Flemish Opera), which formed when the opera companies of Ghent and Antwerp merged.

The stunning interior of the Vlaamse Opera building

🎭 Klein Begijnhof
Lange Violettestraat 209.
☐ *6:30am–10pm (or dusk), daily.*

The Klein Begijnhof (Small Béguinage) is the prettiest of Ghent's three béguinages *(see p53)*. Rows of step-gabled, whitewashed houses – most dating from the 17th century – enclose a small park and Baroque church, creating a refuge of deep and timeless tranquillity. The Klein Begijnhof was founded as a community of single women in about 1235 and has been continuously occupied ever since; however, the residents today are no longer béguines. All Flemish béguinages were listed as UNESCO World Heritage Sites in 1998, and this one is particularly impressive.

A small garden surrounded by step-gabled houses in the Klein Begijnhof

🏛 Stedelijk Museum voor Actuele Kunst (SMAK). Map E5.
Citadelpark. *Tel (09) 221 1703.*
☐ *10am–6pm, Tue–Sun.* ● *Mon.*
🎫 📷 🚻 www.smak.be.

SMAK is one of Europe's most dynamic modern art galleries, a force in the art world that, over the past two decades, has helped to bring the spotlight to the Belgian art scene. Originally the Museum for Hedendaagse Kunst housed in the Museum of Fine Arts, its extensive and challenging permanent collection includes work by artists such as Bacon, Beuys, Broodthaers, Long, Muñoz, Nauman, Panamarenko, Tuymans and Warhol, while temporary exhibitions feature international artists at the cutting edge of contemporary art. The airy and attractive building dates from 1949 but was remodelled in the 1990s.

🏛 Museum voor Schone Kunsten. Map F5.
Ferdinand Scribedreef, Citadelpark.
Tel (09) 240 0700. ☐ *10am–6pm Tue–Sun.* 🎫 www.mskgent.be

Ghent's largest collection of fine art is displayed in this Neo-Classical building. Inside, a rotunda divides the works, with the older exhibits in a series of rooms on the right and 19th- and 20th-century art to the left. Medieval paintings include the *Bearing of the Cross* by Hieronymus Bosch (1450–1516). There are also works by Rubens *(see pp14–15)*, Anthony van Dyck (1599–1641) and Jacob Jordaens (1593–1678).

Visitors planning to also visit the Royal Museum of Fine Arts in Antwerp and the Groeninge Museum in Bruges should invest in the Flemish Art Collection combiticket to save on entry fees.

The grand, Neo-Classical façade of the Museum voor Schone Kunsten

Street-by-Street: Bruges ⑫

Traditional organ grinder

With good reason, Bruges is one of the most popular tourist destinations in Belgium. An unspoilt medieval town, Bruges' winding streets pass by picturesque canals lined with fine buildings. The centre of Bruges is amazingly well preserved. The town's trade was badly affected when the River Zwin silted up at the end of the 15th century. It was never heavily industrialized and has retained most of its medieval buildings. As a further bonus Bruges also escaped major damage in both world wars.

Today, the streets are well maintained: there are no billboards or high rises, and traffic is heavily regulated. All the major attractions are located within the circle of boulevards that marks the line of the old medieval walls.

View of the Rozenhoedkaai
A charming introduction to Bruges is provided by the boat trips along the city's canal network.

Onze Lieve Vrouwekerk
The massive Church of Our Lady employs many architectural styles. It took around 200 years to build, and its spire is Belgium's tallest.

Hans Memling Museum
Six of the artist's works are shown in the small chapel of the 12th-century St Janshospitaal, a city hospital that was still operating until 1976.

0 metres 100

0 yards 100

★ The Markt
Medieval gabled houses line this 13th-century market square at the heart of Bruges, which still holds a market each Saturday.

VISITORS' CHECKLIST

119,000. Stationsplein.
Stationsplein, Markt.
Burg 11, 8000 Bruges, (050) 44 4646. www.brugge.be

Oude Griffie, or Old Recorder's House

Blind Donkey Alley
This narrow, arched alley leads from the Burg to the 18th-century Vismarkt.

BURG

WOLLESTRAAT

ROZENHOEDKAAI

Heilig Bloed Basiliek

DIJVER

★ Stadhuis
One of the oldest and finest town halls in Belgium, this was built between 1376 and 1420. Inside, the beautifully restored Gothic hall is noted for its 1385 vaulted ceiling.

Groeninge Museum
(see pp124–5)

Arentshuis Museum

Gruuthuse Museum
(see pp122–3)

The Belfort
Built in the 13th century, the Belfort or Belfry is a stunning octagonal tower where the city's medieval charter of rights is held.

KEY

– – – Suggested route

STAR SIGHTS

★ The Markt

★ Stadhuis

Exploring Central Bruges

Bruges developed around a 9th-century fortress, built to defend the coast against the Vikings. Despite the vagaries of successive invasions by the French, between the 14th and 16th centuries Bruges became one of northern Europe's most sophisticated cities. Today, it owes its pre-eminent position to the beauty of its historic centre, whose narrow cobbled lanes and meandering canals are lined by an ensemble of medieval build-ings. These are mostly the legacy of the town's heyday as a centre of the international cloth trade, which flourished for 200 years from the 13th century. During this golden age, Bruges' merchants lavished their fortunes on fine mansions, churches and a set of civic buildings of such extravagance that they were the wonder of northern Europe.

Bell maker in market

Bruges' medieval buildings reflected in the River Dijver

Getting Around

The centre of Bruges is compact, and as most major sights are near each other, it is easiest to walk around. However, the bus service is useful for getting from the railway station to the centre. Half-hour boat trips along the canals leave from several jetties. From March to November, boats depart twice every hour.

The Vismarkt

Braambergstraat. **Map** B3. ◯ *daily.*
From the Burg an attractive arched path called the Alley of the Blind Donkey (Blinde Ezelstraat) leads to the open-air fish market with its elegant 18th-century colonnades. Fish is still sold here early each morning and business is brisk.

🏛 The Burg
Map B3.
This pleasant cobbled square a few metres from the Markt, was once the political and religious focus of Bruges. It is also the site of the original fort around which the city grew. Some of the most imposing civic buildings are located here. The beautiful sandstone Stadhuis or town hall has a

façade dating from 1375, and is adorned with turrets and statues. In contrast, the Proostdij or Provost's House was built of grey stone in 1662 in the Baroque style and boasts an ornate entrance.

🏛 Stadhuis
Burg 12. **Map** B3. *Tel* (050) 44 8711. ◯ *9:30am–5pm daily.* 🗹
The intricately carved façade of the Stadhuis was completed in 1375, but the niche statues are modern effigies of the counts and countesses of Flanders. These were added in the 1960s to replace those destroyed by the French army over a century before. The building is still used as a town hall. It is also a popular venue for Bruges weddings. Inside, a staircase leads up from the spacious foyer to the beautiful Gothic Hall, which is open to visitors year round. This magnificent parliamentary chamber was built around 1400. Immaculately restored, the ceiling boasts some lavish woodcarvings including 16 beautiful corbels (brackets) bearing representations of the seasons and the elements. A series of paintings around the hall was completed in 1895, each portraying a key event in the city's history.
In an adjacent building is the Renaissance Hall, which houses a massive wood, marble and alabaster chimney designed by Lanceloot Blondeel. The chimney is one of the best sculptural works of 16th-century Flanders.

🔒 Heilig Bloed Basiliek
Burg 15. **Map** B3. *Tel* (050) 33 6792, 33 3767. ◯ *10am–midday, 2–4pm Tue–Sun.*
The Basilica of the Holy Blood holds one of the most sacred reliquaries in Europe. The basilica divides into two distinct sections, the lower part being the evocative St Basil's chapel with its plain stone-pillared entrance and arches. The upper chapel was rebuilt in the 19th century after the French destroyed it in the 1790s. Here, brightly coloured decorations surround a silver tabernacle of 1611 which houses a sacred phial, supposed to contain a few

drops of blood and water washed from the body of Christ by Joseph of Arimathea. The phial was brought here from Jerusalem in 1150, and is still the object of great veneration. The church also has a museum of paintings, vestments and other artifacts.

⚜ The Markt
Map A3.

A market has been held on Bruges' main square since the 10th century. It is an impressive open space lined with 17th-century houses and overlooked by the Belfort on one side. The oldest façade on the square (dating from the 15th century) belongs to the Huis Bouchotte, which was the home of Charles II of England during part of his exile from 1656–7.

In the middle is a statue of Pieter de Coninck and Jan Breidel, two 14th-century guildsmen who led a rebellion against the French in 1302. Known as the *Bruges Matin*, they led Flemish soldiers to attack the French at dawn on May 18, 1302, killing almost all of them. This bloody uprising paved the way for a form of independence for the Low Countries' major towns. Rights such as the freedom to trade were subsequently enshrined in the towns' charters until the 15th century.

⚜ The Belfort
Markt. **Map** B3. ◯ *daily.* ▨

The Markt is dominated by the belfry, whose octagonal belltower rises 83 m (272 ft) above the square. Built between the 13th and 15th centuries, the belfry is Bruges' most celebrated landmark as it was used to store the town's charter, and is therefore a constant reminder of the city's past as a centre of trade. Inside the tower a winding staircase leads up, past the chamber where the town's rights and privileges were stored, to the roof, where the views across Bruges are delightful.

Bruges' Belfort or belltower overlooking the Markt

Gruuthuse Museum
Map B4. *See pp122–3.*

🏛 Arentshuis Museum
Dijver 16. **Map** B4. **Tel** (050) 44 8763. ◯ *9:30am–5pm daily.* ● *Mon (except Easter Mon and Whit Mon).* ▨

The Arentshuis Museum is housed in an 18th-century mansion overlooking the Dijver Canal. The interior is divided into two sections, with the ground floor devoted to a delightful selection of antique lace. Bruges was a centre of Belgian lace making and, although there were a few local factories, most of the work was done by women at home. The collection focuses on needlepoint and bobbin lace, with several fine examples of Bruges floral or Duchesse lace as well. Upstairs is the work of Frank Brangwyn (1867–1956), a painter and sculptor who was born in Bruges of Welsh parents. Most of Brangwyn's life was spent in Britain, but he bequeathed this collection to Bruges, as well as his drawings, furniture and carpets. The dark and powerful canvases depicting industrial scenes are perhaps the most diverting.

Statue of Breidel and Pieter de Coninck

⚜ Concertgebouw
't Zand. **Map** A4. **Tel** (070) 22 3302.

Built as part of the celebrations for Bruges' European City of Culture, this terracotta concert hall features a 28-m (92-ft) tower that offers great views.

Groeninge Museum
See pp124–5.

🔒 Onze Lieve Vrouwekerk
Mariastraat. **Map** A4. **Tel** (050) 34 5314. ◯ *9am–12:30pm & 1:30–5pm daily (4pm Sat), 1:30–5pm Sun.* ● *during services.* ▨ *mausoleum only.*

The Church of Our Lady took over 200 years to build, starting in 1220, and incorporates a variety of styles. The interior, with its white walls, stark columns and black-and-white tiled floor has a medieval simplicity, while the side chapels and pulpit are lavishly decorated.

One of the church's artistic highlights is Michelangelo's sculpture *Madonna and Child* (1504–5), at the end of the southern aisle. This marble statue was imported by a Flemish merchant, and was the only one of the artist's works to leave Italy during his lifetime. In the choir there are fine paintings by Pieter Pourbus including a *Last Supper* (1562), and the carved mausoleums of the Burgundian prince Charles the Bold and his daughter Mary.

The soaring spire of the Vrouwekerk

Gruuthuse Museum

Facial fireguard

The Gruuthuse Museum occupies a large medieval mansion close to the Dijver Canal. In the 15th century, it was inhabited by the merchant (or Lord of the Gruuthuse) who had the exclusive right to levy a tax on the "Gruit", an imported mixture of herbs added to barley during the beer-brewing process. The mansion's labyrinthine rooms, with their ancient chimneypieces and wooden beams, have survived intact and nowadays hold a priceless collection of fine and applied arts. There are tapestries, wood carvings, furniture and even a medical section devoted to cures of everyday ailments such as haemorrhoids. The authentic kitchen and original 1472 chapel transport visitors back to medieval times.

2nd Floor

1st Floor

Ground Floor

Façade of the Gruuthuis
The museum's Gothic façade, with its elegant tower, stepped gables and fine stone windows, was built in the 15th century.

Entrance

★ Charles V bust
This incredibly life-like terracotta and wood bust of Hapsburg king Charles V was carved in 1520 and is attributed to German sculptor Konrad Meit.

STAR EXHIBITS

★ Charles V bust

★ Chapel

The Seven Free Arts
Dating from around 1675, this exquisite tapestry depicts the "free arts", which included music.

VISITORS' CHECKLIST

Dijver 17, 8000 Bruges. **Map** B4. **Tel** (050) 44 8762. ▦ *Markt.* ◻ 9:30am– 5pm Tue–Sun (tickets sold until 4:30pm). ● 1 Jan, 25 Dec. ▨

GALLERY GUIDE

Laid out over three floors, the collection is organized into types of object from glassware, porcelain and ceramics to medical instruments in a series of 22 numbered rooms. Visitors may view the rooms in sequence from 1–22 and get a good sense of the original uses and layout of the house in doing so.

★ **Chapel**
Built in 1472, this oak-panelled chapel on the museum's second floor overlooks the high altar of the church next door.

KEY

- ▦ Glassware, porcelain and ceramics
- ▦ Kitchen
- ▦ Chapel
- ▦ Musical instruments
- ◻ Coins
- ▦ Tapestries
- ▦ Tools, weights and measures
- ▦ Entrance hall
- ▦ Textiles and lace
- ▦ Household implements
- ▦ Renaissance works
- ▦ Baroque works
- ▦ Reliquary and furniture
- ▦ Medical instruments
- ◻ Great Hall
- ▦ Weaponry

House on the Southern Bridge at Minnewater

🏛 Hans Memling Museum

Mariastraat 38, 8000 Bruges. **Map** A4. **Tel** (050) 44 8771. ◻ *Tue–Sun.* ▨
This small museum (a former 13th-century hospital) contains the works of Hans Memling (1430–94), one of the most talented painters of his era. Among them, *The Mystical Marriage of St. Catherine* (1479), the central panel of a triptych, is superb. The former wards also house a collection of paintings and furniture related to the hospital's history.

🔒 St Salvator-Kathedraal

St Salvatorskof 1, 8000 Bruges. **Map** A4. **Tel** (050) 33 61 88. ◻ *Apr–Sep: daily.* ● 1 Jan, 25 Dec. ▨
Built as a parish church from the 12th and 15th centuries, this large, yellow-brick building became Bruges' cathedral in 1788 when the French army destroyed the existing one. The interior is enormous and quite plain except for a handsome set of Brussels' tapestries hanging in the choir, and a 1682 organ adorned with angels.

Pale brick tower of St Salvator-Kathedraal in Bruges

♣ Minnewater

Map A5–B5.
Just south of the Begijnhof, Minnewater is a peaceful park with a lake. Swans have been here since 1448 when Maximilian of Austria ordered they be kept in memory of his councillor, Pierre Lanchais, who was beheaded by the Bruges citizens.
Once this was a bustling harbour which connected to the canal network and the sea. Today, Minnewater can be visited by one of the tourist barges that take visitors on a tour of Bruges by canal. It is also a popular spot for walkers and picnickers who may view the pretty 15th-century lock gate and house and the 1398 tower (Poedertoren).

🏰 Begijnhof

Wijngaardplein 1, 8000 Bruges. **Map** A4–A5. **Tel** (050) 36 01 40. ◻ *daily.*
Béguines were members of a lay sisterhood founded in 1245. They lived and dressed as nuns but did not take vows and were therefore able to return to the secular world at will. The begijnhof or béguinage is the walled complex in a town that housed the béguines. In Bruges, this is an area of quiet tree-lined canals faced by white, gabled houses, with a pleasant green at its centre. Visitors and locals enjoy strolling here and may visit the small, simple church which was built in 1602. The nuns who live in the houses are no longer béguines, but Benedictine sisters who moved here in the 1930s. One of the houses is open to visitors and displays simple rustic furniture and artifacts that illustrate the women's contemplative lives.

Groeninge Museum

Bruges' premier fine arts museum, the Groeninge, holds a fabulous collection of early Flemish and Dutch masters, featuring artists such as Jan van Eyck (d.1441) and Hieronymous Bosch (1450–94), famous for the strange freakish creatures of his moral allegories. Hugo van der Goes is well represented too, as is Gerard David (d.1523) and Pieter Brueghel the Younger (1564–1638). These early works are displayed on the ground floor of the museum, as well as a collection of later Belgian painters, most notably Paul Delvaux (1897–1994) and René Magritte (1898–1967). Originally built between 1929 and 1930, the museum is small and displays its collection in rotation, along with various temporary exhibitions.

Museum Façade
Originally built in 1930, the gallery was extended in 1994 to a design by architect Joseph Viérin. The old entrance is based on that of a Romanesque convent.

Portrait of Bruges Family *(1645)*
Jacob van Oost the Elder's focus on the affluence of this family surveying their beloved city shows why he was Bruges' most popular artist of the Baroque period.

★ The Moreel Triptych *(1484)*
This panel of the triptych, by German-born artist Hans Memling, was designed to adorn the altar in a Bruges church. It is said to be the first ever group portrait.

Last Judgement
Painted on three oak panels in the early 16th century, this detail from Hieronymous Bosch's famous tryptich depicts scenes of cruelty and torture. The strong moral tone of the work suggests that man's sinful nature has created a hell on earth.

STAR PAINTINGS

★ Virgin and Child with Canon by Jan van Eyck

★ The Moreel Tryptich by Hans Memling

1st Floor

Ground Floor

Main Entrance

VISITORS' CHECKLIST

Dijver 12, 8000 Bruges. **Map** B4.
Tel (050) 44 8743. Markt.
9:30am–5pm Tue–Sun (tickets till 4:30pm). 1 Jan, 25 Dec.

Household Cares (1913)
Rik Wouters used his wife Nel as the model for this statue, cast in bronze. The work's Fauvist style (see p17), *is reflected in the bold planes that enhance the figure's anxious stance.*

★ **Virgin and Child with Canon** (1436)
Jan van Eyck's richly detailed painting is noted for its realism. It shows van Eyck's patron, the canon, being presented to St Donatian by St George.

Serenity (1970)
This unusually representative work by Paul Delvaux was commissioned by the museum, and retains elements of the artist's surrealist style.

GALLERY GUIDE
The Groeninge is on one level with a two-storey extension. To the right of the main entrance there is a series of rooms displaying the early Flemish masters, and works from the 17th to 20th centuries. The extension, which is to the left of the main entrance, has temporary exhibitions on the ground floor, and work by the Bruges-born British artist Frank Brangwyn on the first floor.

KEY

- 15th and 16th centuries
- 17th to 19th centuries
- 19th and 20th centuries
- Frank Brangwyn
- Temporary exhibitions
- Non-exhibition space

Exploring Northeast Bruges

Statue of Jan van Eyck

In the height of the summer and on holiday weekends, tourists pour into Bruges, and parts of the city centre often get too crowded for comfort. Fortunately, the narrow cobbled streets and picturesque canals to the northeast of the Markt never suffer from this, and this fascinating area remains one of the most delightful parts of Bruges. Streets of charming, medieval terraced houses are dotted with grand, yet elegant 18th-century mansions. The best approach is via Jan van Eyckplein, in medieval times the city's busiest harbour, from where it is a short stroll along Spinolarei and Potterierei streets to the many museums and churches that are found in this historic district.

The historic buildings and lovely canals of northeast Bruges

The Jeruzalemkerk, built in 1497

Lace-making skills on show at the Kantcentrum lace centre

⛪ Kantcentrum

Peperstraat 3a. **Map** C2. **Tel** (050) 33 0072. ☐ Mon–Sat. 📷

The area from the white-washed cottages to the east of Potterierei Street is one of several old neighbourhoods where the city's lace workers plied their craft. Mostly, the women worked at home, receiving their raw materials from a supplier who also bought the finished product.

Lace-making skills are kept alive at the Kantcentrum, the Lace Centre at the foot of Balstraat, where local women (and a few men) fashion lace in a variety of styles, both modern and traditional. It is a busy place, and visitors can see the lace-making demonstrations held every afternoon during the summer. Some of the finished pieces are sold in the Kantcentrum shop at very reasonable prices.

⛪ Muur der Doodgeschotenen

Map C3.

Bruges was occupied by the German Army during both world wars. The bullet-marked "Wall of those who were shot dead", as its name roughly translates, is located just south of the Kruispoort and commemorates a dozen men executed by German firing squad in 1916. Eleven of them were Belgian, shot for resisting German rule. The twelfth was Captain Fryatt, a British merchant navy officer. His arrest and execution here caused almost as much outrage around Europe as the death of Edith Cavell in Brussels a year earlier.

⛪ Jeruzalemkerk

Peperstraat. **Map** B3. ☐ Mon–Sat. 📷

Next door to the Kantcentrum, the Jeruzalemkerk is Bruges' most unusual church. The present building dates from the 15th century, and was built on the site of a 13th-century chapel commissioned by a family of wealthy Italian merchants, the Adornes family, whose black marble tomb can be seen inside. Based on the design of the church of the Holy Sepulchre in Jerusalem, the structure possesses a striking tower with two tiers of wooden, polygon-shaped lanterns topped by a tin orb. Inside, the lower level contains a macabre altarpiece, carved with skulls and assorted demons. Behind the altar is a smaller vaulted chapel; leading from this is a narrow tunnel guarded by an iron grate. Along the tunnel, a lifelike model of Christ in the Tomb can be seen at close quarters.

⛪ The Kruispoort and the windmills

Map C2.

Medieval Bruges was heavily fortified. It was encircled by a city wall which was itself protected by a moat and strengthened by a series of massive gates. Most of the wall was knocked down in the 19th century, but the moat has survived and so has one of the gates, the Kruispoort, a monumental structure dating from 1402 that guards the eastern approach to the city. The earthen bank stretching north of the Kruispoort marks the line of the old city wall, which was once dotted with some 20 windmills. Today, only three remain overlooking the canal. The first, the Bonne Chieremolen, was brought here from a Flanders village in 1911, but the second – St Janshuismolen – is original to the city, a restored structure erected in 1770. The northernmost mill of the three is De Nieuwe Papegai, an old oil mill that was relocated here in 1970.

The massive Kruispoort, all that remains of Bruges' old city walls

🛈 English Convent

Carmersstraat 85. **Map** C2. **Tel** (050) 33 2424. ◯ Mon–Sat. 🖼 obligatory.
The English Convent was where dozens of English Catholics sought asylum following the execution of Charles I in 1642, and during Oliver Cromwell's subsequent rule as Lord Protector. The conventual buildings are not open to the public, but the nuns provide a well-informed tour of their beautiful church, which was built in the Baroque style in the 1620s. The interior has a delightful sense of space, its elegant proportions enhanced by its cupola, but the highlight is the altar, a grand affair made of around 20 types of marble.

🏛 Museum voor Volkskunde

Balstraat 43. **Map** B2–C2. **Tel** (050) 44 8764. ◯ 9:30am–5pm Tue–Sun, Easter & Whit Mon. 🖼
The Museum voor Volkskunde is one of the best folk museums in Flanders. It occupies

17th-century almshouses comprising the Museum voor Volkskunde

an attractive terrace of low, brick almshouses located behind an old neighbourhood café called the "Zwarte Kat" (Black Cat), which serves as the entrance. Each of the almshouses is dedicated to a different aspect of traditional Flemish life, with workshops displaying old tools. Several different crafts are represented here, such as a cobbler's and a blacksmith's, through to a series of typical historical domestic interiors.

⚜ Schuttersgilde St Sebastiaan

Carmersstraat 174. **Map** C2. **Tel** (050) 33 1626. ◯ May–Sep: 10am–midday Tue–Thu, 2–5pm Sat; Oct–Apr: 2–5pm Tue–Thu & Sat. 🖼
The Archers' guild (the Schuttersgilde) was one of the most powerful of the militia guilds, and their 16th- and 17th-century red-brick guildhouse now houses a museum.

The commercial life of medieval Bruges was dominated by the guilds, each of

The St Sebastiaan guildhouse, now a museum

which represented the interests of a particular group of skilled workmen. The guilds guarded their privileges jealously and, among many rules and customs, marriage between children whose fathers were in different guilds was greatly frowned upon. The guild claimed the name St Sebastian after an early Christian martyr, whom the Roman Emperor Diocletian had executed by his archers. The bowmen followed orders – medieval painters often show Sebastian looking like a pincushion – but miraculously Sebastian's wounds healed before he was finished off by club-wielding assassins. The guildhouse is notable for its collection of paintings of the guild's leading lights, gold and silver trinkets and guild emblems.

🏛 Museum Onze Lieve Vrouw ter Potterie

Potterierei 79. **Map** B1. **Tel** (050) 44 8731. ◯ 9:30am–midday, 1:30–5:30pm Tue–Sun.
Located by the canal in one of the quietest parts of Bruges, the Museum Onze Lieve Vrouw ter Potterie (Our Lady of Pottery) occupies part of an old hospital that was founded in 1276 to care for elderly women. There is a 14th- and 15th-century cloister, and several of the sick rooms house a modest collection of paintings, the best of which are some 17th- and 18th-century portraits of leading aristocrats. The hospital church is in excellent condition, too; it is a warm, intimate place with fine stained-glass windows and a set of impressive Baroque altarpieces.

A 90-Minute Walk Around Bruges

Almost all the most famous sights of Bruges are in the centre and to the southwest of the centre. But the commercial and residential heart in Bruges' medieval golden age was to the north of the Markt. This is where a cosmopolitan collection of European merchants had their grand national "lodges", which oversaw the trade that passed into the city along a network of canals. Only small traces of this former glory remain, hidden among a collection of waterways, bridges, and residential streets of exceptional tranquillity and charm.

The Provinciaal Hof housing the local government offices ②

Markt and Vlamingstraat

Like most of the old trading cities of Flanders, Bruges clusters around its old market square, the Markt *(see p121)*. The 19th-century statue in the centre celebrates Pieter de Coninck and Jan Breidel ①, the guildsmen who led a revolt against their French overlords in Bruges in 1302. It culminated in victory at the Battle of the Golden Spurs *(see p30)*, a key date in Flemish nationalism. Goods came into the square on a canal, and were unloaded under the roof of the Waterhalle. The canal was filled in during the 1780s and now the site of the Waterhalle has been taken by the Provinciaal Hof ②, the administrative

offices of the province of West Flanders. This Neo-Medieval building was designed by Louis Delacenserie (1838–1909), the architect responsible for much of the restoration of medieval Bruges. On the other side of the Markt, on the corner of St-Amandstraat, is the Huis Bouchotte ③; the compass on the façade, attached to a weathervane, was used by merchants to check the winds for the ships bringing goods to Bruges. Opposite it is the Craenenburg ④ (now a café), where Archduke Maximilian of Austria was imprisoned by the Bruges' authorities in 1488. A walk up Vlamingstraat leads past the Stadsschouwburg ⑤ (Municipal Theatre), a handsome Neo-Classical building from 1868. At No. 33 is the former Genuese Loge ⑥, the lodge of the Genoese traders, dating from 1399. No. 35 was the Huis Ter Beurze ⑦, where merchants and bankers exchanged credit notes as early as the 13th century, making this perhaps the world's first stock exchange, and the origin of the French term for a stock-exchange, "Bourse".

Statue of Pieter de Coninck and Jan Breidel ①

Spiegelrei

On the right-hand side of the Academiestraat stands the Poortersloge ⑧ (Burghers' Lodge), a clubhouse for leading citizens in medieval Bruges. Almost all the city's grand buildings of that era had a tower; this is a rare example where the tower (rebuilt in 1775) has survived. On the other side of the street is the Oud Tolhuis ⑨, the Old Customs House. It overlooked a weighbridge where customs charges were assessed; that area has been replaced by the square, Jan van Eyckplein, named after the city's great artist who is represented by a statue ⑩. The canal that once led to the city centre now stops between Spiegelrei and

KEY

••• Walk Route

Spinolarei. On the corner of Spiegelrei and Genthof is Roode Steen ⑪; this was the home of Georges Rodenbach, the author of the controversial novel *Bruges-la-Morte* (Bruges the Dead, 1892). Koningstraat, off Spinolarei, leads to the St

Walburgakerk ⑫, Bruges' finest Baroque church, built for the Jesuits in 1612–42.

Jeruzalemkerk

Back on Spinolarei, cross the canal on Strooibrug. Straight ahead is Blekersstraat, with Café Vlissinghe ⑬ on the right. This is reputedly Bruges' oldest tavern, dating from 1515. Heading south down St-Annarei, the first left leads to the St Annakerk ⑭, a pretty parish church from 1497. The

A room at Bruges' folk museum, the Museum voor Volkskunde ⑯

Jeruzalemkerk *(see p126)* ⑮ on Peperstraat is very different, built in the 15th century and themed on pilgrimage sites in the Holy Land. Adjoining it is the Kantcentrum, the Lace Centre *(see p126)*. A row of almshouses in Balstraat is now the Museum voor Volkskunde *(see p127)* ⑯, a folk museum that paints a vivid picture of life in old Bruges. The only domed church in Bruges is in the English Convent (Engelsklooster) *(see p127)* ⑰, on Carmersstraat. Head back west along Carmerstraat, cross the canal on the Carmersbrug, and turn right to reach St Gilliskerk ⑱, an attractive church dating from the 13th–15th century. A series of cobbled streets leads to a picturesque section of canal at the Augustijnenbrug. The street on the opposite side called Spaanse Loskaai ⑲ recalls that this was once the Spanish quarter. Cross the

canal on the Vlamingbrug ⑳. At Naaldenstraat 19 is Hof Bladelin ㉑, a mansion built in about 1450 by Pieter Bladelin; after 1469, it was owned by the Medici Bank of Florence. Hotel Lucca ㉒, at Naaldenstraat 30, is on the site of the trading house of the merchants of the Italian city of Lucca. The alley off Naaldenstraat called Boterhuis ㉓ passes beneath the arch of the old Butter House and dairy market, and leads to St Jakobskerk ㉔. This fine Gothic church – with Baroque remodelling – contains art, ornate chapels, and tombs. The route along Moerstraat and Ontvangersstraat marks the bounds of the Prinsenhof, the former palace of the Dukes of Burgundy; its memory survives only in the name of a smart hotel and a small street ㉕. Geldmuntstraat is named after the old mint that stood on the little square called Muntplein; it leads back to the Eiermarkt (Egg Market) ㉖ and the Markt.

The Spinolarei canal, one of Bruges' principal waterways

TIPS FOR WALKERS

Starting point: *The Markt*
Length: *3.7 km (2.3 miles)*
Getting there: *The Markt is within walking distance of almost all hotels in Bruges; bus routes from all directions also go to this hub.*
Stopping off points: *There are a multitude of cafés and restaurants around the Markt, but very few beyond Vlamingstraat. A famous exception is the venerable old tavern called Cafe Vlissinghe in Blekersstraat (No. 13 on this walk).*

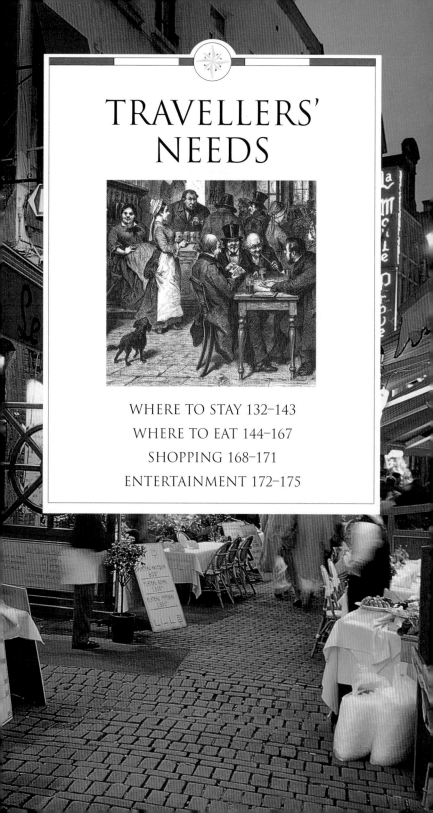

TRAVELLERS'
NEEDS

WHERE TO STAY

For most of the year, Brussels is primarily a business or political destination, and accommodation is often priced accordingly. The wide range of top hotels has one fine advantage for the visitor; weekend and summer deals make it possible even on a modest budget to stay in some of Europe's most luxurious establishments. The midrange of hotels is also well represented

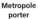
Metropole porter

in the city, with period houses turned into stylish family-run hotels and chain hotels. To keep accommodation costs to a minimum, choose from Brussels' abundance of youth hostels and bed-and-breakfast options. As well as Brussels hotels, there are also listings of establishments in Antwerp, Bruges and Ghent. A detailed description of each hotel is listed on pp136–43.

Hallway in the Hotel Metropole on Place de Brouckère (see p138)

BRUSSELS HOTELS

While Brussels does not have a specific hotel area, there are clusters of hotels in various parts of the city. Centrally, the most fertile ground is between Place Rogier and Place de Brouckère, which is within walking distance of both the Upper and Lower Town and a short bus ride from most major sights. The streets to the west of the Grand Place are also well supplied for those who want to be in the historic centre of town, but road noise can be a problem at night. To the north, Place Ste-Catherine or the streets behind Avenue de la Toison d'Or also have plenty of options. Following the pattern of cities worldwide, hotels generally reduce in price the further they are from the centre. Bed-and-breakfast rooms are also dispersed across the capital and can often be found in residential

districts at very good rates. When arriving in the city from abroad by train or plane, it is worth knowing that the Gare du Midi and the airport both have nearby hotel colonies, although the station surroundings are run down in places. The airport has principally attracted chain hotels, which often offer good value package deals with the national airlines, although sightseeing from here is inconvenient.

ROOM RATES

Hotels at the top end of the market offer exceptional standards of comfort and convenience to their largely corporate clients, and their prices reflect this. In general, prices are higher than in the rest of Belgium, but on a par with other European capitals. For a night in a luxury hotel, expect to pay €250 to €300 for a double room; the price for a room in the city averages in the €150 to €175 bracket.

Façade of the Crowne Plaza Hotel, one of the hotel chain (see p137)

However, there are numerous discounts available *(see Special Rates, p126)*.

Single travellers can often find reasonable discounts on accommodation, although few places will offer rooms at half the price of a double. It is usual to be charged extra if you place additional guests in a double room. Travelling with children is not the financial burden it might be in this child-friendly society *(see p127)*. Youth hostels cater very well to the budget student traveller and some also have family rooms.

TAXES AND CHARGES

Room taxes and sales taxes should be included in the cost of your room, so the price quoted should be what appears as the total. The price of car parking may be added. Some hotels offer free parking, others charge up to €20 a night. In hotels with no private car park, it is worth checking discounts for public parking facilities if these are located nearby. While many hotels are happy to allow pets, many will add a small nightly charge to the bill. Breakfast is not always included in the price of a room, even in very expensive establishments. However, many hotels do offer excellent free breakfasts, so ask when you book. The fare usually consists of continental breakfast, including good coffee, warm croissants and brioche rolls, preserves and fruit juice. Bear in mind that if the expensive place where you are staying is charging €20 for breakfast, there will be plenty of places nearby offering equal quality for much less money. The usual price for a hotel breakfast ranges upwards from €2.50, but coffee and rolls are usually priced at around €6.20. Unusually, youth hostels also offer lunches and dinners at around €9.90 each.

Phone calls from hotel rooms can be extremely expensive, with unit charges of €.60 for even a local call not uncommon. To make a long-distance call, buying a phonecard and using the efficient public payphone service is several times less expensive. Hotel faxes or modem charges, when available, can also mount up.

Minibar charges are usually very high, although no more so than in any other western European city. Watching satellite or pay-TV stations can also be expensive. However, Belgium's advanced cable network and proximity to other countries means that there are usually more than 20 free channels to choose from including the BBC as well as French and German television.

HOTEL GRADINGS AND FACILITIES

Approved hotels are issued with a shield by the Belgian Tourist Board which must be displayed in a prominent position. Hotels carrying this sign conform to official standards set by Belgian law which guarantee certain standards of quality. Some hotels are also graded according to the Benelux

Reception desk at the Hotel Eurostars Sablon *(see p140)*

system, ranging from one to five stars, with one as the minimum. It is worth remembering, however, that membership of this scheme is voluntary and as a result, there may be high-quality hotels which are not graded in this way.

In a city with so many luxury hotels, fierce competition has led to ever more sophisticated gadgets and services for businesspeople. Several private phone lines, screened calls, free wireless internet access, automatic check-out services, 24-hour news via Reuters, secretarial services, free mobile phones and even executive suites designed expressly for women are all on offer. Most of the top hotels also house extensive fitness facilities, including saunas and full gymnasiums, although there are few large swimming pools.

Brussels' reputation as a centre for fine dining is significantly enhanced by the hotel trade, with major hotels

often offering several options, from expert gastronomy to excellent brasserie dining. For snacks and drinks, Brussels'

19th-century courtyard of the Conrad International *(see p142)*

hotels are known for their old-style, entertaining bars with piano music for those guests who prefer not to venture into the city at night. A handful have nightclub facilities where lively crowds meet in the evening for cocktails and dancing.

As one of Europe's major centres for the convention trade, Brussels is not short of meeting and function rooms, with the big hotels offering dozens of spaces for anything from conferences to society weddings and even relatively modest hotels offering good-sized rooms for business seminars and the like. Many expensive hotels have serviced apartments on offer; these can be useful for the greater freedom they provide.

The Hotel Ter Brughe, next to one of Bruges' many canals *(see p143)*

View of the Grand Place from a room at Auberge Saint-Michel *(see p137)*

HOW TO BOOK

Rooms are available in Brussels at most times of the year, but you should book several days in advance to ensure that you get the place you want. In mid- and top-range hotels, a credit card is the usual way to book, giving card details as a deposit; in smaller hotels, bookings can often be made simply by giving your name and details of the day and time of arrival.

The **Tourist Office** offers a free, same-day reservation service on-site. It also publishes a practical guide to Brussels hotels, updated annually, which is available on request. For booking by telephone, **Resotel** provides a free service for visitors and is very helpful.

If you are familar with the technology, internet bookings can be quick and efficient and the information available on hotel websites is often more regularly updated than the hotel brochure.

SPECIAL RATES

Brussels is an exceptional destination, in that relatively few people come for the weekend or in July and August, meaning that often

Porter at the Conrad International

remarkable deals can be acquired at these times.

The cost of staying in one of the top hotels over the weekend or at off-peak times can plummet by as much as 65 per cent (for example, from €300 to €100 for a double room), so checking before booking about any special deals may save a large sum of money. A few hotels also offer discounts for guests who eat in their restaurants.

Some reservation services charge a small fee, but they can usually find competitively priced accommodation. Any deposit given is deducted from the final hotel bill.

Many travel agents also offer packages for visiting Brussels or Belgium, with accommodation working out less expensively than a custom-booked break.

It is worth checking with your airline about possible discounts through its reservation services, and to find out about frequent-flyer bargains for affiliated hotels.

DISABLED TRAVELLERS

Hotels in Brussels and the rest of Belgium take the needs of disabled travellers seriously. Many have one or more rooms designed with wheelchair-bound guests in mind. It is worth remembering that many hotel buildings in Brussels are historic and therefore may not be suitable. Most staff, however, will be helpful. It is wise to ask in

DIRECTORY

RESERVATION AGENCIES

Resotel
Avenue E Van Nieuwenhuyse 6, Brussels 1160.
Tel (02) 779 3939.
www.resotel.be

Tourist Information Board
Town Hall, Grand Place 1, Brussels 1000.
Map 2 D3.
Tel (02) 513 8940.
www.bitc.be

AUBERGES DE JEUNESSE/YOUTH HOSTELS:

Jacques Brel
Rue de la Sablonnière 30, Brussels 1000. **Map** 2 F1.
Tel (02) 218 0187.

Generation Europe
Rue de l'Eléphant 4, Brussels 1080. **Map** 1 A1.
Tel (02) 410 3858.

New Sleep Well
Rue du Damier 23, Brussels 1000. **Map** 2 D1.

Tel (02) 218 50 50.
www.sleepwell.be

BED AND BREAKFAST

Bed and Breakfast Taxi Stop
Rue du Fossé-aux-Loups 28, Brussels 1000. **Map** 2 D2. *Tel* (70) 22 2292.

New Windrose
Avenue de Jette 26, Brussels 1081.
Tel (02) 534 7191.

Bed & Brussels
Rue Kindermans 9, Brussels 1050. *Tel* (02) 646 0737.
www.bnb-brussels.be

GAY AND LESBIAN ACCOMMODATION

The Rainbow House
Rue du Marché au Charbon 42, Brussels 1000. **Map** 1 C3 *Tel* (02) 503 5990.

Tels Quels
Rue du Marché au Charbon 81, Brussels 1000. **Map** 1 C3. *Tel* (02) 512 4587.

The Hilton Brussels, formerly the Albert Premier Rogier *(see p140)*

advance whether the hotel can cater to travellers with special needs. Most hotels will allow the visually handicapped to bring a guide dog onto the premises, although again it is best to make sure that this is the case before you arrive.

YOUTH ACCOMMODATION

Brussels has several central, excellent youth hostels, with modern facilities, reasonably priced food and more privacy than is usually associated with hostel stays. Perhaps the best are the **Jacques Brel**, close to Place Madou, and the **New Sleep Well**, which has disabled access. A bed in a four-person room should cost in the region of €19, rising to around €30 for a single room. Breakfast is sometimes included or costs from €2.50, with lunch and dinner for a charge of around

€9.90. If you are not a member of Hostelling International, rates rise by up to €5 extra per night; membership cards, priced €9–15, are available at most hostels. Joining is worthwhile if you are travelling around Belgium, as there are over 30 hostels across the country and there are discounts at some attractions.

GAY AND LESBIAN ACCOMMODATION

There are no specifically gay or lesbian hotels in the city, but same-sex couples should have few problems finding welcoming accommodation. The **Tels Quels** association, located on the Rue de Marché au Charbon, is the best source of information about good places to choose. It has a documentation centre covering most aspects of gay life in the city and publishes a monthly magazine. **The Rainbow House**, across the road, is a good place to find details of gay and lesbian events taking place in and around the centre of the city.

TRAVELLING WITH CHILDREN

Children are welcome at all hotels in Brussels, with many making a concerted effort to cater for the needs of those travelling with children. Most allow one or two under-12s to stay in their parents' room without extra charge and some hotels will extend this

principle to under-16s and under-18s. When travelling with children, it is worth reserving in advance as the hotel will find the room that best suits your needs. Families planning a long stay in Brussels should consider renting a suite or a self-catering apartment, which are more economical.

SELF-CATERING APARTMENTS

There is no shortage of self-catering accommodation in Brussels, with many places available for a short stay as well as by the week or month. A few places are

The lobby at the Meridien Hotel in Brussels' Lower Town *(see p139)*

attached to hotels as suites, with the rest run by private companies. Prices start at around €600 per week, for a fairly basic but furnished one- or two-bedroom apartment, to €1,000 or more for more luxurious lodgings. Contact Resotel or visit the Tourist Office for a detailed list of suggestions.

BED-AND-BREAKFAST

Bed-and-breakfast, also called *chambre d'hôte*, accommodation can be a very pleasant alternative to staying in a cheap hotel, and rooms can often be found even in the centre of town. You may come across a bargain by wandering the streets, but the easiest way to find bed-and-breakfast lodgings is through the Tourist Office or one of the capital's specialist agencies.

Breakfast room of the George V hotel *(see p137)*

Choosing a Hotel

The hotels on the following pages have been selected across a wide price range for the excellence of their facilities, location or character. The chart below first lists hotels in Brussels by area, followed by a selection in Antwerp, Bruges, and Ghent. Hotels within the same price category are listed alphabetically. Map references refer to the Brussels Street Finders on pp190–193.

PRICE CATEGORIES
The following price ranges are for a standard double room and taxes per night during the high season. Breakfast is not included, unless specified.

€ under 80 euros
€€ 80–130 euros
€€€ 130–180 euros
€€€€ 180–260 euros
€€€€€ over 260 euros

LOWER TOWN

Arlequin   🖥 P   €

Rue de la Fourche 17–19, Greepstraat, 1000 Brussels **Tel** *(02) 514 1615* **Fax** *(02) 514 2202* **Rooms** *92* **Map** *2 D2*

A modern, three-star hotel in the heart of the historical centre. Although not the most historically interesting of Brussels' hotels, it does have a great location. Some of the guest rooms boast great views over the city. Breakfast is included. There are plenty of restaurants and bars in the vicinity. Conference facilities available. **www.arlequin.be**

Astrid Centre   🖥 P 📖   €

Place du Samedi 11, 1000 Brussels **Tel** *(02) 219 3119* **Fax** *(02) 219 3170* **Rooms** *100*   **Map** *1 C1*

A comfortable and efficient hotel in the centre of the city, the Astrid Centre Hotel can be found near the picturesque fish market and the popular restaurants of Place Ste Catherine. The rooms are large with modern furnishings and facilities. Conference facilities. Private parking. Complimentary breakfast. **www.astridhotel.be**

Bedford   🖥 P 🍴 📖   €

Rue du Midi 135–137, 1000 Brussels **Tel** *(02) 507 0000* **Fax** *(02) 507 0010* **Rooms** *326*   **Map** *1 C3*

The rooms in this recently-renovated four-star hotel are spacious and comfortable with plenty of lounge space. Within walking distance of the Grand Place and the area's busy restaurants. The hotel also has 18 sumptuously-decorated executive rooms and 12 suites suitable for families. Breakfast is included. **www.hotelbedford.be**

Grande Cloche   €

Place Rouppe 10, 1000 Brussels **Tel** *(02) 512 6140* **Fax** *(02) 512 6591* **Rooms** *37*   **Map** *1 C4*

A welcoming hotel halfway between the Grand Place and Brussels' Gare du Midi, Grande Cloche occupies a recently renovated 19th-century townhouse. Rooms are comfortable with modern facilities, ideal for budget travellers. Breakfast is included in the price. Free parking on the square in front of the hotel. **www.hotelgrandecloche.com**

Manhattan   €

Boulevard Adolphe Max 132–140, 1000 Brussels **Tel** *(02) 219 1619* **Fax** *(02) 223 2599* **Rooms** *62* **Map** *2 D1*

Situated between the Grand Place and the Botanical Gardens, Hotel Manhattan is very well priced but pretty basic. Rooms have an old-fashioned feel, but are clean and comfortable and the main sights are within walking distance. The price includes breakfast. Plenty of nearby restaurants, which staff can recommend. **www.hotelmanhattan.be**

NH Grand Place Arenberg   🖥 P 🍴 📺 📖 €

Rue d'Assaut 15, 1000 Brussels **Tel** *(02) 501 1616* **Fax** *(02) 501 1818* **Rooms** *155*   **Map** *2 D2*

A modern hotel within sight of Brussels' cathedral and a short stroll away from Place du Grand Sablon, with its famous chocolatiers. All rooms have modern facilities and have recently been renovated to their current spotless state. Breakfast not included in the price. Business-friendly amenities. **www.nh-hotels.com**

Vendôme   🖥 P 🍴   €

Boulevard Adolphe Max 98, 1000 Brussels **Tel** *(02) 227 0300* **Fax** *(03) 218 0683* **Rooms** *135*   **Map** *2 D1*

The rooms of this comfortable, modern and business-friendly hotel, just north of Place de Brouckère, are large and pleasantly decorated with ensuite facilities. Breakfast is included in the price. Stylish bar and brasserie serving traditional Belgian cuisine. Convention facilities. Business club rooms (with Internet connections). **www.hotel-vendome.be**

Aris Grand Place   🖥 📖   €€

Marché aux Herbes 78–80, 1000 Brussels **Tel** *(02) 514 4300* **Fax** *(02) 543 0119* **Rooms** *55*   **Map** *2 D3*

This reasonably-priced hotel in the historical centre is just a minute from the Grand Place. Housed in a late 19th-century building, the rooms are modern and comfortable with double-glazing to keep out exterior city noise. Discounts for weekend bookings. Breakfast included. **www.arishotel.be**

Aristote   🖥 🍴   €€

Avenue de Stalingrad 7, 1000 Brussels **Tel** *(02) 513 1310* **Fax** *(02) 513 8070* **Rooms** *25*   **Map** *1 B4*

Located in a striking-looking building between the Grand Place and the central station, Hotel Aristote occupies a renovated 19th-century townhouse with small, but elegant bedrooms and a popular pizzeria (decorated in medieval style). Breakfast is included. Staff are friendly and offer plenty of sightseeing tips and advice. **www.aristote-hotel.be**

Key to Symbols *see back cover flap*

Auberge Saint-Michel

Grand Place 15, 1000 Brussels **Tel** *(02) 511 0956* **Fax** *(02) 511 4600* **Rooms** *14* **Map** *2 D3*

A former mansion overlooking the Grand Place, the two-star Auberge Saint-Michel is well-placed. Be sure to ask for a room with a view over the square (as only seven have them). Rooms are basic, but clean, with ensuite facilities. Staff are friendly and helpful. Breakfast is included in the price and is served in the rooms.

Carrefour de l'Europe

Rue du Marché aux Herbes 110, 1000 Brussels **Tel** *(02) 504 9400* **Fax** *(02) 504 9500* **Rooms** *64* **Map** *2 D3*

An elegant, four-star hotel in the heart of Brussels, targeted at the business traveller. Eight conference rooms and 10 executive traveller rooms. Lobby bar. Large public parking next to the hotel. All rooms have wi-fi Internet connection and breakfast is included in the price. **www.carrefoureurope.net**

Central Hotel

Rue des Colonies 10, 1000 Brussels **Tel** *(02) 504 9910* **Fax** *(02) 503 1451* **Rooms** *47* **Map** *2 E3*

This historic four-star hotel near the Royal Palace offers comfortable and reasonably-priced accommodation in the centre of Brussels. Efficient staff provide sightseeing advice and restaurant recommendations. Complimentary buffet breakfast. **www.hotusa.com**

Citadines St Catherine

Quai Au Bois A Bruler 51, 1000 Brussels **Tel** *(02) 221 1411* **Fax** *(02) 221 1599* **Rooms** *169* **Map** *1 C1*

This apartment hotel just north of the Grand Place (near the church of Ste-Catherine) offers studio apartments with a peaceful communal garden on a self-catering or half-board basis. A good choice for visitors coming for a week or more, the apartments come with all modern facilities. **www.citadines.com**

Congres

Rue du Congres 42, 1000 Brussels **Tel** *(02) 217 1890* **Fax** *(02) 217 1897* **Rooms** *70* **Map** *2 F2*

This peaceful three-star hotel occupies four renovated 19th-century townhouses and is within walking distance of all the main sights. Rooms are modern but elegant, with business-friendly facilities. Complimentary buffet breakfast. Polite and friendly staff. **www.hotelducongres.be**

Crowne Plaza Hotel

Rue Gineste 3, 1210 Brussels **Tel** *(02) 203 6200* **Fax** *(02) 203 5555* **Rooms** *354* **Map** *2 E1*

An Art Nouveau hotel dating back to 1908, combining turn-of-the-century style with modern facilities. Rooms are clean and comfortable, and some have recently been refurbished. Generous buffet breakfast. Helpful and friendly staff. Book in advance in the busy summer season. **www.crowneplaza.com**

George V Hotel

Rue T'Kint 23, 1000 Brussels **Tel** *(02) 513 5093* **Fax** *(02) 513 4493* **Rooms** *20* **Map** *1 B3*

This friendly, very reasonably priced three-star hotel within walking distance of the Grand Place occupies an old English-inspired 19th-century townhouse. Rooms are large and opulently decorated with period furnishings and plenty of old-world charm. Hotel bar. Complimentary breakfast included in price. **www.george5.com**

IBIS Grand Place

Rue du Marché aux Herbes 100, 1000 Brussels **Tel** *(02) 514 4040* **Fax** *(02) 514 5067* **Rooms** *184* **Map** *2 D3*

The best thing about this modern hotel, just off Grand Place, is its location. Rooms are basic, but comfortable and clean. The bar serves some food. Staff are friendly and efficient. Rooms can be expensive in high season, but look out for off-peak weekend offers. **www.ibishotel.com**

La Legende

Rue du Lombard 35, 1000 Brussels **Tel** *(02) 512 8290* **Fax** *(02) 512 3493* **Rooms** *26* **Map** *1 C3*

La Legende isn't the most modern of Brussels' two-star hotels but, given its central location, it is reasonably-priced and welcoming. Rooms are clean and functional, with four-bed family rooms on offer. A good choice for budget travellers. Guests can use a private car park for 20 euros per day. **www.hotellalegende.com**

La Vieille Lanterne

Rue des Grands Carmes 29, 1000 Brussels **Tel** *(02) 512 7494* **Fax** *(02) 512 1397* **Rooms** *6* **Map** *1 C3*

Centrally-located, La Vieille Lanterne is a good value hostel with six rooms. All are brightly decorated, with ensuite, and benefit from great views onto Manneken Pis. Breakfast is included in the price and is served in the rooms. No check-in after 10pm, when the doors are closed for the night. Book in advance in summer seasons.

Madeleine

Rue de la Montagne 20–22, 1000 Brussels **Tel** *(02) 513 2973* **Fax** *(02) 502 1350* **Rooms** *52* **Map** *2 D3*

Behind its slightly shabby exterior, Hotel La Madeleine is quite charming and offers rooms to meet all budgets – from small and cosy to executive suites. Double-glazing keeps out the exterior noise. Not all rooms have ensuite facilities. Complimentary buffet breakfast. **www.hotel-la-madeleine.be**

Matignon

Rue de la Bourse 8–12, 1000 Brussels **Tel** *(02) 511 0888* **Fax** *(02) 513 6927* **Rooms** *37* **Map** *1 C2*

A small, reasonably-priced, three-star hotel in a good location with simple, but thoughtfully-decorated rooms. The price includes breakfast and a minibar. The Matignon also has a welcoming brasserie. Not all rooms have ensuite facilities. Friendly staff are on hand to offer sightseeing advice. **www.hotelmatignon.be**

Mozart

Rue du Marché-aux-Fromages 23, 1000 Brussels **Tel** *(02) 502 6661* **Fax** *(02) 502 7758* **Rooms** *50* **Map** *2 D3*

A three-star budget hotel in a fabulous location, Hotel Mozart is a great choice for young travellers looking to stay in the thick of the action. The hotel is fantastically decorated with a luxurious reception and plenty of personal touches in each of the 47 rooms. Breakfast is included in the price. Book early to avoid disappointment. **www.hotel-mozart.be**

Noga

Rue du Béguinage 38, 1000 Brussels **Tel** *(02) 218 6763* **Fax** *(02) 218 1603* **Rooms** *19* **Map** *1 C1*

A friendly hotel near the church of St-Jean-Baptiste, Noga feels like a home away from home with its comfy lounge, popular games room with billiard table, library and music room with piano, not to mention the eclectic furnishing in its bedrooms. Bicycles for rent. Internet access and laundry facilities. **www.nogahotel.com**

Novotel (off Grand Place)

Rue du Marché Aux Herbes 120, 1000 Brussels **Tel** *(02) 514 3333* **Fax** *(02) 511 7723* **Rooms** *138* **Map** *2 D3*

Sister hotel to the nearby Novotel Tour Noire, this two-star hotel has been designed and decorated in 16th-century Spanish style. Though not the most luxurious of the central hotels, rooms are a good size and well-furnished, given the price and location. **www.novotel.com**

Novotel Tour Noire

Rue de la Vierge Noire 32, 1000 Brussels **Tel** *(02) 505 5050* **Fax** *(02) 505 5000* **Rooms** *217* **Map** *1 C2*

A welcoming hotel with plenty of family-friendly facilities – including gym and pool – the Novotel Tour Noire offers an efficient and well-priced base in the heart of the city. Paid parking. Friendly staff. Generous buffet breakfast. Rooms have triple-glazing to keep out the noise. **www.novotel.com**

Opera

Rue Grétry 53, 1000 Brussels **Tel** *(02) 219 4343* **Fax** *(02) 219 1720* **Rooms** *49* **Map** *2 D2*

Situated just off the Grand Place, the two-star Hotel Opera is clean, quiet, friendly and well-located. Rooms are modern, comfortable and simply decorated. Reasonably priced for the location with discounts available if rooms are booked online. Complimentary buffet breakfast. **www.hotel-opera.be**

Queen Anne

Boulevard Emile Jacqmain 110, 1000 Brussels **Tel** *(02) 217 1600* **Fax** *(02) 217 1838* **Rooms** *60* **Map** *2 D1*

Close to the De Brouckère metro station, the welcoming Hotel Queen Anne is small, but friendly, with clean, comfortable rooms and a generous buffet breakfast. All rooms have ensuite facilities. Eleven apartments are available for longer stays. The peaceful location and relaxed atmosphere is perfect for families. **www.queen-anne.be**

Scandic Grand Place

Rue d'Arenberg 18, 1000 Brussels **Tel** *(02) 548 1811* **Fax** *(02) 548 1820* **Rooms** *100* **Map** *2 D2*

This luxury hotel in the Scandic chain is situated behind the facades of two listed townhouses and boasts a popular bar and restaurant, sauna, fitness room, "recreation area" and conference facilities. Close to Gare Centrale train station, it is well placed for exploring the city. **www.scandic-hotels.com**

Welcome Hotel

Quai au Bois à Brûler 23, 1000 Brussels **Tel** *(02) 219 9546* **Fax** *(02) 217 1887* **Rooms** *15* **Map** *1 C1*

Situated in a peaceful location to the north of Place Ste Catherine (the city's old fish market), Hotel Welcome sits in the midst of some fabulous fish restaurants. Recently renovated rooms. Complimentary breakfast is served in the Art Deco breakfast room. Metro stop just in front of the hotel. Shuttle bus from the airport. **www.hotelwelcome.com**

Art Hotel Siru

Place Rogier 1, 1210 Brussels **Tel** *(02) 203 3580* **Fax** *(02) 203 3303* **Rooms** *101* **Map** *2 D1*

A three-star hotel with an impressive collection of contemporary Belgian art and some wonderful futuristic décor, the Art Hotel Siru is a veritable museum-hotel. The corridors feature original comic strips and verses by Flemish poets on the walls. The building stands on the former base of French poets Verlaine and Rimbaud. **www.comforthotelsiru.com**

Atlas

Rue du Vieux Marché aux Grains 30, 1000 Brussels **Tel** *(02) 502 6006* **Fax** *(02) 502 6935* **Rooms** *88* **Map** *1 C2*

Modern, three-star hotel just to the north of Grand Place. Offers basic, but comfortable rooms with free wi-fi Internet connection and breakfast included in the price. Six suite rooms have a mini-kitchenette. Families can rent duplex rooms, sleeping four (daily supplement applies). **www.atlas.be**

Hotel Metropole

Place de Brouckère 31, 1000 Brussels **Tel** *(02) 217 2300* **Fax** *(02) 218 0220* **Rooms** *305* **Map** *1 D2*

Built 1895, this plush hotel boasts striking architecture and a mix of French Renaissance, Empire and Art Deco styles. High ceilings, stained-glass restaurant and crystal chandeliers in the lobby, bar and gourmet restaurant. Not all rooms are period decorated. Complimentary breakfast. **www.metropolehotel.be**

Royal Embassy

Boulevard Anspach 159–163, 1000 Brussels **Tel** *(02) 512 8100* **Fax** *(02) 514 3097* **Rooms** *54* **Map** *1 C3*

A modern four-star hotel in a classical townhouse on one of Brussels' most picturesque boulevards, the Royal Embassy is a popular resting place for business travellers. Rooms are quite small, but clean and comfortable, with modern facilities. The main sights are only a short walk away. **www.hotel-royal-embassy.be**

Key to Price Guide *see p136* **Key to Symbols** *see back cover flap*

Amigo

Rue de l'Amigo 1–3, 1000 Brussels **Tel** *(02) 547 4747* **Fax** *(02) 513 5277* **Rooms** *174*   **Map** *1 C3*

This newly-restored five-star hotel in the Rocco Forte Hotel chain provides an elegant setting and great location just near the Grand Place. Rooms have king-size beds and marble bathrooms. Family suites. Award-winning restaurant. Meeting room, spa and fitness facilities. **www.hotelamigo.com**

Floris Grand Place

Rue des Harengs 6–8, 1000 Brussels **Tel** *(02) 514 0760* **Fax** *(02) 548 9039* **Rooms** *12*   **Map** *2 D3*

Between the Grand Place and the Marche aux Herbes, this three-star Floris hotel is well located near some of Brussels' most popular restaurants and bars, which is reflected in the rather pricey room rates, although substantial discounts are available when booking online. Rooms are modern and there is a communal lounge area. **www.florishotels.com**

Meridien

Carrefour de l'Europe 3, 1000 Brussels **Tel** *(02) 548 4211* **Fax** *(02) 548 4080* **Rooms** *224*   **Map** *2 D3*

A modern luxury hotel just south of the Grand Place, the Meridien offers a classy place to stay in the heart of old Brussels if you don't mind its proximity to the more seedy area around the Gare Centrale train station. Rooms are designed in Victorian/English style. The hotel organizes golf, canoeing and sightseeing trips. **www.brussels.lemeridien.com**

Radisson SAS Royal Hotel

Rue du Fosse-aux-Loups 47, 1000 Brussels **Tel** *(02) 219 2828* **Fax** *(02) 219 6262* **Rooms** *281*   **Map** *2 D2*

A fabulous five-star hotel behind a glorious Art Deco façade (designed by famed Belgian designer, Michel Haspers), Radisson is one of the best places to stay in the city. Stunning garden and two restaurants, along with Bar Dessiné filled with Tintin illustrations. The hotel will organize city tours. **www.radisson.com**

Van Belle

Chaussée de Mons 39, 1070 Brussels **Tel** *(02) 521 3516* **Fax** *(02) 527 0002* **Rooms** *105*   **Map** *1 A3*

The Van Belle is a three-star hotel situated just off Brussels' busy Boulevard du Midi. Welcoming and efficient, it has rooms that are comfortable and well furnished, and the communal lounge area has a large open fire. Breakfast is included in the price. Underground garage. Free transportation to the Grand Place. **www.hotelvanbelle.be**

Le Plaza

Boulevard Adolphe Max 118–126, 1000 Brussels **Tel** *(02) 278 0100* **Fax** *(02) 278 0101* **Rooms** *193*   **Map** *2 D1*

An opulent five-star hotel which regularly provides accommodation to visiting stars and gentry, Le Plaza even has its own theatre. The building itself dates back to 1930 when it was built to model Paris' famous George V hotel. Rooms were renovated in 1996 to provide modern facilities. Business- and tourist-friendly. **www.leplaza-brussels.be**

Marriott Brussels

Rue Auguste Orts 3–7, 1000 Brussels **Tel** *(02) 516 9090* **Fax** *(02) 516 9000* **Rooms** *202*   **Map** *1 C2*

Five-star Marriott in the centre of Brussels, this hotel is perfectly placed for a shopping break. It lies near the top designer stores on Antoine Dansaert, the antique district is just a short walk away and if you arrive in the winter months, it is also in the midst of Brussels' famed Christmas market. Price includes breakfast. **www.marriott.com**

Royal Windsor

5 Rue Duquesnoy, 1000 Brussels **Tel** *(02) 505 5555* **Fax** *(02) 505 5500* **Rooms** *266*   **Map** *2 D3*

A characterful hotel near the Grand Place, the Royal Windsor is as luxurious as its name would suggest. Despite their rather smallish size, the rooms are sumptuously decorated (including four-poster beds and French antiques), with marble bathrooms. The restaurant has a stunning stained-glass ceiling. **http://royalwindsorbrussels.com**

UPPER TOWN

Les Bluets

Rue Berckmans 124, 1060 Brussels **Tel** *(02) 534 3983* **Fax** *(02) 543 0970* **Rooms** *9*

Charming, family-run, non-smoking hotel in a 19th-century bourgeois townhouse. The nine rooms are decorated with a laidback mix of antique furnishings, objets d'art and modern facilities, making it an interesting place to stay. The hotel has been refurbished and some rooms now have kitchenettes. Small plant-covered annex. **www.bluets.be**

Chambord

Rue De Namur 82, 1000 Brussels **Tel** *(02) 548 9910* **Fax** *(02) 514 0847* **Rooms** *70*   **Map** *2 E4*

The Penthouse Suite of this hotel has a stunning view from its terrace and even some of the standard rooms have their own balconies. There is also a terrace bar. Good promotional rates for off-peak tourists and breakfast is included. The hotel does not have parking facilities but can find a place for your car nearby. **www.hotel-chambord.be**

The White Hotel

Avenue Louise 212, 1000 Brussels **Tel** *(02) 644 2929* **Fax** *(02) 644 1878* **Rooms** *40*

Located on Brussels' luxury shopping street Avenue Louise, this four-star hotel is now part of the Design hotel group. It is modern and friendly with a cosy bar and a pool room. Rooms are spacious and recently redecorated with all mod cons. Private car park (at a small charge). Complimentary buffet breakfast. **www.thewhitehotel.be**

Best Western Hotel Royal Centre 　　　　　　　　🖼 🅿 📋　　€€€
Rue Royale 160, 1000 Brussels **Tel** *(02) 219 0065* **Fax** *(02) 218 0910* **Rooms** *73*　　　　**Map** *2 F1*

A four-star hotel within walking distance of the Royal Palace, the President Centre has elegant rooms, luxurious hotel bar, business centre with meeting room and private garage (at a fee). Continental breakfast included in the price. Good last-minute rates available online. **www.bestwestern.be**

Jolly Hotel du Grand Sablon 　　　　　　　　　🖼 🅿 🍴　　€€€
Rue Bodenbroek 2–4, 1000 Brussels **Tel** *(02) 518 1100* **Fax** *(02) 512 6766* **Rooms** *193*　　　**Map** *2 D4*

Flagship Brussels establishment of the Italian Jolly chain, the Hotel du Grand Sablon boasts a fantastic location on the Place du Grand Sablon. Rooms are large and carefully decorated, with great amenities and free Internet connection. Mini Baroque art gallery in the lobby. **www.nh-hotels.com**

Dixseptième 　　　　　　　　　　　　　　　　€€€€
Rue de la Madeleine 25, 1000 Brussels **Tel** *(02) 517 1717* **Fax** *(02) 502 6424* **Rooms** *24*　　　**Map** *2 D3*

The former home of a 17th-century Spanish ambassador, this small, friendly hotel is a great choice for art aficionados. All rooms are named after famous Belgian artists and the lounge has its own art library! Communal rooms have opulent decorations, including crystal chandeliers and a Louis XVI staircase. Breakfast is included. **www.ledixseptieme.be**

Four Points Sheraton 　　　　　　　　🖼 🅿 🍴 📺 📋　　€€€€
Rue Paul Spaak 15, 1000 Brussels **Tel** *(02) 645 6111* **Fax** *(02) 646 6344* **Rooms** *128*

The deluxe Four Points is a Sheraton hotel just off Avenue Louise. It has luxurious rooms which are newly renovated, as well as a fitness room with indoor "whirlpool" and a gourmet restaurant. Popular with business travellers for its conference facilities. Paid parking. **www.four-points.be**

Hilton Brussels 　　　　　　　　　　🖼 🅿 🍴 📺 📋　　€€€€
Boulevard de Waterloo 38, 1000 Brussels **Tel** *(02) 504 1111* **Fax** *(02) 504 2111* **Rooms** *434*　　**Map** *2 E5*

This recently-refurbished five-star hotel has the luxury facilities and efficient service that you would expect from a Hilton. The lobby is decorated with a frieze of the Grand Place. The hotel offers sightseeing tours as well as conference facilities. **www.brussels.hilton.com**

Hotel Café Pacific 　　　　　　　　　　　　　🖼 🍴　　€€€€
Rue Antoine Dansaert 57, 1000 Brussels **Tel** *(02) 213 0080* **Fax** *(02) 213 0083* **Rooms** *12*　　**Map** *1 B2*

This newly opened boutique hotel is located in one of the trendiest areas of Brussels. Just five minutes' walk from Grand Place and the main shopping streets, guests can retreat to this little oasis complete with restaurant after taking in the nearby sights. It is ideal for both couples and families alike. Breakfast is included. **www.hotelcafepacific.com**

New Hotel Charlemagne 　　　　　　　　　　🖼 🅿 🍴　　€€€€
Boulevard Charlemagne 25–27, 1000 Brussels **Tel** *(02) 230 2135* **Fax** *(02) 230 2510* **Rooms** *66*　　**Map** *3 B2*

In the heart of the European district (next to the headquarters of the EU Commission), New Hotel Charlemagne is slightly distant from the historical centre, but well connected by metro. Close to the Parc du Cinquantenaire. Rooms are modern but comfortably furnished. A good choice for business travellers. **www.new-hotel.com**

Hotel Eurostars Sablon 　　　　　　　　　　🖼 📺 📋　　€€€€€
Rue de la Paille 2–8, 1000 Brussels **Tel** *(02) 513 6040* **Fax** *(02) 511 8141* **Rooms** *32*　　　**Map** *2 D4*

A friendly boutique hotel with sauna and relaxation centre, the Sablon boasts a fantastic location beside the city's main art galleries and is within walking distance of the characterful cafés on Place du Grand Sablon. Rooms are large with split-level suites and plenty of facilities. The staff are particularly helpful. **www.eurostarshotels.com**

Stanhope 　　　　　　　　　　　　🖼 🅿 🍴 📺 📋　　€€€€€
Rue du Commerce 9, 1000 Brussels **Tel** *(02) 506 9111* **Fax** *(02) 512 1708* **Rooms** *108*　　**Map** *2 F4*

Providing deluxe Belgian hospitality in three converted townhouses, the five-star boutique Hotel Stanhope is decorated in English country style and delivers old-fashioned service that even stretches to chauffeur-driven cars. Elegant rooms, beautiful interior garden and gourmet restaurant. Extensive conference facilities. **www.stanhope.be**

GREATER BRUSSELS

Holiday Inn Garden Court 　　　　　　　　　　🖼 🅿 🍴　　€
Avenue Imperatrice Charlotte 6, 1020 Brussels **Tel** *(02) 478 7080* **Fax** *(02) 478 1000* **Rooms** *79*

This standard Holiday Inn near the Brussels Exhibition Centre is well-located for reaching central Brussels thanks to the nearby metro station. Rooms are basic but comfortable. Meeting and conference facilities. Hotel restaurant and bar. Complimentary breakfast and parking. **www.holiday-inn.com**

Gresham Belson 　　　　　　　　　　　　🖼 🅿 📺 📋　　€€
Chaussee de Louvain 805, 1140 Brussels **Tel** *(02) 708 3100* **Fax** *(02) 708 3166* **Rooms** *135*

A welcoming hotel on the outskirts of central Brussels, the Belson offers standard and deluxe rooms with business amenities and a popular bar and restaurant. Small fitness centre. Close to Brussels airport. Meeting room and conference facilities. **www.gresham-hotels.com**

Key to Price Guide *see p136* **Key to Symbols** *see back cover flap*

Husa President Park

Boulevard du Roi Albert II 44, 1000 Brussels **Tel** *(02) 203 2020* **Fax** *(02) 203 2440* **Rooms** *302*

This modern but luxurious hotel next to a wide stretch of public park is a popular choice for business travellers and is within driving distance of central Brussels. The 302 rooms are spacious and family friendly. Delightful red-brick hotel restaurant. Impressive fitness centre. **www.husa.es**

Les Tourelles

Winston Churchill Avenue 135, 1180 Brussels **Tel** *(02) 344 9573* **Fax** *(02) 346 4270* **Rooms** *21*

A fantastically atmospheric hotel with fake medieval turrets and a faux rustic façade, the three-star Les Tourelles has an old-fashioned feel with old stone fireplaces and antique wooden furnishings. Located south of the centre, the hotel benefits from good transport links. Welcoming staff. **www.lestourelles.be**

Best Western County House

Square des Heros 2–4, 1180 Brussels **Tel** *(02) 375 4420* **Fax** *(02) 375 3122* **Rooms** *102*

A comfortable and efficient hotel in a peaceful, park-side location south of central Brussels and close to the financial district. Rooms are spacious and modern with business-friendly facilities. Complimentary buffet breakfast. Meeting and conference centre. **www.bestwestern.be**

Bristol Stephanie

Avenue Louise 91–93, 1050 Brussels **Tel** *(02) 543 3311* **Fax** *(02) 538 0307* **Rooms** *142*   **Map** *2 D5*

The luxurious rooms in this five-star hotel on Brussels' fashionable Avenue Louise have been decorated in traditional Norwegian style – one even has its own private sauna! Suites have four-poster beds and dainty antique furnishings. Elegant restaurant serving tasty French cuisine. **www.bristol.be**

Eurostars Montgomery

Avenue de Tervueren 134, 1150 Brussels **Tel** *(02) 741 8511* **Fax** *(02) 741 8500* **Rooms** *63*   **Map** *4 E4*

A five-star hotel with a relaxed atmosphere and plenty of period furnishings, the elegant rooms in the Montgomery are individually decorated in diverse colours and styles. The restaurant is well-reputed and the staff are happy to provide sightseeing advice. **www.eurostarshotels.com**

Hotel Capital

191 Chaussée de Vleurgat, 1050 Brussels **Tel** *(02) 646 6420* **Fax** *(02) 646 3314* **Rooms** *62*

Located near Avenue Louise, Hotel Capital is just south of the historical centre of Brussels. Rooms are modern and comfortable with more luxurious suites also available, including longer-stay suites with kitchenettes. The restaurant has a terrace that opens in the summer. Private underground parking. **www.hotelcapital.be**

Kasteel Gravenhof

Alsembergesteenweg 676, 1653 Dworp **Tel** *(02) 380 4499* **Fax** *(02) 380 4060* **Rooms** *26*

The Kasteel Gravenhof is a stately castle hotel in the middle of a magnificent stretch of parkland, south of the city centre, that offers an elegant break in a peaceful setting. Built in 1649, the castle rooms have all the period fittings and luxurious furnishings you would expect from its genteel surroundings. **www.gravenhof.be**

Leopold

Rue de Luxembourg 35, 1050 Brussels **Tel** *(02) 511 1828* **Fax** *(02) 514 1939* **Rooms** *111*   **Map** *3 A4*

An elegant four-star hotel near the European Parliament and Parc Leopold, Hotel Leopold also has a well-reputed gourmet restaurant. Rooms are designed for tourists and business travellers, with half-board and self-catering apartments available for longer-term visitors. The price includes breakfast. **www.hotel-leopold.be**

Monty Hotel

101 Brand Whitlock Boulevard, 1200 Brussels **Tel** *(02) 734 5636* **Fax** *(02) 734 5005* **Rooms** *18*   **Map** *4 F3*

A small "design hotel" to the east of central Brussels, the Hotel Monty's rooms are carefully decorated to contemporary tastes with luxurious bathrooms and colourful, modern furnishings. Communal lounge, bar and private gardens. Breakfast is included. All furniture is individually produced by local designers. **www.monty-hotel.be**

Marriott Courtyard

Avenue des Olympiades 6, 1140 Brussels **Tel** *(02) 337 0808* **Fax** *(02) 337 0800* **Rooms** *191*

The Marriott Courtyard is a modern hotel in the city's financial district near Brussels airport, and is a good choice for business travellers. Built at the end of 2004, rooms are comfortable and spacious with business amenities. Brasserie serving Belgian and French fare. 24-hour fitness centre. **www.courtyardbrussels.com**

Park Hotel

Avenue de L'Yser 21–22, 1040 Brussels **Tel** *(02) 735 7400* **Fax** *(02) 735 1967* **Rooms** *53*   **Map** *4 D3*

A Best Western hotel just in front of the Parc du Cinquantenaire, the Park Hotel occupies a renovated, 1903 mansion. Rooms are spacious and elegant with antique furnishings and modern facilities. The price includes breakfast. Health club and sauna. Business centre. Private garden. Transport network close by. **www.parkhotelbrussels.be**

Sofitel Toison d'Or

Rue Capitaine Crespel 5, 1050 Brussels **Tel** *(02) 514 2200* **Fax** *(02) 514 5744* **Rooms** *170*   **Map** *2 D5*

South of the Grand Place, near Avenue Louise, the Sofitel Toison d'Or is well-placed for exploring the city's antique shops and museums. Rooms are modern and comfortable. Bar, four meeting rooms for up to 200 people and fitness centre. Baby-sitting service by request. Good transport links to centre of town. **www.sofitel.com**

Conrad International
Avenue Louise 71, 1050 Brussels **Tel** *(02) 542 4242* **Fax** *(02) 542 4200* **Rooms** *269*   **Map** *2 D5*

A grand hotel on Brussels' main shopping street, Avenue Louise, the Conrad Brussels has large, luxurious rooms, extensive leisure facilities (including a spa with six treatment rooms) and business-friendly facilities. The Grand Place is just a 20-minute walk away. Excellent restaurant and lounge bar. Baby-sitting service. **www.conradhotels.com**

Manos Premier
Chaussée de Charleroi 100–106, 1060 Brussels **Tel** *(02) 537 9682* **Fax** *(02) 539 3655* **Rooms** *50*

Close to its sister hotel, Manos Stephanie near Avenue Louise, the five-star Manos Premier is full of character and charm. Rooms and suites are individually decorated with elegant Louis XV and XVI period furniture. Spa and fitness centre. Peaceful private garden. Luxury restaurant. The price includes breakfast. **www.manoshotel.com**

Manos Stephanie
Chaussée de Charleroi 28, 1060 Brussels **Tel** *(02) 539 0250* **Fax** *(02) 537 5729* **Rooms** *55*

An elegant four-star hotel, Manos Stephanie is situated just south of the centre in a converted townhouse near Avenue Louise. The rooms are spacious with some charming features, including antique furnishings and marble bathrooms. The Duplex Suite has a circular wooden stairwell. Breakfast included. Meeting facilities. **www.manoshotel.com**

ANTWERP

Antwerp Hilton
Groenplaats, 2000 Antwerp **Tel** *(03) 204 1212* **Fax** *(03) 204 8688* **Rooms** *211*

Well-located next to the historical cathedral, the Antwerp Hilton has some great views over the city's sights. An architectural landmark (it sits behind a listed Baroque façade), the hotel occupies part of the former Grand Bazar department store. Rooms are business-friendly with fax machines and wi-fi Internet connections. **www.hilton.com**

Firean
Oomsstraat 6, 2018 Antwerp **Tel** *(03) 237 0260* **Fax** *(03) 238 1168* **Rooms** *15*

A welcoming, four-star hotel in an early-20th century Art Deco mansion. With crystal chandeliers in the lounge, antique furnishings in the rooms and a secluded garden, the hotel offers its own unique version of luxury. Well-reputed hotel restaurant. Breakfast is included in the price. **www.hotelfirean.com**

Rubens
Oude Beurs 29, 2000 Antwerp **Tel** *(03) 222 4848* **Fax** *(03) 225 1940* **Rooms** *36*

This quietly-situated four-star hotel, just a short walk from the Grand Place, offers deluxe accommodation, including spacious double rooms and a romantic junior suite with private terrace. Rooms have views into the hotel garden or over to the city cathedral. Complimentary buffet breakfast. Paid parking. **www.hotelrubensantwerp.be**

Villa Mozart
Handschoenmarkt 3, 2000 Antwerp **Tel** *(03) 231 3031* **Fax** *(03) 231 5685* **Rooms** *25*

Three-star Best Western hotel within a short stroll of Antwerp cathedral offers a reasonably-priced base in the city's medieval centre. Modern facilities, including large bathrooms and guest sauna. Ask for a room with a cathedral view. Complimentary buffet breakfast. Paid parking. **www.bestwestern.be**

Hyllit
De Keyserlei 28–30, 2018 Antwerpen **Tel** *(03) 202 6800* **Fax** *(03) 202 6890* **Rooms** *127*

Hotel Hyllit has all the facilities you would expect from a modern four-star hotel, including pool, fitness centre, sauna and solarium. Well-located on Antwerp's major shopping avenue, De Keyserlei. Fantastic rooftop restaurant with views over the historical centre. Underground parking. **www.hyllithotel.be**

Plaza
Charlottalei 49, 2018 Antwerp **Tel** *(03) 287 2870* **Fax** *(03) 287 2871* **Rooms** *80*

Priding itself on its personal touch, the four-star Plaza Hotel has rooms that have each been individually decorated by the owner – some even have a walk-in dressing room. Staff are on hand to offer tourist information and restaurant advice. Complimentary buffet breakfast. Paid parking. **www.plaza.be**

Radisson SAS Park Lane
Van Eycklei 34, 2018 Antwerp **Tel** *(03) 285 8585* **Fax** *(03) 285 8586* **Rooms** *174*

A plush hotel near the historical centre, the rooms of the Radisson SAS Park Lane boast glorious views over the city park and the nearby diamond sector. Reasonably-priced hotel restaurant serving French and Belgian cuisine. Family suites available. Fitness room free for guests in suites and business-class rooms. **www.radisson.com/antwerpbe**

't Sandt
Zand 13–19, 2000 Antwerp **Tel** *(03) 232 9390* **Fax** *(03) 232 5613* **Rooms** *29*

A cosy four-star hotel in Antwerp's historical centre, 't Sandt occupies a protected Neo-Rococo building from the mid-19th century that was the site of the city's first customs duty office. The rooms and apartments are individually decorated. The Cathedral Penthouse has one of the city's best views. Breakfast included. **www.hotel-sandt.be**

Key to Price Guide *see p136* **Key to Symbols** *see back cover flap*

De Witte Lelie

P €€€€€

Keizerstraat 16–18, 2000 Antwerp **Tel** *(03) 226 1966* **Fax** *(03) 234 0019* **Rooms** *10*

An atmospheric five-star B&B in Antwerp's historical core, the whitewashed De Witte Lelie ("The White Lily") is constructed out of three converted 17th-century canal houses. Rooms have great city views and a luxurious mix of white-linen sofas, antique furnishings and modern facilities. Breakfast buffet included. **www.dewittelelie.be**

BRUGES

de Pauw

P ⅋ €

Sint Gilliskerkhof 8, 8000 Bruges **Tel** *(050) 33 7118* **Fax** *(050) 34 5140* **Rooms** *8*   **Map** *B2*

The welcoming de Pauw is a family-run two-star hotel in a quiet area just outside Bruges' historical centre. Rooms are basic, but spacious and comfortably furnished, with modern bathrooms. Breakfast included. Good restaurant serving traditional Belgian cuisine. Parking on the street beside the hotel. Half-board available. **www.hoteldepauw.be**

Bourgoensch Hof

P ⅋ €€

Wollestraat 39, 8000 Bruges **Tel** *(050) 33 1645* **Fax** *(050) 34 6378* **Rooms** *17*   **Map** *B3*

Situated in Bruges' historical centre near the central market, this three-star hotel boasts some fabulous canal-side views. Rooms are simple, but well presented; most visitors to both the hotel and its bistro come for the views. Hotel bistro with outdoor terrace. The price includes breakfast. Paid parking available on request. **www.bourgoensch-hof.com**

Hotel Heritage

P €€€

Niklaas Desparsstraat 11, 8000 Bruges **Tel** *(050) 44 4444* **Fax** *(050) 44 4440* **Rooms** *20*   **Map** *A3*

A four-star hotel which aims to pamper its visitors: some rooms have their own Jacuzzi baths; others are decorated with fine Italian fabrics. State-of-the-art technology in each room. Prices do not include breakfast, fitness facilities, Internet connection or underground parking. **www.hotel-heritage.com**

Ter Brughe

P €€€

Oost Gistelhof 2, 8000 Bruges **Tel** *(050) 34 0324* **Fax** *(050) 33 8873* **Rooms** *46*   **Map** *B2*

This charming hotel in a converted 16th-century family home has luxury rooms with private terraces, antique furnishings and great canal views. Even the standard rooms have wood-beamed ceilings. Breakfast takes place in the hotel's medieval basement. Garage parking must be reserved in advance. **www.hotelterbrughe.com**

Hotel de Tuilerieën

P €€€€€

Dyver 7, 8000 Bruges **Tel** *(050) 34 3691* **Fax** *(050) 34 0400* **Rooms** *45*   **Map** *B4*

A luxurious four-star hotel with indoor pool, the Hotel de Tuilerieën offers a deluxe break in the heart of Bruges' medieval centre. Rooms are spacious and elegantly decorated with four-poster beds and antique furnishings. Stately breakfast dining room with banquet tables and crystal chandeliers. **www.hoteltuilerieen.com**

GHENT

Cour St Georges

P €€

Hoogpoort 75–77, 9000 Ghent **Tel** *(09) 224 2424* **Fax** *(09) 224 2640* **Rooms** *32*   **Map** *F2*

This well-priced and superbly-located Best Western hotel in the centre of Ghent occupies a historic building, which explains the establishment's unique décor (including painted panels in the breakfast room). The rooms in the attic have great views over the historical centre. (Note: there is no elevator). Breakfast included. **www.bestwestern.be**

Gravensteen

P €€

Jan Breydelstraat 35, 9000 Ghent **Tel** *(09) 225 1150* **Fax** *(09) 225 1850* **Rooms** *49*   **Map** *E1*

An elegant hotel in a converted 19th-century mansion, the Gravensteen has been decorated in keeping with its stately exterior, including an impressive marble stairwell. Rooms are simple but comfortable with modern facilities. Bicycles for rent. Fitness room with sauna. Dinner by request. **www.gravensteen.be**

The Boatel

P €€

Voorhoutkaai 44, 9000 Ghent **Tel** *(09) 267 1030* **Fax** *(09) 267 1039* **Rooms** *7*

The two-star Boatel is a floating hotel constructed from a converted canal boat! Moored in Portus Ganda, a short walk from the centre of town, its seven cosy rooms (five standard and two luxury) are carefully decorated in various styles. Great river views! Breakfast is included. Evening entertainment with barbecue when weather permits. **www.theboatel.com**

Ghent River Hotel

€€€

Waaistraat 5+, 9000 Ghent **Tel** *(09) 266 1010* **Fax** *(09) 266 1015* **Rooms** *77*   **Map** *F1*

This four-star riverside hotel occupies a mid-19th century rice mill on the banks of the River Leie. Although the entrance is modern, the rooms are more in keeping with the building's rich history, including wood-beamed ceilings and wooden floors. Fitness room with sauna. Bicycles for rent. **www.ghent-river-hotel.be**

For Bruges and Ghent map references *refer to the inside back cover*

WHERE TO EAT

I t is almost impossible to eat badly in Brussels. Some say one can eat better here than in Paris, and even meals in the lower- to mid-price bracket are always carefully prepared and often innovative. Venues range from top gastronomic restaurants to unpretentious local taverns where you can find generous

Thai chef in Brussels

servings of local specialities such as *moules-frites* (mussels and French fries). If you tire of Belgian fare, try the variety of excellent local seafood and the range of ethnic cuisine that reflects the city's lively cultural diversity. The listings on pp152–61 give recommendations on where to eat in Antwerp, Bruges and Ghent.

Brasserie Horta in Centre Belge de la Bande Dessinée *(see p154)*

WHERE TO EAT

The Belgian love affair with dining out makes for an astonishing concentration of restaurants and eateries: a 10-minute stroll from almost anywhere in Brussels should bring you to a decent, and often almost undiscovered, tavern or brasserie. However, superb dining is to be had without leaving the Ilôt Sacré, the area around the central Grand Place, where many

very good and surprisingly reasonable restaurants abound. Beware the tourist traps around the Grand Place that make their living from gulling unwary visitors into spending far more than they intended to. The impressive displays of seafood adorning the pavements of Rue des Bouchers northwest of the Grand Place and Petite Rue des Bouchers can promote rather touristy restaurants, but those on p154 are recommended.

TYPES OF CUISINE

Elsewhere in the city centre is a wealth of quality fish restaurants, especially around the former fish market at Place Ste-Catherine, while the city's trendiest eateries can be found on Rue Dansaert and in the Place Saint-Géry district. If you are planning to explore other parts of Brussels, or if you are staying outside the city centre, you will find plenty of good Belgian fare on offer in the southern communes of Ixelles and Saint-Gilles, and in Etterbeek, where the European Commission buildings are

located. Ixelles also boasts the largest concentration of Vietnamese and Southeast Asian restaurants, especially around Chaussée de Boondael. This student area in the Matonge district is also home to several African restaurants, serving food from the Congo (formerly Zaire), Senegal and Rwanda.

North of the city centre, in the communes of Schaerbeek and Saint-Josse, Turkish and North African communities have sprung up, and excellent Moroccan and Tunisian cuisine is commonplace. There is also a growing trend for "designer couscous", with Belgian restaurateurs exploiting the popularity of North African food in spectacularly ornate venues, often featuring ethnic music in the evenings.

Spanish and Portuguese restaurants can be found in the Marolles district and in Saint-Gilles, reflecting the wave of immigration in the 1950s and 1960s when many southern Europeans chose to settle in Brussels. The city is also liberally sprinkled with Greek restaurants, although many veer on the over-touristy side. A better bet are the modern Latin American eateries.

VEGETARIANS

Despite a marked upturn in recent years, Brussels is far from being a vegetarian-friendly city, since there are only a handful of specialist vegetarian restaurants. However, those who eat fish will find mainstream restaurants cater generously to their needs; Brussels is very strong on fish and seafood. Also, the traditional dish, *stoemp*, mashed potatoes

Tables at the popular restaurant Aux Armes de Bruxelles *(see p154)*

mixed with root vegetables, is a classic vegetarian speciality. North African restaurants usually offer vegetarian couscous courses, and there are plenty of Italian options. Indian restaurants are few and far between, but most offer vegetable curries. Vegans may struggle, particularly in European restaurants.

HOW MUCH TO PAY

Most restaurants, taverns and cafés display a menu in the window and the majority take credit cards. Prices usually include VAT (21 per cent) and service (16 per cent), although it is worth checking the latter before you tip. A meal at the city's most luxurious restaurants can cost up to €150 per head, but you can eat superbly for around €50 per head (including wine) and a hearty snack in a tavern should cost no more than €15. The mark-up level on wine can be very high, especially in most Mediterranean restaurants and in obviously touristic areas, but most taverns do a reasonable *vin maison* and serve myriad varieties of beer.

Service in all but the most expensive restaurants can be erratic by British and US standards. But beneath the sometimes grumpy exterior, you will often find warmth and an earthy, cheerfully self-deprecating sense of humour that is unique to Belgium. There are no hard and fast rules, but some diners leave an additional tip of up to 10 per cent if they are especially

The opulent Belle Epoque dining room of the Belga Queen *(see p153)*

satisfied with the quality of the meal and the service. Note that some restaurants cannot take service on a credit card slip, and this, plus the tip, will have to be paid in cash, as do other gratuities in the city.

Stall selling freshly made snacks in Saint-Gilles at the weekend

DINING ON A BUDGET

Many restaurants offer bargain, fixed-price or rapid lunchtime menus for under €12.50, plus reasonably priced dishes of the day. Even the city's most expensive

eateries have similar deals, meaning you can sample haute cuisine for less than €37. In the evening, look out for set menus with *vin compris* (wine included), which are often a way to save a large part of the dining bill.

At the other end of the scale, Brussels has most of the usual fast-food outlets, and sandwiches are sold at most butchers or delicatessens *(traiteurs)*, usually with tuna, cheese or cold meat fillings. Some of the latter offer sit-down snacks too. Alternatively, take advantage of Belgium's national dish, *frites/frieten* (French fries, hand-cut and double-fried to ensure an even crispiness). There are *Friteries/Frituurs* all over town, serving enormous portions of French fries with mayonnaise and dozens of other sauces, plus *fricadelles* (sausages in batter), lamb kebabs, fish cakes or meatballs. Inevitably, these establishments vary in quality; one sure bet is Maison Antoine on Place Jourdan in Etterbeek, where they have been frying for over half a century.

Most cafés and taverns offer *petite restauration* (light meals) on top or instead of a regular menu. These simple, traditional snacks include croque monsieur, shrimp croquettes, chicory baked with ham and cheese, salads, spaghetti bolognaise and *américain* (raw minced beef with seasoning). Do not be fooled by the word "light" – most of these dishes will keep you going from lunchtime well into the evening.

The contemporary interior of Lola, a fashionable Brussels brasserie *(see p156)*

Entrance of the historic tavern
In 't Spinnekopke *(see p152)*

BUDGET FOOD

Brussels is home to a sizeable Turkish community which means that kebab, gyros and pitta restaurants are ubiquitous, especially in Saint-Josse and on the gaudy Rue du Marché aux Fromages, just off the Grand Place. The nearby L'Express, a Lebanese takeaway specializing in chicken and felafel pittas, generously crammed with fresh salad, is perhaps a better bet.

Ethnic food can work out at a very reasonable price; large portions of couscous, pizzas and African specialities are often to be found at good rates in student areas and at stands throughout the city.

BREAKFAST & SNACKS

Especially good breakfasts – as well as inventive light lunches and snacks – with an emphasis on vegetarian dishes are the staple of L'Ultime Atome *(see p157)*, a bustling brasserie situated in the St Boniface quarter. Breakfasting in a café or brasserie is recommended if breakfast is not included in your hotel accommodation. For snackers who are sweet-toothed, waffle stands or vans appear on almost every corner of the city, while cafés and taverns offer a tempting variety of waffles (topped

Open-air tables outside fish restaurants in Rue des Bouchers

with jam, cream or chocolate). Pancakes *(crêpes)* are just as popular – and filling – although you can cut down the calories with a savoury wholewheat pancake at one of the city's crêperies.

OPENING TIMES

Time-consuming business lunches are still part of the culture in Belgium and most restaurants serve lunch from noon until 2 or 3pm. Dinner is generally served from 7pm onwards and last orders are taken as late as 10pm. Late-night restaurants, serving until midnight, can be found in the side streets of downtown Brussels and a handful provide meals after 1am. Breakfast bars usually open around 7am. For details of café and bar opening times, see pp162–7.

MAKING A RESERVATION

When visiting one of the more celebrated restaurants, it is always wise to book in advance. The listings indicate where booking is advisable. If you plan on going to the legendary Comme Chez Soi, you should reserve weeks ahead rather than hope for a last-minute cancellation. Trendy designer restaurants are often crowded but usually take reservations well in advance.

READING THE MENU

Menus at most restaurants are written in French, sometimes in Dutch and French. Some,

The Art Nouveau interior of Comme Chez Soi, often praised as Brussels' best restaurant *(see p154)*

The 16th-century cellar of 't Kelderke in the Grand Place *(see p153)*

especially in tourist areas, may have explanations in English. Dishes of the day or suggestions are often illegibly scribbled on blackboards. Fortunately, most waiters speak at least a little English. You may find a food dictionary useful. For details of some of the most popular Belgian specialities, see pp148–9. The phrasebook on pp205–208 also gives translations of many menu items.

The logo of a Latin American restaurant

ETIQUETTE

Brussels is less relaxed than, say, Amsterdam and, although casual or smart-casual dress is acceptable in most restaurants, you will probably feel more at home dressing up for upmarket places. A few formal restaurants will insist on a jacket and tie for men. The dress code for women is more flexible, but smartness is appreciated.

PETS

Do not be suprised to see a dog sat beneath the next-door table. The Belgians are great dog lovers and many bars and cafés have a relaxed attitude to clients bringing their pets.

CHILDREN

In general, Brussels is child-friendly, perhaps because Belgian children tend to be well behaved in restaurants.

Many establishments have children's menus, although they are not always a bargain, and several offer free meals for children under 12. High-chairs should be available on request, and some restaurants have inside play areas, including some of the big hotels, where children are usually welcome. On the outskirts of Brussels or near one of the parks, eateries can offer extensive outside playgrounds. Ethnic restaurants, in particular Vietnamese, Greek and the less formal Italian ones, tend to be especially accommodating. They do not always have children's menus, but are happy for adults to share their meal with youngsters. Children are usually allowed in cafés and bars although they are forbidden to drink

Place settings at the restaurant La Truffe Noire *(see p158)*

alcohol. Some restaurants may be too formal for children to feel comfortable.

SMOKING

Brussels is still very much a smokers' city. Although a new law requests all but the smallest establishments to provide non-smoking areas plus ventilation, many do not conform to this regulation. If you are truly adverse to cigarette smoke, make sure you ask about arrangements when reserving, or before you take a seat. Many cafes and taverns can be very smoky, and some locals do not take kindly to being asked to put out a cigarette. Smokers should know that most restaurants do not sell cigarettes.

The modest facade of Comme Chez Soi in the Lower Town *(see p154)*

DISABLED FACILITIES

Facilities for the disabled are poor in Brussels, although there have been some recent improvements. The cobbled streets and hilly areas may be difficult to negotiate, but most people will go out of their way to help There is a limited number of restaurants with ramps and ground-floor bathrooms, so do check the extent of the access before making a reservation or taking a seat. A list of restaurants and cafés with disabled facilities is published by a Walloon charity; contact AWIPH at Rue de la Rivelaine 21, 6061 Charleroi (071 205 711). www.awiph.be.

The Flavours of Brussels

Most Belgians are passionate about food and standards are generally very high. The many first-class grocers, greengrocers, butchers, fishmongers, bakers and pâtissiers, including Belgium's noted chocolatiers, are held in high public esteem, alongside the nation's top chefs and restauranteurs. In Brussels, the culinary heart of the country, there are a wide range of fine eateries to suit all budgets, serving both sophisticated Walloon (Belgian-French) dishes alongside more basic, hearty Flemish fare. A history of invasion has also added a dash of other European culinary traditions, particularly those of Spain and Austria.

Belgian chocolates

Bunches of white asparagus, some of Belgium's finest produce

THE NORTH SEA

Brussels, being only 60 km (40 miles) from the North Sea, has a good supply of really fresh fish and seafood. In Place Sainte-Catherine, just to the west of the Grand Place, there used to be a bustling fish market and the area remains a centre for fish restaurants. The best sole, cod, turbot, skate, hake and

monkfish, simply grilled or fried in butter, or swathed in a well-judged sauce, are always on the menu, along with huge platters of *fruits de mer* (mixed seafood).

A uniquely Belgian fish dish that is well worth seeking out and is *anguilles au vert (paling in't groen)*, which consists of large chunks of eel, cooked with a mass of finely chopped, fresh herbs.

PASTURE AND WOODLAND

The flat, reclaimed land of northern Belgium and the hills of the south are home to herds of cattle. Quality beef is the stock-in-trade of any Belgian butcher, and *steak-frites* (steak and chips) is a classic dish on bistro menus. Belgians are so confident in their beef that they are happy to eat it raw: minced

Oysters   **Cockles**   **Lobster**   **Langoustine**   **Whelks**

Selection of fine quality North-Sea seafood

LOCAL DISHES AND SPECIALITIES

Although Belgian chefs produce some of the world's most complex and sophisticated cooking, many of Belgium's great classic dishes are relatively simple, striking a healthy balance between nourishment and pleasure. Fine examples include steaming platefuls of *moules-frites* and warming stews such as *carbonnade flamades* and *waterzooï* (which is made with either fish or chicken) all dishes that might well be labelled as "comfort" food. However, the quality of the ingredients and the skill put into the making of such dishes in Belgium invariably turns such homely fare into a feast. Desserts include a host of sweet tarts and the ever-popular waffles. Endive, almost the national vegetable, gets in here too, as a flavouring for ice cream.

Endives

Moules-frites *Mussels, steamed in their own juices with onion and white wine, are served with chips and mayonnaise.*

Fish restaurant in the elegant Galéries St-Hubert shopping arcade

must be the potato, in the form of chips (French fries). *Frites* (*frietjes*), served with a dollop of mayonnaise, are a favourite street-food.

THE PÂTISSIER

No Belgian community is without a pâtisserie, selling superlative tarts, cakes and biscuits, and many pâtissiers double-up as chocolatiers. *Gaufres* (waffles) are another great sweet treat, sold at specialist shops and street stalls. Enjoyed freshly made, topped with knobs of butter and a sprinkling of sugar, they may be raised to perfection with spoonfuls of jam or fruit and fresh cream.

in *steak à l'américaine* (or *steak tartare*) and on toast as the snack, *toast cannibale*. Dairy cattle are the source of fine cheeses, such as Herve, Chimay and Maredsous.

Pork products include a range of sausages, patés and the noted Ardennes ham. In autumn and winter, look out for game, such as wild boar, pheasant and venison, often served in a rich fruity sauce. Quail, guinea fowl, pigeon and rabbit are also popular.

THE VEGETABLE PATCH

Not long ago, most Belgian householders toiled to fill their gardens with tightly-packed rows of top-class vegetables – beans, leeks, lettuces, carrots, potatoes and onions. This tradition may be waning, but the same quest for quality lives

on in commercial market-gardens. In the 1840s, Belgian gardeners created *chicon* (*witloof*) by forcing the roots of the chicorée lettuce. It is now one of Belgium's most widely used vegetables, although the most popular

Freshly made waffles on a street stall, a familiar sight in the city

ON THE MENU

White asparagus An early summer speciality, it is usually served with melted butter or hard-boiled egg and parsley.

Jets d'houblon Spring menus feature this dish of young hop shoots in a creamy sauce.

Crevettes grises Tiny but big on flavour, these "grey" shrimps are a popular snack.

Stoemp Mashed potato, with flecks of vegetables or meat, make up this pub favourite.

Garnaalkroketten Deep-fried croquettes, filled with shrimp.

Speculoos These buttery, spicy biscuits are available in festive shapes for Christmas.

Carbonnades flamandes *Beef is cooked in Belgian beer, with a touch of sugar, to make this hearty casserole.*

Waterzooî *This classic stew from Ghent consists of fish or chicken and vegetables, poached in a creamy broth.*

Flamiche aux Poireaux *Leeks, fried in butter and whisked with cream and eggs, are baked in a crisp pastry shell.*

Belgian Beer

Gambrinus,
legendary
Beer King

Belgium makes more beers, in a greater mix of styles and flavours, than any other country in the world. The Belgian citizen drinks on average 100 litres (200 pints) a year, and even small bars will stock at least 20 varieties. The nation's breweries produce over 400 different beers. The cheerful peasants in Brueghel the Elder's 16th-century medieval village scenes would have been drinking beer from their local brewery, many of which had been active since the 11th century, as every small town and community produced its own beer. By 1900 there remained 3,000 private breweries throughout Belgium. Today, more than 100 still operate, with experts agreeing that even large industrial concerns produce a fine quality beer.

Detail from *The Wedding Dance*
by Pieter Brueghel the Elder

TRAPPIST BEERS

Chimay label with
authentic Trappist mark

Label for Westmalle
Trappist beer

The most revered of refreshments, Belgium's Trappist beers have been highly rated since the Middle Ages when monks began brewing them. The drink originated in Roman times when Belgium was a province of Gaul, Gallia Belgica. Beer was a private domestic product until the monasteries took over and introduced hops to the process. Today's production is still controlled solely by the five Trappist monasteries, although the brewers are mostly laymen. Trappist beers are characterized by their rich, yeasty flavour. They are very strong, ranging from 6.2 to 11 per cent in alcohol content by volume. The most celebrated of the 20 brands is Chimay, brewed at Belgium's largest monastic brewery in Hainaut. This delicate but potent bottled beer has three different strengths, and is best kept for many years before drinking. The strongest Trappist beer is Westvleteren, from Ypres.

Chimay served in its
correct glass

LAMBIC BEERS

Made for centuries in the Senne Valley around Brussels, the unique family of lambic beers are made using yeasts naturally present in the air to ferment the beer, rather than being added separately to the water and grain mix. Containers of unfermented wort (water, wheat and barley) are left under a half-open roof in the brewery and wild airborne yeasts, only present in the atmosphere of this region of Belgium, descend to ferment it. Unlike the sterility of many breweries and officially exempt from EU hygiene regulations, lambic cellars are deliberately left dusty and uncleaned in order for the necessary fungal activity to thrive. Matured in untreated wooden casks for up to five years, the lambic is deliciously sour to drink, with a moderate strength of 5 per cent alcohol.

Young and old lambic beers are blended together to produce the variant of gueuze. A tiny bead, distinctive champagne mousse and a toasty, slightly acid flavour, are its main characteristics. Bars and restaurants lay down their gueuze for up to 2 years before it is drunk.

Lambic
cherry beer

Brewer sampling beer from the vat at a
brewery outside Brussels

SPECIALITY BELGIAN BEERS

Duvel

Chimay

Brugse Tripel

De Verboden
Frucht

Kwak

Speciality beers are common in Belgium, where the huge variety of brands includes unusual tastes and flavours. Fruit beers are a Brussels speciality but are available throughout the country. The most popular, kriek, is traditionally made with bitter cherries grown in the Brussels suburb of Schaerbeek; picked annually, these are added to the lambic and allowed to macerate, or steep. The distinctive almond tang comes from the cherry stone. Raspberries are also used to make a framboise beer, or frambozen.

For a characterful amber ale, Kwak is good choice. Strong beers are also popular; apart from the Trappist beers, of which Chimay is a popular variety, the pilseners De Verboden Frucht (meaning "forbidden fruit") and Duvel ("devil") are almost as strong as red wine. Brugse Tripel, from Bruges, is also popular. Even Belgium's best-sellers, Jupiler and Stella Artois, are good quality beers.

Fruit beer mat of
Chapeau brewery

The façade of a beer emporium in Brussels

BLANCHE BEERS

Hoegaarden

Belgium's refreshing wheat beers are known as "blanche", or white beers, because of the cloudy sediment that forms when they ferment. Sour, crisp and light, they are relatively low in alcohol at 5 per cent. Blanche is produced in the western region of Hoegaarden, after which the best-known blanche is named. Many people now serve them with a slice of lemon to add to the refreshing taste, especially on warm summer evenings.

HOW TO DRINK BELGIAN BEER

There are no snobbish distinctions made in Belgium between bottled and casked beer. Some of the most prestigious brews are served in bottles, and, as with casks, bottles are often laid down to mature. The choice of drinking glass, however, is a vital part of the beer-drinking ritual. Many beers must be drunk in a particular glass, which the barman will supply, ranging from goblets to long thin drinking tubes. Beers are often served with a complementary snack; cream cheese on rye bread and radishes are a popular accompaniment.

The traditional drinkers' snack of
fromage blanc on rye bread

Choosing a Restaurant

The restaurants in this guide have been selected for their good value, food, character and location. Restaurants in Brussels are listed by area, followed by a selection in Antwerp, Bruges, and Ghent. Restaurants within the same price category are listed alphabetically. For map references see pp190–193.

PRICE CATEGORIES
The following price ranges are for a three-course evening meal for one, including a half-bottle of house wine, tax and service.

€ under 25 euros
€€ 25–37 euros
€€€ 37–50 euros
€€€€ 50–62 euros
€€€€€ over 62 euros

LOWER TOWN

Comocomo   €

Rue Antoine Dansaert 19, 1000 **Tel** *(02) 503 0330*   **Map** *1 C2*

In the middle of downtown Brussels, a stone's throw from trendy St Géry, Comocomo combines a Basque tapas restaurant with a sushi-bar-style conveyor belt. After shopping on Rue Antoine Dansaert, retire to this modern establishment and pick out generously portioned *pintxos* (pronounced "pintchos") as they slowly pass you by.

Den Teepot   €

Rue des Chartreux 66, 1000 **Tel** *(02) 511 9402*   **Map** *1 B2*

In a town not famed for its vegetarian options this Flemish vegetarian restaurant is a welcome addition. Located above its sister health-food shop, although not completely vegan, the owners try to minimize the amount of animal products used. Many of the dishes feature beans and pulses. Open for lunch only, noon–2pm, Monday to Saturday.

EXKi   €

Chaussée d'Ixelles 12, 1050 **Tel** *(02) 502 7277*

For fast yet healthy food, look no further than EXKi, the chain of fast-food eateries with the motto "natural, fresh and ready". EXKi offers both hot and cold dishes, along with a wide choice of vegetarian meals. For something a little naughtier, indulge in the special cheesecake made with speculoos biscuits. Closed Sunday.

Arcadi   €€

Rue d'Arenberg 1B, 1000 **Tel** *(02) 511 3343*   **Map** *2 D2*

Producing arguably the best quiches in a city that has some outstanding quiche-making outlets, Arcadi has an enormous selection of these egg flans, although the salmon and broccoli variety is the most popular. The rochefort and cauliflower quiche is spectacular among the vegetarian options, and they don't skimp on portions. Great cakes too.

Bifanas   €€

Rue des Dominicains 30, 1000 **Tel** *(02) 502 2548*

If you've missed the numerous Portuguese-run street markets in the commune of St Gilles during August weekends, the inexpensive Bifanas serves a cheerful representation of the cuisine of the city's large Portuguese community. Fish is the order of the day, above all, the *bacalhau* (salt cod).

Bonsoir Clara   €€

Rue Antoine Dansaert 22, 1000 **Tel** *(02) 502 0990*   **Map** *1 C2*

From the same stable as the collection of hip bars in St Géry owned by Brussels' famed impresario, Frederic Nicolay, Bonsoir Clara is situated right in the middle of the fashion district. One of the prettiest restaurants in town, Clara is high on style and a honeypot for fashionistas. Closed Saturday lunch, Sunday.

Den Talurelekker   €€

Rue de l'Enseignement 25, 1000 **Tel** *(02) 219 3025*   **Map** *2 E2–F2*

This Dutch-Belgian eatery offers up hearty stews that are perfect for that grey autumn or winter weekend. One of the notable dishes on Den Talurelekker's menu is its rich, velvety *carbonade de la gueuze* – a casserole made with Belgian gueuze beer.

In 't Spinnekopke   €€

Place du Jardin aux Fleurs, 1000 **Tel** *(02) 511 8695*

A superb example of quality Belgian food can be found in this intimate former 17th-century coaching inn. In 't Spinnekopke (In the Spider's Head) has a strong range of unusual local brews and items on the menu that are cooked in them. Friendly service and a lovely terrace in an area that's off the beaten track. Closed Saturday lunch, Sunday.

L'Achepot   €€

Place Ste-Catherine 1, 1000 **Tel** *(02) 511 6221*   **Map** *1 C2*

This small, family-run Brussels tavern off the Vismarkt (fish market) serves fish simply but very well. Apart from the seafood, try the traditional *stoemp* (a coarse mash with vegetables and sausages) and *chèvre* (goat cheese) salad; if you're feeling more adventurous, there is a wide range of offal dishes, including kidneys, brain, tripe and liver.

Key to Symbols *see back cover flap*

La Cantina

Rue du Jardin des Olives 13–15, 1000 **Tel** *(02) 513 4276*

Customers to La Cantina come for the restaurant's *feijoada*, the rather heavy Brazilian national dish of rice, red beans, pork, smoked bacon and spicy sausage. In fact, just about every last part of the pig is thrown in the pot, along with oranges and a traditional sauce. Closed Sunday.

La Fin de Siècle

Avenue Louise 423, 1050 **Tel** *(02) 648 8041*

A favourite with young Eurocrats working in the nearby Commission buildings, La Fin de Siècle is an inexpensive Italian bistro with an extensive menu. Fast service, a Baroque-style décor, candles and soft classical music all combine to produce a restful atmosphere. Closed Saturday lunch, Sunday.

La Iberica

Rue de Flandre 8, 1000 **Tel** *(02) 511 7936*

Map *1 B1*

A friendly, inexpensive, traditional Spanish restaurant, with the patron looking after the front of the house and his wife taking care of the kitchen. The paella is excellent, while the meat dishes – especially the Spanish ham and chorizo starters – are recommended. Impressive selection of Spanish wines. Closed Wednesday, three weeks in August.

La Kasbah

Rue Antoine Dansaert 20, 1000 **Tel** *(02) 502 4026*

Map *1 C2*

Next door to achingly cool Bonsoir Clara, La Kasbah is another of Frederic Nicolay's stylish dining projects. This time, however, the food really is something to write home about. The interior is dark and decked out with North African knick-knacks, and the attentive service and decent Moroccan wines ensure that it is always busy but intimate.

L'Element Terre

Chaussée de Waterloo 465, 1050 **Tel** *(02) 649 3727*

This little vegetarian restaurant aims to convert even the fiercest of carnivores by offering a mouth-watering array of world cuisine from Brazil to Senegal and Japan to Greece. There is a great selection of homemade patisserie to top it off. Closed Sunday and Monday.

Le Paon Royal

Rue du Vieux Marché-aux-grains 6, 1000 **Tel** *(02) 513 0868*

Map *1 C2*

This handsome 17th-century house encloses a temple to traditional Belgian cuisine without pretensions or faddish fusion twists. In particular, the customers roll in for the veal in *kriek* (cherry) beer with Belgian endive. Good wine list, but a superb beer list. Vasco the family dog will welcome you with or without reservations. Closed Sunday, Monday.

Les Larmes du Tigre

Rue de Wynants 21, 1000 **Tel** *(02) 512 1877*

The peaceful, elegant surroundings of Les Larmes du Tigre (The Tears of the Tiger) stand in a marked contrast to the rather explosive variety of flavours found in one of the city's most impressive Asian restaurants. As is usually the case for a Thai eaterie, Les Larmes offers extremely friendly service. Closed Saturday lunch.

Strofilia

Rue du Marché aux Porcs 11–13, 1000 **Tel** *(02) 512 3293*

One of the best Greek restaurants in town also happens to be one of the most atmospheric of Brussels' many eateries. Amid candlelight and brick walls, the chef creates a new take on the Greek salad that includes spinach, capers, scampi and calamari. Mains include aubergine (eggplant) minced-meat roulade and suckling pig. Closed Saturday lunch, Sunday.

't Kelderke

Grand Place 15, 1000 **Tel** *(02) 513 7344*

Map *2 D3*

On the Grand Place, this cellar restaurant is as busy as you may expect but the feel is decidedly genuine. *Moules-frites* (mussels and French fries) are served in their traditional, huge black pails at a fast and furious pace. Expect to wait for a table, but not for too long.

Vismet

Place Sainte-Catherine 23, 1000 **Tel** *(02) 218 8545*

Map *1 C2*

Wood panelling, old-school green-stemmed wine glasses and paper tablecloths give Vismet a 1970s Germanic feel, but the open concept kitchen is of a more contemporary era. Seafood specialist head chef and owner Tom Decroos is known to wander the dining room. Closed Sunday, Monday.

A la Recherche du Temps Perdu

Rue du Lombard 25, 1000 **Tel** *(02) 513 7884*

Map *1 C3*

The ornate Art Nouveau façade of this building hides a space that truly is of a previous era. The rich patina on the gorgeous carved woodwork and the splendid ancient chimney take you back to a much older Brussels, even as chef Alain Pessemier offers decidedly agreeable flavours of today. French-based cuisine.

Belga Queen

Rue Fossé aux Loups 32, 1000 **Tel** *(02) 217 2187*

Map *2 D2*

The chic Belga Queen, with its two bars – one for fancy beverages, the other for oysters – and cigar lounge, is located in the completely transformed former Hôtel de la Poste, a cavernous Belle Epoque bank. However, the food is not quite as impressive as the setting. A special beer and tasting menu is available.

Big Mama

*Place de la Vieille Halle aux Blés 41, 1000 **Tel** (02) 513 3659*

Just a short walk from Grand Place is Big Mama. The warm and cosy décor adds to the friendly atmosphere and children are well catered for with their own menu. The monthly changing four-course set menu with an aperitif offers great value at 32 euros. Closed Monday, Tuesday.

Brasserie Horta

*Rue des Sables 20, 1000 **Tel** (02) 217 7271*   **Map** *2 E2*

This brasserie doubles as the cafeteria in the lobby of the Centre Belge de Bande Desinée, yet its cuisine is as strong as any of Brussels' best restaurants. The building itself is a spectacular example of Art Nouveau architecture. If you tire of the comic book exhibits before the youngsters, there's also a bar.

Brussels Café

*Place Ste-Catherine 3, 1000 **Tel** (02) 502 3573*   **Map** *1 C2*

Set in picturesque Place Ste-Catherine, Brussels Café serves simple, tasty dishes. Specialities include rabbit cooked in *kriek* (cherry beer) and *stoemp* (a coarse mash with vegetables and sausages). The four-course menu offers good value. On a warm evening, grab one of the sought after tables on the small terrace.

La Manufacture

*Rue Notre-Dame du Sommeil 13, 1000 **Tel** (02) 502 2525*   **Map** *1 B2*

A hundred years ago, this venue northwest of the city was a printer's workshop, replaced 40 years later by the Delvaux leather factory. Now it is a very 21st-century dining establishment complete with polished wood and iron pillars. Cuisine leans towards the international with a French base. Good value two-course set lunch served Monday to Friday.

La Moule Sacrée

*Rue des Chapeliers 11, 1000 **Tel** (02) 511 5334*   **Map** *1 D3*

Needless to say, the "Sacred Mussel" specializes in mussels, as well as other *fruits de mer*. In fact, this is one of the more inexpensive hostelries supplying *moules frites* (mussels and French fries) in the capital. Its location, a short walk from the Grand Place, means that it is generally busy.

Le Variétés

*Place Ste-Croix 4, 1050 **Tel** (02) 647 0436*

Located on the ground floor of a magnificent Art Deco building, Le Variétés has totally recreated the atmosphere of a 1930s brasserie. The centrepiece of the dining room is the open kitchen complete with an impressive grill, hence the wide range of rotisserie and grilled dishes. The beef tartare with fresh herbs is particularly recommended.

Les Ateliers de la Grande Ile

*Rue de la Grande Ile 33, 1000 **Tel** (02) 512 8190*   **Map** *1 C3*

If you are with a large-ish number of people looking for a convivial evening where the meal constitutes the entire night's merriment, Les Ateliers is an ideal location. Specialities at this Russian bistro include the grilled pork and goulash, but the restaurant is most proud of its range of caviars.

Aux Armes de Bruxelles

*Rue des Bouchers 13, 1000 **Tel** (02) 511 5550*   **Map** *2 D2*

In the heart of the Ilôt Sacré restaurant area, Aux Armes de Bruxelles was a favourite haunt of Brussels' most famous *chanteur*, Jacques Brel, and remains popular for its seafood. The lobster, mussels and game are the key recommendations. Try the Belgian endive salad to start.

Aux Deux Couleurs

*Place Sainte-Catherine 3, 1000 **Tel** (02) 502 3573*   **Map** *1 C2*

"At the Two Colours" is indeed colourful, both in its red and blue décor and its variety of inventive seafood offerings, which marks out this quality establishment in the seafood restaurant quarter of Ste-Catherine. If you're feeling a bit of a gourmand, best go for the half lobster with morille mushrooms and fresh pasta.

Aux Arcades

*Rue des Bouchers 36, 1000 **Tel** (02) 514 0819*   **Map** *2 D2*

One of the better establishments in the often-busy restaurant alley next to the Grand Place, Aux Arcades is decorated in the style of 17th-century Flemish art and is famous for its prawn croquettes. The à la carte menu is expensive, but as with most places along Rue des Bouchers, stick to the fixed menu and you will grab yourself a relative bargain.

Chez Ma Douce Provence

*Rue de la Presse 21–23, 1000 **Tel** (02) 217 3831*   **Map** *2 F2*

Provençale cooking is the order of the day at this recently opened restaurant. The owners have a robust vision of what they are trying to achieve, resulting in an enticing menu. Indeed, their smooth *crème de langoustine* and house foie gras could not be bettered in Avignon.

Comme Chez Soi

*Place Rouppe 23, 1000 **Tel** (02) 512 2921*   **Map** *1 C4*

Widely regarded as the city's best restaurant, Comme Chez Soi, with its three Michelin stars, is particularly strong in the game department. A mahogany bar, a bookcase and over-stuffed leather couches all feature in the lounge area. The dessert trilogy is unmissable. Book well in advance. Closed Sunday, Monday, Wednesday lunch.

Key to Price Guide *see p152* **Key to Symbols** *see back cover flap*

Jaloa ⬛⬛ €€€€€
Place Ste-Catherine 5–7, 1000 **Tel** *(02) 512 1831*

Located near the charming *Vismarkt* area, site of the former fish market, in an 18th-century house once inhabited by Vincent van Gogh is Jaloa. The restaurant serves modern European cuisine, offering both à la carte dishes and a wide range of monthly changing set menus. Closed Sunday.

Le Dauphin ⬛⬛⬛ €€€€€
Quai aux Briques 34, 1000 **Tel** *(02) 514 2258*   **Map** *1 C1*

Le Dauphin's chef, formerly of St Catherine seafood mainstay Vismet, delivers his Belgian compositions, such as green eel or roast turbot, at his new address with its bright, contemporary decoration. The mussels are also done with a pinch more creativity than most of the city's numerous *moules-frites* establishments. Closed Sunday.

L'Ogenblik ⬛ €€€€€
Galeries des Princes 1, 1000 **Tel** *(02) 511 6151*   **Map** *2 D2*

In the centre of the stunning Saint Hubert's Galleries, this thirty-year-old Parisian-style bistro with a relaxed ambience is a gastronomic wonder. Dishes such as duck magret carpaccio with parmesan cuttings, or sea bass filet with aubergine (eggplant) caviar are a gourmand's delight. Closed Sunday.

Resource ⬛⬛⬛⬛ €€€€€
Rue du Midi 164, 1000 **Tel** *(02) 514 3223*   **Map** *1 C3*

Resource's clean, light, modern interior, with contemporary art and intelligent music, reflects both the taste and ethics of the offerings, which include a set "Slow Food" menu of a selection of vegetables, shellfish, fish, a variable main course and dessert or cheese. The wine list has an organic bias. Closed Sunday, Monday.

Vincent ⬛⬛ €€€€€
Rue des Dominicains 8–10, 1000 **Tel** *(02) 511 2607*

Brussels may be landlocked, but that hasn't stopped the proprietors of Vincent from indulging their maritime fantasies in the decoration of their restaurant. With a surfeit of dark-wood panelling and sea-themed murals, it is no surprise that their speciality is turbot served in a mussel sauce with apples. Closed first two weeks in August.

UPPER TOWN

Aux Bons Enfants ⬛⬛⬛ €€
Place du Grand Sablon 49, 1000 **Tel** *(02) 512 4095*   **Map** *2 D4*

This restaurant takes its name from the young singers of the choir of Sainte-Gudule who practised here in the 16th century. Rustic interior, classical music and a range of simple, Italian staples – pasta and pizza – at prices that are reasonable for the Sablon. Closed Tuesday evening, Wednesday.

De Ultieme Hallucinatie ⬛⬛ €€
Rue Royale 316, 1000 **Tel** *(02) 217 0614*   **Map** *2 F1*

Constructed in 1850 and transformed in 1904, this is the city's only remaining restaurant with an original Art Nouveau interior. Recommended specialties include the pike in Cantillon gueuze beer. The venue hosts a trilingual "Afterwork Party" from 5pm on the first Thursday of every month. Closed Sunday.

Het Warm Water ⬛⬛ €€
Rue des Renards 25, 1000 **Tel** *(02) 513 9159.*   **Map** *1 C5*

A pleasant little Flemish café at the top of the narrow Rue des Renards, this is the perfect rendezvous point at the end of an afternoon of antique hunting in the shops and jumble of the centuries-old *marché aux puces* (flea market). With cake, a glass of gueuze and a nice sit-down, you can relax while the antique dealers pack up their wares.

La Grande Porte ⬛ €€
Rue Notre-Seigneur 9, 1000 **Tel** *(02) 512 8998*   **Map** *1 C4*

The Marolles district, where the old but dying Bruxelaire patois can still occasionally be heard, is often described as the most Bruxellois of Brussels districts. The convivial La Grande Porte, which offers mostly regional specialities such as *jambonneau* (pig's knuckle), *waterzooi* (stew)) and *stoemp* (mashed potato) in huge portions. Closed Sun.

Le Grain de Sable ⬛⬛ €€
Place du Grand Sablon 15–16, 1000 **Tel** *(02) 514 0583*   **Map** *3 D4*

Regarded as having one of the best terraces in Brussels, the Sablon's Grain de Sable ("Grain of Sand") is a popular coffee-spot among the city's young and well-to-do. It is also popular for brunch, a meal that is otherwise quite hard to locate in the city. Essentially, though, it's all about the terrace.

Au Stekerlapatte ⬛ €€€
Rue des Pretres 4, 1000 **Tel** *(02) 512 8681*   **Map** *1 C5*

This unpretentious yet high-quality brasserie near the Palais de Justice is owned by a film producer and attracts a mixture of business types as well as tourists. The tasty fare leans towards Belgian favourites such as grilled fish and chicken dishes as well as steaks and ribs. Friendly atmosphere with a wide selection of beers and wines.

Au Vieux Saint-Martin

Place du Grand Sablon 38, 1000 **Tel** *(02) 512 6476* **Map** 2 D4

Another sharp, modernist eatery on the Sablon, Au Vieux Saint-Martin is also a gallery for contemporary painters, a number of whose works hang on the walls. Whether you come here for a coffee and a read of the trilingual magazines or to ingest in something more substantial, you'll definitely be made very welcome. Closed Monday.

Havana

Rue de l'Epée 4, 1000 **Tel** *(02) 502 1224*

For dinner and dancing with a Latin flavour, take the outside lift that descends from Avenue Louise to Marolles. Here you will find Havana, a colourful establishment that is very welcoming during the grey northern European winter, but just as enticing on one of Belgium's long summer evenings. Closed Monday, Tuesday.

L'Atelier Europeen

Rue Franklin 28, 1000 **Tel** *(02) 734 9140* **Map** 3 C2

Some twenty years ago, owner Michel Prévot gave up journalism and opened a restaurant. Situated in the European quarter, L'Atelier is a favourite for those who remain in his former profession. It has large but welcoming rooms, and highlights of the Belgian-inflected French cuisine include the veal escalope with Roquefort butter.

Le Cap

Place de la Vieille Halle aux Blés 28, 1000 **Tel** *(02) 512 9342*

A jazzy, lofty brasserie in the heart of Brussels with a good selection of old and new world wines at decent prices, Le Cap is perhaps more a place for friends to meet for drinks than one of Brussels' top dinner venues. The daily suggestions are more than substantial, however – the knuckle of ham is particularly recommended.

Le Loup Voyant

Avenue de la Couronne 562, 1050 **Tel** *(02) 640 0208*

This restaurant in the student area offers Belgian favourites as well as a good selection of Italian pasta dishes. Smaller snacks, such as *croque monsieur* (toasted cheese and ham) are also available for those in need of a quick pit-stop. Children are warmly received and well catered for.

L'Estrille du Vieux Bruxelles

Rue de Rollebeek 7, 1000 **Tel** *(02) 512 5857*

This old establishment just off the Place du Grand Sablon has something of a venerable literary pedigree: La Tribune Poétique (the Poetic Tribune) once held their meetings here. The eatery specializes in traditional, substantial, beer-soaked Belgian cuisine. Try the eel or game when in season. Closed Monday, Tuesday.

Les Trois Chicons

Rue des Renards 9, 1000 **Tel** *(02) 511 5583* **Map** 1 C5

Down the quaint and narrow Rue des Renards and above the antique shops and flea markets of Rue Haute and Rue Blaes, the proprietors of Les Trois Chicons (The Three Belgian Endives) have successfully attempted just about everything that can be done with the nation's beloved endive. The braised ham and endives with Ardennes apples is a must.

Lola

Place du Grand Sablon 33, 1000 **Tel** *(02) 514 2460* **Map** 2 D4

A brasserie so fashionably and contemporarily fitted out in white wood, stone and glass that the place would seem cold were it not for the warmth and open friendliness of the staff. Expect healthy, light fusion dishes such as yellow curry scampi and cashew nuts with Thai vegetables.

Orphyse Chaussette

Rue Charles Hanssens, 5, 1000 **Tel** *(02) 502 7581*

Orphyse Chausette's chef crosses the cuisine of the Languedoc-Roussillon in the south of France with that of Catalonia. He uses only seasonal regional produce, although the menu always carries its most popular dish, Indian-style red tuna tartare. A strong wine list of some 250 French wines. Closed Sunday, Monday.

Café Maris

Chaussée de Waterloo 1260, 1180 **Tel** *(02) 374 8834*

This splendid Parisian-style brasserie complete with an Art Deco interior and a warm atmosphere has a strong following. Fish and seafood dishes are the order of the day with a variety of oyster platters available. Carnivores will be satisfied with the wide choice of meat dishes as well.

La Tortue du Zoute

Rue de Rollebeek 31, 1000 **Tel** *(02) 513 1062*

While the menu at the Tortue is solidly based around the lobster – for which the chefs offer ten different preparations – other wonders of the sea receive no less consideration. The bistro is located on a delightful, descending cobbled pedestrian street filled with boutiques and other restaurants. Go for one of the alfresco tables in the summer.

Les Petits Oignons

Rue Notre-Seigneur 13, 1000 **Tel** *(02) 512 4738* **Map** 1 C4

In the Marolles quarter, family-friendly Les Petits Oignons offers up classical, seasonal French cuisine in charming 17th-century surroundings. Although not the strongest kitchen in Brussels, the restaurant has an ambience that more than makes up for it. Nonetheless, the fried goose liver with caramelized onions is recommended.

Key to Price Guide *see p152* **Key to Symbols** *see back cover flap*

L'Esprit de Sel Brasserie

Place Jourdan 52–54, 1000 **Tel** (02) 230 6040

Map 3 B4

The beef, stewed in Belgian beer, is as warming as the soft wood and velvet décor. The walls are partly but deliberately left unfinished, while elsewhere bear a message written in over-size copperplate from the Marquise de Sévigné, describing the restaurateur's art form.

L'Idiot du Village

Rue Notre-Seigneur 19, 1000 **Tel** (02) 502 5582

Map 1 C4

The fifteen-year-old Village Idiot is reportedly a favoured establishment of foreign ministers and even Belgian royalty. No wonder, with such intriguing concoctions as the escalope of hot *foie gras*, pepper and vanilla, served on the earthy crockery. Reservations are recommended at this extremely popular eaterie. Closed Saturday, Sunday.

GREATER BRUSSELS

Amazone

Rue du Méridien 10, 1210 **Tel** (02) 229 3800

Amazone is a Flemish non-profit association founded in 1995 aimed at establishing equality between the sexes. Its restaurant is situated in a grand 19th-century townhouse where you can have possibly the cheapest quality meal in Brussels. Booking advisable. Open Monday–Friday lunch only.

Tout Près, Tout Prêt

Chaussée de Boondael 413, 1050 **Tel** (02) 640 8080

Between the twin universities of the ULB and VUB, this sandwich bar offers quick, inventive snacks to a largely student crowd. Cheap coffee and cakes also bring in the crowds as does the fact this is one of the few outlets in town that sells bagels. Closed Sunday.

Café des Spores

Chaussée d'Alsemberg 103, 1060 **Tel** (02) 534 13 03

If you don't like mushrooms, Café des Spores is not for you – the entire cuisine is based around fungus. The café is also an example of the gentrification that is slowly taking hold of St Gilles, with its stylish interior, blackboards instead of menus and downtown prices. An exciting wine list. Closed Saturday lunch, Sunday, Monday lunch.

Copenhagen Tavern

Boulevard de Waterloo 6A, 1050 **Tel** (02) 513 5062

Map 2 E5

This high-class Anglo-Danish establishment isn't really a tavern at all, but a restaurant with a soft, fashionable ambience. Naturally, it is very popular amongst the Scandinavian Euro-expats who come here for a spot of gastronomic nostalgia.

Guru Bar

Chaussée de Boondael 8, 1050 **Tel** (02) 644 5434

The black and zebra patterned interior is a knowing throwback to the 1980s, but the generous tapas dishes at reasonable prices belie the painful chicness of the place. Meat- and fish-oriented, but with such a hip clientele there is also a good selection for vegetarians. Closed Saturday lunch, Sunday.

La Buvette

Chaussée d'Alsemberg 108, 1060 **Tel** (02) 534 1303

Opposite Café des Spores lies its twin wine bar, La Buvette. The focus, is on the quality wine list, but the rustic dishes that accompany your degustation are more than generous, especially the *table d'hôte*. The venue is a transformed 1930s' Art Deco butcher's shop, with original hooks, tiles, mirrors and steel shelving serving as décor.

Le Bonnet d'Ane

Avenue Brugmann 522, 1180 **Tel** (02) 345 6105

The "Donkey Bonnet" (a dunce's cap) is adorned like a schoolroom from the 1900s. While reading the menu, bread and butter appears in a lunchbox. But it is no theme restaurant, as illustrated by the hearty servings of caramelized spare ribs or the knuckle of ham in mustard sauce and rich, grandmotherly desserts.

L'Ultime Atome

Rue St Boniface 14, 1050 **Tel** (02) 511 1367

The key venue in the gentrified St Boniface quarter, L'Ultime Atome is popular amongst the young Euro-set. Cavernous, bustling and noisy, this busy brasserie serves fantastic crêpes at breakfast, and there is a good range of vegetarian options.

Mille-et-une Nuits

Rue de Moscou 7, 1060 **Tel** (02) 537 4127

This undiscovered gem – decorated to give the impression of the inside of a Bedouin tent – lies hidden away in bohemian St Gilles, and has friendly service and reasonable prices. If one person at your table orders the lamb tagine with prunes and almonds, everybody else will wish they had as well.

Brasserie Georges   🅿️🚶‍♂️♿🏠   €€€
Avenue Churchill 259, 1180 **Tel** *(02) 347 2100*

Gorgeous Parisian-style seafood brasserie with numerous waiters in floor-length aprons and a conspicuous, showy shellfish stall at the front doors. The terrace overlooks the entrance to the Bois de la Cambre park (but also the number 23 tramline). The *fruits du mer* (seafood) platter is the restaurant's showpiece. Immaculate customer service.

Le Fils de Jules   ♿🏠   €€€
Rue du Page 35, 1050 **Tel** *(02) 534 0057*

An Art Deco Basque bistro off Ixelles' happening Place du Châtelain. The well-heeled clientele come here for the house *foie gras*, tartare of tuna, spicy squid and the rest of the menu's resolutely Basque repetoire. If the Basque country had an ambassador to Belgium, it would be Le Fils de Jules. Closed Saturday lunch, Sunday lunch, Monday.

Relais St-Job   🚶‍♂️♿🏠   €€€
Place Saint-Job 1, 1180 **Tel** *(02) 375 5724*

It really is so much quieter, greener and more relaxed out in suburban Uccle, where you'll find the Relais just off the St-Job tram stop. If you want to get away from the bustle of the city, sit on the roof of the Relais in August, with your chilled rosé and awaiting your knuckle of ham and creamy mustard sauce. Have the nougat glacé for dessert.

Salon 58   🅿️🏠   €€€
Avenue de l'Atomium 6, 1020 **Tel** *(02) 479 8400*

The "vision-of-the-future" building of Salon 58 was originally called the Tuilier Pavillion when it was built for the 1958 Brussels Universal Exhibition. It was constructed by the same architect as the Atomium and its renovation in 2002 set it out in retro-futuristic pink and gold. An extraordinary dining experience. Closed Sunday evening.

En Face de Parachute   ♿🏠   €€€€
Chaussée de Waterloo 578, 1050 **Tel** *(02) 346 4741*

Manly navy-blue and brown décor envelopes this Corsican-Marseillaise fusion establishment that sits across the road from Parachute, a men's clothing outlet (that also sells Vespa scooters). Try the tartar of Japanese tuna or the veal chop with boletus and crystallized tomatoes.

Touareg   🚶‍♂️📋♿🏠   €€€€
Chaussée de Charleroi 80, 1060 **Tel** *(02) 534 5400*

Touareg offers the traditional Moroccan mix of Berber, Arab and Andalousian cuisines, concocted from ancient recipes. A short walk up from boutique-filled Avenue Louise, this refined establishment offers a smart welcome to those made weary and, most especially, hungry from a hard day's shopping. Closed Saturday lunch.

La Truffe Noire   €€€€€
Boulevard de la Cambre 12, 1050 **Tel** *(02) 640 4422*

The menu at this renowned truffle restaurant is extravagant, with prices to match. It includes such items as a Périgord truffle cooked in a Porto jus, or warm duck foie gras with honey-roasted carrots. In summer, guests can eat in the garden. Closed Saturday lunch, Sunday.

Le Pain et Le Vin   🏠   €€€€€
Chaussée d'Alsemberg 812a, 1180 **Tel** *(02) 332 3774*

Le Pain et Le Vin prides itself on sourcing local ingredients. The frequently changing menu aims to provide diners with a balanced meal rich in vegetables. A new twist is added to common dishes such as lobster and prawn lasagne with a ginger sauce. The terrace is perfect for alfresco dining in good weather. Closed Saturday lunch, Sunday, Monday.

Rouge Tomate   ♿🏠   €€€€€
Avenue Louise 190, 1050 **Tel** *(02) 647 7044*

If you were in London or New York, you would feel at home with Rouge Tomate's health-conscious philosophy (only two meat dishes on the menu) and high prices. The restaurant prides itself on the quality of its produce and its seasonal menu. Not the place for a hearty stew, but you will go away satisfied that you have eaten exceptional food.

ANTWERP

Amadeus   🚶‍♂️♿   €€
Sint-Paulusplaats 20, 2000 **Tel** *(03) 232 25 87*

This former glass-factory mecca for spare rib fans is extremely good value. Despite the Art Nouveau interior, the menu, including all-you-can-eat ribs, is more American in tone. Drink as much or as little of the litre of red wine that is plonked atop the table in advance of your sitting there – you only pay for what you consume.

Ciro's   ♿🏠   €€
Amerikalei 6, 2000 **Tel** *(03) 238 1147*

The best steaks in Antwerp, along with the rest of the traditional Belgian menu, are served up at Ciro's with little regard for pretence, fashion, or ambience – which is perhaps its most endearing quality. The last redecoration happened in 1962. It's rough and ready, but ever popular.

Key to Price Guide *see p152* **Key to Symbols** *see back cover flap*

De Foyer
€€

Komedieplaats 18, 2000 **Tel** *(03) 233 5517*

This opulent space is in the foyer of the 19th-century Bourla Theatre. Red velvet drapes and marble columns add to the sumptuous feel. Prices are reasonable however, with a good value daily lunch buffet consisting of hot and cold dishes, making this one of Antwerp's most popular venues. Closed Sunday evening.

Hippodroom
€€€

Leopold De Waelplaats 10, 2000 **Tel** *(03) 248 5252*

Across from the Musées Royaux des Beaux-Arts, the early 20th-century building that houses the Hippodroom is itself home to an enviable collection of art and photography. The restaurant's menu is as modern as its contemporary fittings, offering sushi, traditional Belgian meat dishes and vegetarian options. Closed Saturday lunch, Sunday.

Mie Katoen
€€

Kleine Kraaiwijk, 2000 **Tel** *(03) 231 1309*

Mie Katoen is a popular little fondue house located in a farm in central Antwerp. Choose a traditional fondue or try something different – the Japanese fondue served with tempura. Grilled dishes are also available. The inner courtyard is perfect for a summer's evening. Open for dinner only, closed Wednesday.

De Kleine Zavel
€€€€

Stoofstraat 2, 2000 **Tel** *(03) 231 9691*

The old furniture and the wooden crates filled with bottles remind customers that this was once a hotel for shipping industry workers. The bistro's affordable inventions have made the site popular once again with travellers, and also with locals, who appreciate such intriguing creations as fillet of hare with wild mushroom ravioli. Closed Saturday lunch.

Gin-Fish
€€€€€

Haarstraat 9, 2000 **Tel** *(03) 231 3207*

Located over two floors, Gin-Fish is undoubtedly one of Antwerp's finest seafood restaurants. Many of the items on the menu are based on that morning's catch from the North Sea, and the open kitchen allows diners to see the chef at work. Advance booking is essential. Open evenings only. Closed Sunday, Monday.

Het Pomphuis
€€€€€

Droogdok, Siberiastraat 7, 2030 **Tel** *(03) 770 8625*

The Antwerp docklands drydock pumphouse was remade as Het Pomphuis in 2003, a Pacific Rim bistro that is in keeping with the city's appetite for industrial resto-bar conversions. The large, very dramatic restaurant has kept much of the original hydraulic machinery. Rare for Belgium, it also offers wi-fi access.

Pazzo
€€€€€

Oudeleeuwenrui 12, 2000 **Tel** *(03) 232 8682*

This old warehouse has been updated with contemporary decoration but has still retained much of its original character, especially the wood beams and intimate cavern beneath the main floor. This wine bar offers most wines by the glass, each intended to match the various tapenades, stir-fries, tempuras and risottos. Closed Saturday, Sunday.

P. Preud'Homme
€€€€€

Suikerrui 28, 2000 **Tel** *(03) 233 4200*

Providing a memorable dining experience in the grand surroundings of a beautiful Art Nouveau building, P. Preud'Homme is one of Antwerp's finest restaurants. Its menu includes fine fare such as lobster, game, terrine and scallops, and the wine list to accompany it is of suitably high quality.

Rooden Hoed
€€€€€

Oude Koornmarkt 25, 2000 **Tel** *(03) 233 2844*

As the oldest restaurant in Antwerp – it first served food back in around 1750 – the Rooden Hoed is one of the city's most renowned eateries. It specializes in seafood, especially mussels, of which there are at least half a dozen ways of having them cooked. You can have a pre-dinner drink in the restaurant's medieval cellar.

BRUGES

Sacré Coeur
€

Langestraat 137, 8000 **Tel** *(050) 341093*

Map *C3*

With a menu featuring local meat and fish specialities along with a wide choice of pizza and pasta dishes, Sacré Coeur caters for everyone. Alternatively, you can opt for a light snack accompanied by one of the many Belgian beers on offer, while enjoying one of the restaurant's live music nights.

Bhavani
€€

Simon Stevinplein 5, 8000 **Tel** *(050) 339025*

Map *A4*

Bruges may not be the most cosmopolitan of places, but it does at least have a decent Indian restaurant. Moreover the pleasant contemporary decor is quite a change to the typical Bruges brown café. Cosy but colonial Bhavani serves a wide range of Indian dishes and the Kashmiri Rogan Josh is one of its best. Closed Wednesday.

For Bruges map references *refer to the inside back cover*

Brasserie Erasmus

Wollestraat 35, 8000 **Tel** *(050) 335781*   **Map** *B3*

The tiny Brasserie Erasmus is found in the centrally located hotel of the same name and stocks over 150 beers – ten on draught. What's more, every single dish on the menu is made with the stuff. Try the rabbit in beer sauce or the fish *waterzooi*.

Lotus

Wapenmakersstraat 5, 8000 **Tel** *(050) 331078*   **Map** *B3*

On any given day, there will be just two options on the menu at this vegetarian café. These two dishes come in three sizes – small, medium and large – but lunch (the only meal served) is hearty no matter what size chosen. The value for money is the real attraction. Closed Sunday.

De Stove

Kleine Sint-Amandsstraat 4, 8000 **Tel** *(050) 337835*   **Map** *A3*

The very intimate De Stove has room for just 20 patrons, so with its simple furnishings and eponymous iron stove, is the perfect place for a romantic evening. The *foie gras* and duck are exceptional, but don't miss what the house does with fresh North Sea fish, supplied daily – particularly the breaded cod in butter sauce. Closed Wednesday, Thursday.

De Gouden Meermin

Markt 31, 8000 **Tel** *(050) 333776*   **Map** *A3*

Perhaps the best café in the Grote Markt. Because the square is so beautiful and such a tourist honeypot, few establishments on the Markt do right by their customers, but not here at the Golden Mermaid. The service is attentive and the café's mussels and frites are excellent.

De Karmeliet

Langestraat 19, 8000 **Tel** *(050) 338259*   **Map** *B3*

Regarded as the best restaurant in Bruges. In 1996 chef Geert Van Hecke became the first Flemish chef to be awarded three Michelin stars. The servings are substantial, as is common in Flanders. Many dishes are made with Belgian genever, and the potato bouillon with shrimp and cod is a favourite. Closed Sunday, Monday.

De Visscherie

Vismarkt 8, 8000 **Tel** *(050) 330212*   **Map** *B3*

Thirty years ago, Mr and Mrs Tillo Declercq opened De Visscherie, a seafood restaurant overlooking the centuries-old Vismarkt (fish market). The house's signature dish is the monkfish waterzooi with saffron, but try any of the turbot variations. The establishment is a popular destination for locals, so book ahead. Closed Tuesday.

Den Dijver

Dijver 5, 8000 **Tel** *(050) 336069.*   **Map** *B4*

Opened in 1992, this stylish restaurant makes creative use of regional Belgian beers in many of its dishes, which are served in cosy surroundings. Three-, four- or five-course set menus are available in addition to an impressive à la carte selection. Booking is essential. Closed Wednesday, Thursday lunch.

Den Gouden Harynck

Groeninge 25, 8000 **Tel** *(050) 337637*   **Map** *B4*

Chef Philippe Serruys and his wife have run this restaurant – located in a 17th-century building in the museum district – for 25 years. The sea bass with coarse sea salt and rosemary for two people is a must. Alternatively, try other creative concoctions such as pigeon with apples or lobster with fig chutney. Closed Saturday lunch, Sunday, Monday.

Duc de Bourgogne

Huidenvettersplein 12, 8000 **Tel** *(050) 332038*   **Map** *B3*

As it overlooks a canal in the historical city centre, the Duc may be heaving with customers, but the service is friendly and the menu is more than passable, with strong interpretations of traditional Belgian cuisine such as *waterzooi*. The charming interior is decorated with tapestries and linen tablecloths. Closed Monday.

't Pandreitje

Pandreitje 6, 8000 **Tel** *(050) 331190*   **Map** *B4*

On the Quai of the Rosaries, 't Pandreitje dates back to the Renaissance. Today, it is a conservative establishment, with linen tablecloths, an extensive wine list and a cosy lounge with a fireplace. If money's no object, go for the four-course set meal. Otherwise, try the sea bass with watercress and artichoke. Closed Sunday–Wednesday.

GHENT

Kapittelhuis

Lange Kruisstraat 4, 9000 **Tel** *(09) 233 7744*

Located in the heart of Ghent near St Baafskathedraal, Kapittelhuis offers a wide choice of dishes, ranging from steaks to pasta. Children are well catered for, with their own menu and play corner. The lunch menu is good value with a daily special. The adjoining tea room serves great waffles and pancakes. Closed Saturday evening, Sunday.

Key to Price Guide *see p152* **Key to Symbols** *see back cover flap*

Amadeus 🏃 €€
Patershol-Plotersgracht 8–10, 9000 **Tel** *(09) 225 1385*

Vegetarian and fish dishes are served at Amadeus, but the main attraction here is the all-you-can-eat spare ribs meal, served with a choice of sauces and a baked potato. Pay for what you drink from the bottle of wine on the table. A Ghent institution with an Art Nouveau interior. Open for lunch only.

Graaf van Egmond €€
Sint-Michielsplein 21, 9000 **Tel** *(09) 225 0727* **Map** E2

The 13th-century building that houses Graaf van Egmond is one of the most beautiful and oldest in the city. The house, overlooking the River Leie, was the residence of 16th-century Dutch hero Earl Lamoraal van Egmond. The contemporary restaurant offers an extensive menu with fish and meat dishes. Closed Sunday evening, Monday.

Keizershof 🏃♿🖻 €€
Vrijdagmarkt 47, 9000 **Tel** *(09) 223 4466* **Map** F1

Located in a narrow, 17th-century building on the market square. The exposed beams and plain wood tables play as humble backdrop to a local lunchtime work crowd, who consume well-priced Belgian staples and salads. A convivial atmosphere. Paintings by local artists line the walls. Closed Sunday, Monday.

Magazijn 🗒🏃♿ €€
Penitentenstraat 24, 9000 **Tel** *(09) 234 0708* **Map** F1

Trendy seafood fusion dinner-and-dancing restaurant popular both for its range of flavours and its late opening. The two-storey house dates back to 1800 and was used initially as a warehouse for the iron shop run by the Rubens family. There is also a good selection of vegetarian options. Closed Sunday, Monday.

Brasserie Pakhuis 🗏🏃♿🖻 €€€
Schuurkenstraat 4, 9000 **Tel** *(09) 223 5555* **Map** E2

Antwerp's obsession with industrial resto-bar conversions seems to have infected Ghent somewhat too, judging by this ultra-hip renovated 19th-century warehouse. Sit on oak and marble tables amongst exposed giant cast-iron pillars, pipes and tubing. The menu features seafood platters and Flemish favourites such as *waterzooï*. Closed Sunday.

Coeur d'Artichaut ♿🖻 €€€
Onderbergen 6, 9000 **Tel** *(09) 225 3318* **Map** E2

A renowned restaurant in the centre of Ghent, Coeur d'Artichaut has a menu that changes every month. Featuring classic European dishes with a twist in addition to inventive Asian selections, it is housed in an impressive mansion building that also incorporates a patio area. A lunch menu is also available. Closed on Sundays and Mondays.

La Malcontenta 🏃♿🖻 €€€
Haringsteeg 7–9, 9000 **Tel** *(09) 224 1801* **Map** E1

Despite its name, you'll not walk away from this Spanish eatery that offers specialities from the Canary Isles and Latin America feeling anything but content. The seafood pancake is recommended, but their best item is the paella. Popular with students. Closed lunchtime, Sunday, Monday, Tuesday.

't Buikske Vol 🏃🖻 €€€
Kraanlei 17, 9000 **Tel** *(09) 225 1880* **Map** E1

One of the city's best mid-range bistros, 't Buikske Vol has a friendly atmosphere and a dark, modern décor. Chef Peter Vyncke's creativity comes out best with the Canadian lobster or crisp veal sweetbread with spinach in a curry cream sauce. Stylish and sometimes humourous food presentation. Closed Wednesday, lunch Saturday and Sunday.

Valentijn €€€
Rodekoningstraat 1, 9000 **Tel** *(09) 225 0429* **Map** E1

A feature of Ghent's restaurant scene since 1996, Valentijn is a favourite with the city's locals, who enjoy the value-for-money four-course menu in a building situated down a cobbled street next to the River Leie. Priding itself on always using the freshest ingredients, the eaterie serves dishes with a French bias. Closed lunchtime, Thursday, Sunday.

Georges 🗏🏃♿ €€€€
Donkersteeg 23–27, 9000 **Tel** *(09) 225 1918* **Map** E2

A Ghent institution, this friendly seafood restaurant is now over eighty years old, having remained in the same family the whole time. Georges, a father-and-son operation, is one of Ghent's pricier addresses, but offers superior, far from indifferent service. The oysters, crab and mussels of Lélande are the main attraction here. Closed Monday, Tuesday.

Tête à Tête 🗏🏃♿🖻 €€€€
Jan Breydelstraat 32–34, 9000 **Tel** *(09) 233 9500* **Map** 3B3

Tête à Tête, the only wooden house left in Ghent, is the home of a remarkable *bouillabaisse* and an intriguing take on the traditional Flemish dish of *waterzooi*. The cosy bistro is a regular hit with local critics, but is considered by some to be a little expensive.

De Blauwe Zalm 🏃♿ €€€€€
Vrouwebroersstraat 2, 9000 **Tel** *(09) 224 0852* **Map** E1

With the kitchen visible from the street, it's no wonder De Blauwe Zalm ("The Blue Salmon"), in the Patershol district, has quickly made a local name for itself for its atypical way of doing things. Chef Daniel de Cleyn is responsible for one of the best fish and shellfish menus in town. Closed Saturday lunch, Sunday, Monday lunch.

For Ghent map references *refer to the inside back cover*

Cafés and Bars

This section lists the best and most colourful cafés and bars in Brussels, Antwerp, Bruges and Ghent, including both the traditional and the new. Most cafés serve a small selection of alcoholic drinks as well as soft drinks, and most bars offer coffee in addition to alcohol. Light snacks and even larger meals can be found at both.

PRICE CATEGORIES
The following price ranges are for a three-course evening meal for one, including a half-bottle of house wine, tax and service.

€ under 25 euros
€€ 25–37 euros
€€€ 37–50 euros
€€€€ 50–62 euros
€€€€€ over 62 euros

LOWER TOWN

Gecko
Place St Gery 16, 1000 **Tel** *(02) 502 2999*   **Map** *1 C2*

Although not particualry trendy in comparison to the "fashionable" end of St Gery, Gecko successfully teams a calm and relaxed atmosphere with great and charming service. Very reasonable, hot sandwiches are available, as well as larger dishes such as quiche, lasagne and stoemp. The Lindemans draught is the drink of choice.

Kafka
Rue de la Vierge Noire 15, 1000 **Tel** *(02) 513 5489*   **Map** *1 C2*

Where other Belgian cafés have extensive beer lists, Kafka, which is just around the corner from the seafood restaurant alley of Ste-Catherine, also has a directory of vodkas, genevers and other spirits. The atmosphere here is unpretentious and mellow.

Le Greenwich
Rue des Chartreux 7, 1000 **Tel** *(02) 511 4167*   **Map** *1 C2*

At Le Greenwich, the game of chess is taken extremely seriously and the town's players gather to battle it out over the board. As a result, it is quiet, with no music and whispered conversation. An Art Nouveau gem that has retained its charm.

Le Roy d'Espagne
Grand Place 1, 1000 **Tel** *(02) 513 0807*   **Map** *2 D3*

A drink on the Grand Place is an essential part of any visit to Brussels. One of the best places to visit, and one of the best priced, is Le Roy d'Espagne, a huge two-tiered bar housed in the bakers' guildhouse with prime views from its terrace.

Mappa Mundo
Rue du Pont de la Carpe 2–6, 1000 **Tel** *(02) 513 5116*   **Map** *1 C2*

This Latin-flavoured hangout is arguably the best café, with the best terrace, in St Géry. It has its bars spread over three floors and the seating booths are actually old wooden train seats. They serve some of the best mojitos you are likely to find this side of Havana.

Monk
Rue Ste-Catherine 42, 1000 **Tel** *(02) 503 0880*   **Map** *1 C2*

Monk is a relatively large, Flemish-language café in what is otherwise a French-speaking quarter. Step off the Francophone street and into a dark-wood-panelled Fleming stronghold. Although mixed, the crowd here tends to be predominantly younger. One of the few cafés in town to sell the superb Mort Subite Faro on tap. No food here.

Viva Sara
Rue du Marché aux Poulets 2, 1000 **Tel** *(02) 218 0101*   **Map** *1 C2*

With decent coffee available in almost every single restaurant and café in town, Viva Sara gives a refreshing twist to the modern café concept. The tempting chocolate cookies that accompany the coffees and teas are sublime and worth a try. No alcohol is served here.

UPPER TOWN

A La Mort Subite
Rue Montagne aux Herbes Potagères 7, 1000 **Tel** *(02) 513 1318*   **Map** *2 D2*

Cavernous former old haunt of Brussels' favourite son, Jacques Brel, and origin of the Mort Subite brand, "To the Sudden Death" is an Art Deco wonder. However, its proximity to the Grand Place means that prices are extortionate, with some of the most expensive beers in Brussels. The only snacks on offer here are sandwiches.

Key to Symbols *see back cover flap*

Café Metropole
Place de Brouckère 31, 1000 **Tel** *(02) 219 2384*

Map 2 D2

Located at the Hotel Metropole, this slightly pricey cafe has a beautiful Belle Epoque interior and an enormous terrace. Here, locals and hotel guests sit, facing the street, surveying Place de Brouckère and the shoppers descending escalators to the metro station that lies beneath.

Delirium
Impasse De La Fidélité 4A, 1000 **Tel** *(02) 514 4434*

Down the narrow lane by the Grand Place, where Manneken Pis' lesser known little sister statue resides, lies Delirium, a subterranean tourist magnet that claims to carry over 2,000 beers. These can be enjoyed with a selection of meats or cheeses. Beautifully decorated and a cosy place for a beer or glass of wine, though slightly on the expensive side.

L'Archiduc
Rue Antoine Dansaert 6, 1000 **Tel** *(02) 512 0652*

L'Archiduc is conveniently located on one of the hippest shopping streets in Brussels. The bar staff here know their music as well as they do their cocktails. Live jazz acts play every weekend in this beautiful Art Deco room with high ceilings, complete with a grand piano. Rumour has it that Miles Davis used to come here to jam. No snacks available.

Le Cirio
Rue de la Bourse 18–20, 1000 **Tel** *(02) 512 1395*

Map 1 C2

In the shadow of La Bourse, the interior of Le Cirio is a marvel of Art Nouveau ostentatiousness. It was formerly an Italian delicatessen and its location, right in the middle of town, makes it a perfect meeting place to start, or end, the day. Simple dishes on offer include pasta and waterzooï.

Le Perroquet
Rue Watteau 31, 1000 **Tel** *(02) 512 9922*

Map 2 D4

This classic Brussels Art Nouveau bar at the bottom of the Sablon has a terrace that is popular in summer. Serving a variety of beers as well as an assortment of bar snacks and salads, it is one of the more inexpensive hostelries in the dearest area of the city.

The Old Hack
Rue Joseph II 176,1000 **Tel** *(02) 230 8118*

Map 3 B2

The Old Hack lies in the shadow of the Berlaymont EU Parliament building. Although it is rather small it does seem to have been around forever. A reasonably-priced lunch is available, offering a choice of seven main dishes including vegetarian options, but note that it is closed at weekends and throughout August.

Falstaff
Rue Henri Maus 19, 1000 **Tel** *(02) 511 8789*

With its beautiful Art Nouveau interior and Neo-Classical detailing, the Falstaff is something of a Brussels' institution. As well as a wide range of beers, the bar-café also serves food ranging from omelettes to steaks. A pianist plays every Thursday.

The James Joyce
Rue Archimede 34, 1000 **Tel** *(02) 230 9894*

Map 3 B2

A few paces away from the Old Hack is the The James Joyce. It is an Irish pub that plays host to quiz nights. The interior is more authentic than most Irish theme establishments and it serves the traditional Irish Guinness, Beamish and Murphys.

GREATER BRUSSELS

Brasserie de L'Union
Parvis de St Gilles 55, 1060 **Tel** *(02) 538 15 79*

Cornerstone of St Gilles bohemia, L'Union is the place to waste a lazy Sunday reading and listening to some of the best, more experienced, accordion buskers in the business. The kitchen produces a really rather good lasagne, but the service can be questionable.

Brasserie Verscheuren
Parvis St Gilles 11–13, 1060 **Tel** *(02) 539 4068*

Brasserie Verscheuren could possibly be described by some as the Art Deco headquarters of Brussels' down-and-out intellectual left. However, it is worth a visit as here you can find the rare Mort Subite Faro, as well as the rarer-still bottled Pecheresse. Light meals are available.

Café Belga
Place Flagey 18, 1050 **Tel** *(02) 640 3508*

On the corner of the popular Place Flagey, Café Belga is located in an Art Deco building complex, which also houses a cinema. It has a similar bohemian feel to St Gery favourite Mappa Mundo and Le Roi des Belges. Provides a good place to choose which films to see at any of the numerous film festivals held in the cinema. Serves light meals.

Chez Moeder Lambic

Rue de Savoie 68, 1060 **Tel** *(02) 539 1419*

Although Chez Moeder Lambic's stock of 800 beers is impressive, it is considerably less than downtown's more famous Delirium, which stocks 2,000. "Mother" Lambic makes up for this with its array of deadly house beer cocktails that are also on offer.

Le Tavernier

Chausée de Boondael 445, 1050 **Tel** *(02) 640 7191*

Between the VUB and ULB twin universities, Le Tavernier is often busy with students. Although no meals are available and there is not much of a selection of beers, the Vedett lager is cheap and keeps you cool while dancing along to the musical selection of house-jazz and world beats.

Michael Collins

Rue de Bailli 1, 1050 **Tel** *(02) 735 7544*

Michael Collins is an Irish pub, named after the infamous Irish revolutionary leader. It has none of the Emerald Isle kitsch you usually expect to find in such venues and is a smart and relaxed pub. There are performances of live music on Fridays.

The Bank

Rue de Bailli 79, 1050 **Tel** *(02) 537 5265*

Down the road from the Michael Collins lies this other Irish pub. It attracts many different nationalities and is actually a converted bank – the toilets have been carved out of the old vault and original features (such as the numbered brass lock-boxes above the urinals) still remain. The Bank serves brasserie-style food and grilled dishes.

ANTWERP

An Sibhin

Nationalestraat 44, 2000 **Tel** *(03) 226 7251*

As an Irish pub, An Sibhin makes a good attempt at being slightly less predictable and stereotyped than the average Irish-themed Guinness outlet. A nice change when you consider the fact that there are another seven to be found in Antwerp. A range of snacks and salads is served.

Bar Tabac

Waalse Kaai 43, 2000 **Tel** *(03) 238 1937*

Bar Tabac is a favourite retro hangout in the trendy, redeveloped Zuid district. The music played here ranges from 1980s new wave to electro and back again. It is famous for its strawberry margaritas and is an extremely popular venue for New Year's Eve celebrations. Bar Tabac doesn't serve meals.

Berenbak

Minderbroedersstraat 17, 2000 **Tel** *(03) 231 1173*

Not far from the Koninklijk Museum voor Schone Kunsten is Berenbak, a typical Antwerp brown café that is home to a varied clientele. One condition – you can't enter wearing a tie. Should you do so, it will be cut off and added to the collection, of which Berenbak has thousands! Its stock of 70 beers is almost as impressive. Children's menu.

Billenkletser

Hoogstraat 22, 2000 **Tel** *(03) 231 3448*

Billenkletser is a tiny brown cafe at the crossroads of Hoogstraat and Haarstraat. There is a bar window from which terrace-dwellers can order their next round of *witbiers met citroen* (white beer with lemon) in the summer, without having to squeeze themselves inside.

Café Beveren

Vlasmarkt 2, 2000 **Tel** *(03) 231 2225*

The Beveren organ was built by the Decap brothers in 1937 and this cafe is home to one of only two Decap organs that are still actually played in a bar (with all other remaining examples being found only in museums). As well as a selection of drinks, you can also purchase Decap organ CDs.

De Fiets

Vrijdagmarkt 52, 2000 **Tel** *(03) 231 4599*

De Fiets ("The Bicycle") is an easy-going bar. The music played here tends to be pop, that is when it isn't playing host to local bands who perform a wider variety of music. It is not overly noisy and has a calm and relaxed vibe, catering to a fun and mixed crowd.

De Volle Maan

Oude Koornmarkt 7 **Tel** *(03) 232 0140*

Just off the Grote Markt, De Volle Maan ("The Full Moon") is a lively place to hangout throughout the week. Though not overtly fashionable, it's a perfect place to have a quiet sit-down, a snack and a read of the newspapers. Thursday is a dedicated student night.

Key to Price Guide *see p162* **Key to Symbols** *see back cover flap*

Den Engel 🖥️♿ €

Grote Markt 3, 2000 **Tel** *(03) 233 1252*

The city's most famous tavern, and one of the oldest cafés in Antwerp, Den Engel ("The Angel") is extremely popular with local business regulars from the town hall, just across on the Grote Markt. It is also more than welcoming to new guests.

Kassa 4 🖥️♿🎵 €

Ossenmarkt 21, 2000 **Tel** *(03) 227 2165*

Kassa 4 is a small, alternative, student bar, which hosts Kassant (an open mike night for poets, comics, songwriters and musicians) every third Sunday. Anyone can climb on stage for 15 minutes, whether they can hold a tune or not. No intimidation here – everyone gets at least a polite round of applause. Snacks are available.

Kulminator 🖥️♿ €

Vleminckveld 32, 2000 **Tel** *(03) 232 4538*

A classic old Antwerp brown café, with one of the best selections of beers in town – some 519 Belgian and 250 foreign bottles. The draught beers change regularly and the staff are knowledgeable guides to the various brews. Widely regarded as the best specialist beer bar in the city and, some would argue, the country.

't Elfde Gebod 🖥️♿🍴 €

Torfbrug 10, 2000 **Tel** *(03) 289 3466*

A stone's throw from the cathedral, 't Elfde Gebod ("The Eleventh Commandment") is a mandatory pit-stop on any wander through town. However, the kitsch displays of saint figurines, angels and pictures of Jesus – along with the classical music – may dissuade you from ordering a Lucifer or a Duvel ("devil"). Good value three-course set lunch.

Axxes 🖥️ €€

Groendendallaan 396, 2000 **Tel** *(03) 541 4411*

This massive salsa bar on the outskirts of the city doesn't open until 11pm, when it appears to fill with half the city's amateur and professional dancers. However, there is no need to feel intimidated as Axxes also offers salsa and merengue lessons. Dress smartly. There is also a restaurant open for lunch and dinner.

Bar 2 🖥️♿🍴 €€

Vrijdagmarkt 19, 2000 **Tel** *(03) 227 5436*

The Vrijdagmarkt is the city's major flea market and has been held every Friday since the 16th century. Here everything (from antiques to technological relics) are sold by auction. The action can be watched from Bar 2's street terrace in the summer. Closed Monday.

Berlin ♿ €€

Kleine Markt 1–3, 2000 **Tel** *(03) 227 1101*

Extremely hip Berlin is located in the Sint-Andries neighbourhood. The soundtrack here leans towards the jazzy-house end of the music spectrum. However, if you are not in the mood for dancing, you can make use of the bar's wi-fi connection instead. Berlin serves brasserie-style dishes.

Borghese 🖥️🍴 €€

Verschansingstraat 24, 2000 **Tel** *(03) 257 3970*

A fashionable 't Zuid hostelry, often frequented by college students, Borghese is a great place to spend the afternoon reading newspapers. Films are screened here weekly in winter and tend to be of the arty and world cinema type, rather than well-known blockbusters.

De Vagant 🖥️🍴 €€

Reyndersstraat 25, 2000 **Tel** *(03) 233 1538*

De Vagant is a genever bar just off the Groenplaats, with a terrace and over 200 varieties of Dutch gin, including walnut, vanilla and chocolate. (You can now buy a copy of the genever menu for 1.25 euros; the free version used to be regularly stolen.) The restaurant upstairs serves Belgian food.

Hangar 41 ♿🎵 €€

Sint-Michielskaai 41, 2000 **Tel** *(03) 257 0918*

Massively popular venue that serves as a hangout for Antwerp's "fashionable" crowd. Its features include a cool, industrial interior and a terrace. Here the drink of choice for most are the stiff cocktails, of which there are many to choose from. Hangar 41 also serves Belgian cuisine.

't Karveel 🖥️♿🍴 €€€

Vlaamse Kaai 11, 2000 **Tel** *(03) 237 3623*

This theme bar is styled on a 16th-century ship and includes portholes, ropes, barrels, rigging and cannon. The beer is ordered at the rudder, as are any of the 15 different whiskys that 't Karveel stocks. Bar food is available, and the menu changes monthly. There's also a children's menu.

Velvet Lounge €€€€€

Luikstraat 6, 2000 **Tel** *(03) 237 3978*

Leading the charge of new design bars that have invaded Antwerp, following the world's discovery of the city as a fashion capital, is Velvet Lounge. This is a swish establishment in the happening, but still slightly run-down, docklands area. Playing lounge music with a smattering of afro-beats. There's a full à la carte menu.

BRUGES

Café Vlissinghe

Blekerstraat 2, 8000 **Tel** *(050) 34 37 37*

Map B2

The genuinely medieval Vlissinghe dates back to 1515 and is one of the city's oldest hostelries still in existence. At the turn of the 20th-century, the building was the meeting place for a number of different artist groups, not least of which was the Kunstgenegen. The interior is an historical marvel.

Cellar Pub De Zolder

Vlamingstraat 53, 8000 **Tel** *(0477) 244905*

Map A3

Cellar Pub De Zolder is an actual cellar, windowless and dark, but it is all the more cosy for it. Watch your head on the steps on the way down and have a seat on one of the mismatched wooden chairs with their decades-old wax patina – perhaps in the snug shared by a large plaster Madonna or next to the massive and sooty stone fireplace.

De Republiek

St Jacobsstraat 36, 8000 **Tel** *(050) 340229*

Map A3

A medium-sized brown café, popular with students and artists who drink in the courtyard at night, De Republiek is also part of a cinema and theatre complex. It has live music late at night and is a good location to find out what's going on in town after the sun sets.

Est Wijnbar

Noordzandstraat 34, 8000 **Tel** *(050) 333839*

Map A3

A wine bar with the atmosphere of a brown café, Est has a range of more than 90 different wines, specializing in New World wines from Chile, South Africa and California, all of which can be ordered by the glass. Also try the melted cheese *raclette*. Free live music on Sundays.

Het Bargehuis

Bargeweg 2, 8000 **Tel** *(050) 332604*

Map B5

"The Barge House", overlooking a canal, may once have been quite rustic and welcoming, but it has since become rather more cafeteria-esque. It is, nonetheless, something of a specialist in local and regional beers – not merely Belgian ones – of which it stocks 125.

Lokkedize

Korte Vuldestraat 33, 8000 **Tel** *(050) 334450*

Map A4

Offering live music in the form of jazz and rhythm 'n' blues nights – with an occasional dose of rock 'n' roll thrown in – Lokkedize is a great place to spend an evening. With a range of beers on tap and light snacks available, the bare-brick and open-fire surroundings create a lovely, relaxed ambience.

Staminee De Garre

De Garre 1, 8000 **Tel** *(050) 341029*

Map B3

Down a narrow lane off the Breidelstraat, this quaint pub is rather easy to miss and remains a real bar for locals. Worth a visit for cheese lovers, as it stocks many of the regional cheeses with an accompanying beer made in the same area.

Straffe Hendrik Brewery Tavern

Walplein 26, 8000 **Tel** *(050) 332697*

Map A4

In the heart of the old town, The De Halve Maan home-brewery is the only remaining family brewery still operating in the centre of Bruges. The current favourite brew is the Brugse Zot ("Bruges Lunatic"), named after the celebration organized by locals to welcome Maximilian of Austria to their city.

't Brugs Beertje

Kemelstraat 5, 8000 **Tel** *(050) 339616*

Map A4

Attracting locals and tourists alike, 't Brugs Beertje is a great red-brick beerhouse located in central Bruges that is renowned for its friendly atmosphere. Choose from 300 different Belgian beers, including five on tap. Belgian cheese plates are also served to keep hunger at bay. Closed on Wednesdays.

Café Craenenburg

Markt 16, 8000 **Tel** *(050) 333402*

Map A3

On the corner of Markt Square and St Amandstraat is this bar and brasserie with friendly waiters who are happy to make beer recommendations. Situated in the north-west of the square, this bar is a little away from the more tourist-heavy bars and therefore attracts locals too. A limited menu includes pasta dishes, salads and sandwiches.

De Versteende Nacht

Langestraat 11, 8000 **Tel** *(050) 333666*

Map C3

De Versteende Nacht ("The Petrified Night") is a downtown cafe whose walls are covered with jazz posters and comic strips. It has free concerts or jazz jam sessions every Wednesday night that last until the early hours and attract a mixed crowd.

For Bruges and Ghent map references *refer to the inside back cover*

GHENT

Café Fatima
🖼️&🎵 €

Struifstraat 3, 9000 **Tel** *(09) 233 9333* **Map** *E2*

Situated near the university, Café Fatima is a student hangout and art space, complete with poetry readings, local bands and a gallery for Ghent artists and photographers to exhibit their work. Not pretentious, the café has a very relaxed ambience.

De Dulle Griet
🖼️ €

Vrijdagmarkt 50, 9000 **Tel** *(09) 224 2455* **Map** *F1*

De Dulle Griet is heaven for a beer fan. One of the 200 beers available is the "Drink Max", an oversized, two-pint version of the famous Kwak beer served in an ornamental glass. But you must first hand over your shoes, which are then placed in a basket that is hoisted to the ceiling. When you return their glass, they return your shoes!

De Gentenaar
🖼️ €

Vlaanderenstraat 68, 9000 **Tel** *(09) 233 4870* **Map** *F3*

There is no phone-book-thick extensive beer list at De Gentenaar, just a comfy old pub for the card-playing, blue-collar locals (one of the last of its kind left in the centre of Ghent). Juicy gossip, jokes and political opinions are served gratis.

Gainsbar
🖼️& €

Oudeburg 51, 9000 **Tel** *(09) 225 1969* **Map** *F1*

Gainsbar, a play on the name of the famous French singer from the 1960s, Serge Gainsbourg, is a slice of swinging France. However, the crowd in this bar are all certainly too young to have caught the chansons Française played at Gainsbar the first time around.

Galgenhuisje
🖼️ €

Groentenmarkt 5, 9000 **Tel** *(09) 233 4251* **Map** *E1*

The Galgenhuisje ("Little Gallows House") has a selection of 60 beers. It is officially the smallest pub in Ghent and dates back to the 17th century. They also brew their own *galgenbier* ("gallows beer"), a brown 6.3% ale. (Due to its size, the Galgenhuisje can get quite smoky.) There's a fine restaurant in the basement.

Gents Geestenrijk
🖼️ €

Kammerstraat 23, 9000 **Tel** *(0475) 589620* **Map** *F1*

A genever and whiskey bar, open from 8pm until late. Oddly, the genever can be charged by weight (at 0.03 euro/gr) or per glass. Whiskey is sold by the bottle. This friendly outlet, where the music hews towards the 1950s, also stocks more than 200 types of brandy.

Kinky Star
🖼️&🎵 €

Vlasmarkt 9, 9000 **Tel** *(09) 223 4845* **Map** *F1*

This alternative music bar is the headquarters of the Ghent-based Kinky Star record label, which is home to Belgian groups such as Sexmachines, De Bossen and Starfighter. There are theme parties on Sundays and free live shows every Tuesday. There's no food available at this bar.

Trappistenhuis
🖼️ €

Brabantdam 164, 9000 **Tel** *(09) 224 2937* **Map** *F3*

Trappistenhuis has 150 beers available and the owner also writes a beer column for a Belgian weekly, which you can read framed on the walls of the pub. At Trappistenhuis, the beer menu comes with extensive descriptions for each item available. Snacks can be ordered to accompany the beers.

Hasta Mañana
🖼️& €€

Lammerstraat 19, 9000 **Tel** *(09) 233 5400* **Map** *F3*

A Spanish bar popular for its sangria and homemade tapas. The sangria is served in carafes that strike the right balance between alcohol and fruit, and there is also a wide variety of Spanish wines that can be tasted by the glass. It is just down the street from sister establishment Gringo Bar, a Mexican cantina.

Het Waterhuis aan de Bierkant
🖼️&🏠 €€

Groentenmarkt 9, 9000 **Tel** *(09) 225 0680* **Map** *E1*

Het Waterhuis aan de Bierkant ("The Waterhouse at the Beerside") has more than 150 kinds of beer, 14 of which are on tap, and boasts one of the finest terraces in Ghent, stretching along the banks of the Leie. A lovely place to be in the summer when the terrace is lit up. Chez Leontine next door serves Belgian specialities.

Oliver Twist
🖼️& €€€

St-Baafsplein 8, 9000 **Tel** *(09) 225 6922* **Map** *F2*

For something a bit closer to home and for a break from the Belgian beer, visit Oliver Twist. It is the first English pub in Ghent and has all the favourite clichéd UK and Ireland beer favourites, including Newcastle Brown Ale, as well as some classic British anthems spilling from the stereo.

SHOPPING

Brussels may traditionally be known for its high-quality chocolate shops but this great shopping city has much more to offer. It is fast gaining on fashion capital Antwerp for its own collection of cutting-edge designers, and the city also happens to be the world capital of comic books, with almost as many shops selling comics as there are

Belgian chocolates

vending chocolate. Throw in department stores selling luxury goods and street markets for bargain-hunters and you have a city that caters for all shopping styles and budgets. Of the other cities, Antwerp is renowned for its diamond and fashion outlets, Ghent offers vibrant music and clothes shops, while you can find beer and classical music in Bruges.

Designer fashion boutique on Rue Neuve

WHERE TO SHOP

Brussels' Grand Place is surrounded by lace vendors, chocolate shops and souvenir outlets, but just one street south is Rue des Éperonniers, with shops selling vintage clothing, posters and specialist teas. North-west of the Grand Place is Avenue Antoine Dansaert, centre of the Bruxellois fashion scene.

To the south-west of the Grand Place is the Rue du Midi, where you can find shops selling second-hand records, clothing, comic books, stamps and coins. Between the Lower and Upper Towns lies the antiques district of Rue Haute and Rue Blaes, leading into the Place du Grand Sablon, where exquisite chocolate shops can be found alongside high-end florists and antique shops.

South of the Palais du Justice lies Avenue Louise and Boulevard de Waterloo, where you can find top boutiques such as Gucci and Louis Vuitton. Perpendicular to Avenue Louise is Rue du Bailli, with its art boutiques,

game shops and tea importers. To the west of the Avenue lies the Matonge, the city's most multi-cultural area, where street markets are held on some weekends, and where you can find skatewear, rare vinyl and vintage denim in the St Boniface area. It is a pleasant district to wander around on a Sunday afternoon.

For all the major high-street chains, head to pedestrianized Rue Neuve, a short walk from the Grand Place.

Renowned Dandoy biscuit shop on Rue au Beurre

OPENING HOURS

Most shops open from around 10am to 6pm, but at a few of the arcades, and in the Rue Neuve area, there is late-night shopping on Fridays until 8pm. Apart from the ubiquitous "night shops" (or corner stores), almost all shops are closed on Sundays, and many also close on Mondays as well. The night shop chain White Nights is the best option for Sunday and late-night convenience shopping.

Sales in Belgium are regulated, with summer sales running from 1 to 31 July, and winter sales taking place from the first weekday after New Year's Day through to the end January.

HOW TO PAY

There is a noticable lack of ATMs in Brussels and cash is still the predominant form of payment. No restaurants accept debit cards, and there are a number that do not accept credit cards. This is also true of a number of the smaller shops and certainly of supermarkets, cafés and newsagents. When you do manage to find an ATM, it is wise to take out more cash than you would usually.

Visitors from outside the EU are entitled to a refund on VAT of purchases of more than €125 in one store. As the sales tax on items can be as much as 21 per cent, this can be a considerable saving. Look out for for the "Tax-Free Shopping" logo on a shop door, request a tax-free cheque and redeem it at customs on your way out of the EU.

Galéries Saint-Hubert historic
19th-century shopping arcade

of the traditional markets is the **Marché du Midi** (Sundays 6am to 1pm) near the Gare du Midi that reflects the tastes of the area's North African community.

The eclectic **Marolles Marché aux Puces** (flea market) in Place du Jeu de Balles (daily 6am to 2pm, but best at weekends) dates back to 1873 and is the starting point for any antiques hunter. While it can take time to sort through the various boxes of items, there are definitely bargains to be found. For pre-sorted antiques, head instead for the more expensive market in the Sablon.

DEPARTMENT STORES AND ARCADES

Brussels has a selection of shopping malls, though they differ little from those found in other cities. However, **City 2** at the northern end of Rue Neuve, is host to the exhaustive French book and CD emporium, **Fnac**, and the Belgian department store **Inno**. Further south on the same street lies **Hema**, a Dutch low-cost store, selling everything from clothes to kitchen utensils. Closer to the Grand Place is the **Centre Anspach**, though a number of outlets are closed while a refit is taking place. Possibly the most impressive collection of shops is the delightful **Galéries Saint-Hubert**, an opulent 19th-century covered arcade – Europe's first – housing a selection of upscale outlets.

MARKETS AND ANTIQUES

Brussels is blessed with markets. Most weekends you can find a "brocante" – a glorified car boot sale combined with street party – somewhere in the city. These are listed in most of the city's free events magazines, as are the various farmers' markets found across the city where you can try some remarkable local breads and cheeses. Cheapest and most extensive

FASHION

Though Antwerp has long been regarded as Belgium's international fashion centre, these days it is the capital city itself that is creating a stir.

Downtown's Rue Antoine Dansaert is at the heart of Brussels' thriving fashion industry, and the principal outlet remains **Stijl**. Since 1984 it has sold the work of fashion graduates from the Antwerp Art Academy such as Dries van Noten, and still offers the best wares – for males and females – produced by domestic talent.

Further down the street, peruse the dresses and womenswear of **Nicolas Woit**, the beautiful knitwear of **Annemie Verbeke**, and **Martin Margiela**'s shop in Rue de Flandre, which offers the apparel of one of Belgium's most talked about designers.

A Dries van Noten design

CHOCOLATES

There are 81 chocolatiers listed in the Brussels phone book – not including franchise outlets – almost all of high quality. The three biggest chains in Belgium are **Godiva, Neuhaus** and **Leonidas. Galler** and **Corné Port-Royal** are also excellent and have numerous outlets throughout the city.

While the area around the Grand Place has many chocolate shops – including the impressive **Dandoy** on Rue au Beurre – it is worth trekking to Rue des Minimes for better quality and service. There you will find **Pierre Marcolini** (who also happens to be a champion pastry-maker) and the **Wittamer** shop *(see p79)* and café, which are probably the best – and most expensive – in Brussels.

BEER

Having fallen in love with Belgium's beers, you may want to take a few bottles home with you. Most local supermarkets, such as **Delhaize**, GB and Match, have quite comprehensive selections of many of the country's finest beers. However, for rarer finds – as well as appropriate glasses for each beer, gift boxes and other beer paraphernalia – visit **Beer Mania** in Ixelles where you can try the beer before you buy it. Also recommended are **De Bier Tempel** and **Delices et Caprices**, both near the Grand Place.

Specialist beer glasses can be found at the Marolles flea market on Saturday mornings.

Browsers at the Marolles flea market

Brüsel, one of Brussels' many comic bookshops

COMICS

Brussels is the world capital for comic books, and the best of its many shops is **Brüsel**, which has a vast collection of comics in French, Dutch and English; it also has a gallery of framed original art for sale on the second floor. In Rue des Renards is **Utopia**, which leans towards American super-hero strips and science fiction but also has a selection of Japanese anime titles. **La Boutique Tintin** is a short walk from the Grand Place and offers a variety of Tintin-imprinted knick-knacks.

A more economical bet is the well-stocked comic shop on the ground floor of the **Centre Belge de la Bande Desinée** *(see pp50–1)*. Separate from the musuem itself, it is free to enter, and despite being a main tourist destination, is one of the better stocked comic shops in the city.

BOOKSHOPS

The Brussels outlet of the English bookstore, **Waterstone's**, and **Sterling** both have a wide selection of English-language books. Nestled among the high-fashion boutiques of Rue Antoine Dansaert is **Passa Porta**, which calls itself a trilingual bookstore and "International House of Literature". **Bibliopolis**, a popular and cheap French second-hand bookstore, has a number of outlets in the city. Its Flemish equivalent is **De Slegte**.

ANTWERP

Apart from the city's diamond district – located west of the railway station – modern jewellery outlets can be found in Schutterhofstraat. Then try **Nadine Wijnants**' shops for clever but inexpensive contemporary pieces from one of the country's most exciting young jewellery designers. The Brussels-based **Christa Reniers**, regarded as Belgium's premier jeweller, has a shop at Vrijdagsmarkt.

Cutting-edge fashion can be found just a few streets away from Antwerp's main high-street shopping district, the Meir. **Ann Demeulemeester**, Dries van Noten's **Het Modepaleis** and Walter van Beirendonck and Dirk van Saene at **Walter** are all must-sees for fashionistas.

Het Modepalis in Antwerp, housing Dries van Noten's collections

GHENT

Ghent is a university town, so it has a high number of hip record stores, streetwear outlets and second-hand shops to service the youthful population. The pedestrianized main shopping area, the Veldstraat, also has all the typical chain stores. For jumble-sale bargains, visit **N'Importe Quoi**; for more organized bargain-hunting, go to **De Kaft**, where you will find used CDs, vinyl and other second-hand goods. **Music Mania** covers three floors and specializes in drum 'n' bass, reggae and jazz. **Het Oorcussen** is another outlet for Antwerp's famed fashion designers, as is the men's boutique **Hot Couture**.

Ghent's quirkiest shop may be **Vve Tierenteijn-Verlent**, a mustard shop dating back to 1858. The recipe for the mustard sold here was first concocted by a Madame Tierenteijn-Verlent in 1790, and it remains a firm favourite over 200 years later.

Bruges' Bottle Shop has a range of beers

BRUGES

While Bruges is considered less of a shopping destination than Belgium's other major cities, the main shopping thoroughfare of Steenstraat is a little quieter and less stressful than Brussels' Rue Neuve or Antwerp's Meir. What's more, the Belgian fashion scene has spilled over into this quaint city. There's the boutique of Brussels' designer **Olivier Strelli**, and L'Heroine, which sells works by a number of Antwerp's famed young designers and their contemporaries.

The Bottle Shop has a more comprehensive range of Belgian beer than its Brussels-based competitors, with an array of some 850 beers and genevers.

Medieval Bruges is the perfect setting for **Rombaux**, which has been selling classical records and sheet music for three generations.

DIRECTORY

DEPARTMENT STORES AND ARCADES

Centre Anspach
Boulevard Anspach 30–36.
Map 2 D2.
Tel (02) 214 2000.

City 2
Rue Neuve 123.
Map 2 D2.
Tel (02) 218 1876.
www.city2.be

Fnac
City 2, Rue Neuve 123.
Map 2 D1.
Tel (02) 275 1111.
www.fnac.be

Galéries Saint-Hubert
Galérie de la Reine.
Map 2 D2.
Tel (02) 512 2061.

Hema
Rue Neuve 13.
Map 2 D2.
Tel (02) 227 5210.
www.hema.be

Inno
Rue Neuve 111–123.
Map 2 D2.
Tel (02) 211 2111.

MARKETS AND ANTIQUES

Marché du Midi
Gare du Midi.
Map 1 A5.

Marolles Marché aux Puces
Place du Jeu de Balle.
Map 1 C5.

FASHION

Annemie Verbeke
Rue Antoine Dansaert 64.
Map 1 C2.
Tel (02) 511 2171.
www.annemieverbeke.be

Martin Margiela
Rue de Flandre 114.
Map 1 B1.
Tel (02) 223 7520.
www.maisonmartin
margiela.com

Nicolas Woit
Rue Antoine Dansaert 80.
Map 1 C2.
Tel (02) 503 4832.
www.nicolaswoit.com

Stijl
Rue Antoine Dansaert 74.
Map 1 C2.
Tel (02) 512 0313.

CHOCOLATES

Corné Port-Royal
Rue de la Madeleine 9.
Map 2 D3.
Tel (02) 512 4314.
www.corne-port-royal.be

Dandoy
Rue au Beurre 31.
Map 2 D3.
Tel (02) 511 0326.
www.biscuiteriedandoy.be

Galler
Rue au Beurre 44.
Map 2 D3.
Tel (02) 502 0266.
www.galler.com

Godiva
Grand Sablon 47–48.
Map 2 D4.
Tel (02) 502 9906.
www.godiva.be

Leonidas
Rue au Beurre 34.
Map 2 D3.
Tel (02) 512 8737.
www.leonidas.com

Neuhaus
Galerie de la Reine 25–27.
Map 1 C3.
Tel (02) 512 6359.
www.neuhaus.be

Pierre Marcolini
Rue des Minimes 1.
Map 1 5C.
Tel (02) 514 1206.
www.marcolini.be

Wittamer
Place du Grand Sablon 6, 12 & 13.
Map 2 D4.
Tel (02) 512 3742.
www.wittamer.com

BEER

Beer Mania
Chausée de Wavre 174–176.
Map 2 F5.
Tel (02) 512 1788.
www.beermania.be

De Bier Tempel
Rue Marché aux Herbes 56
Map 2 D3.
Tel (02) 509 1906.

Delices et Caprices
Rue des Bouchers 68.
Map 2 D3.
Tel (02) 512 1451.

COMICS

Brüsel
Boulevard Anspach 100.
Map 1 C3.
Tel (02) 502 3552.

Centre Belge de la Bande Desinée
Rue des Sables 20.
Map 2 F5.
Tel (02) 219 1980.

La Boutique Tintin
Rue de la Colline 13.
Map 2 D3.
Tel (02) 514 4550.

Little Nemo
Rue de Trône 132.
Map 1 C3.
Tel (02) 646 5345.

Utopia
Rue des Renards 16.
Map 1 C5.
Tel (0475) 817510.

BOOKSHOPS

Bibliopolis
Rue du Midi 93.
Map 1 C3.
Tel (02) 502 4676.
www.bibliopolis.be

De Slegte
Rue des Grands Carmes 17.
Map 1 C3.
Tel (02) 511 6140.
www.deslegte.com

Passa Porta
Rue Antoine Dansaert 46.
Map 1 C2.
Tel (02) 502 9460.
www.passaporta.be

Sterling
Fossé aux Loups 38.
Map 2 D2.
Tel (02) 223 6223.
www.sterlingbooks.be

Waterstone's
Boulevard Adolphe Max 71–75.
Map 2 D1.
Tel (02) 219 2708

ANTWERP

Ann Demeulemeester
Verlatstraat 38.
Tel (03) 216 0133.

Christa Reniers
Vrijdagmarkt 8.
Tel (03) 233 2602.
www.christareniers.com

Het Modepaleis
Nationalestraat 16.
Tel (03) 470 2510

Nadine Wijnants
Kloosterstraat 26 & Nationalestraat 14.
Tel (03) 226 4569.
www.nadinewijnants.be

Walter
St Antoniusstraat 12.
Tel (03) 213 2644.
www.waltervan
beirendonck.com

GHENT

De Kaft
Kortrijksepoortstraat 44.
Map E4.
Tel (09) 329 6439

Het Oorcussen
Vrijdagmarkt 7.
Map F1.
Tel (09) 233 0765.

Hot Couture
Gouvernementstraat 34.
Tel (09) 233 7407.

Music Mania
Bagattenstraat 197.
Tel (09) 225 6815.
www.musicmaniarecords.com

N'Importe Quoi
Burgstraat 11.
Map D/E1.
Tel (09) 223 0617.

Vve Tierenteijn-Verlent
Groentenmarkt 3.
Map E1.
Tel (09) 225 8636

BRUGES

Olivier Strelli
Eiermarkt 3.
Map A3.
Tel (050) 343837.
www.strelli.be

The Bottle Shop
Wollestraat 13.
Map B3.
Tel (050) 349980.

Rombaux
Mallebergplaats 13.
Tel (050) 332575.
www.rombaux.be

For Ghent and Bruges map references *refer to the inside back cover*

ENTERTAINMENT

Lying at at the crossroads of London, Paris, Amsterdam and Cologne, Brussels benefits from the best international touring groups passing through the city. In its own right, Brussels is one of the top destinations in Europe for modern dance and jazz, is host to a world-renown classical musical competition, and has a knowledgeable,

Ecran Total Cinema poster

cinephilic population. The visitor really is spoilt for entertainment choice. Knowingly hip Antwerp, the country's clubbing and fashion capital, offers a similar range of options, while Ghent's large student population gives the city a lively urban scene. Bruges, although quieter, is equipped with a clutch of cosy pubs and jazz bars to while away the evening.

The 19th-century interior of La Monnaie Opera House

LISTINGS AND TICKETS

Expatriates in the Belgian capital depend on the weekly English-language listings magazine *The Bulletin* costing around €2.70. The magazine's pull-out section, *What's On*, is distributed free to hotels. There is also a twin website, www.xpats.com which includes cultural information, news, weather reports and other useful information and links.

More up-to-date and in tune to the city's goings-on is *Agenda*, a trilingual listings magazine that can usually be found freely distributed in boxes outside supermarkets and in cafés. The French newspapers *La Libre Belgique* and *Le Soir* both publish their entertainment supplements every Wednesday. For cinema times online, check www.cinenews.be

Magazines on sale in Brussels

or www.cinebel.be. Visit www.jazzinbelgium.com for a trilingual schedule of jazz gigs throughout the country. If you are interested in reggae, ska and dancehall, visit www.irielion.com. The best online arts agenda is found at www.netevents.be (although the information is only available in French and Dutch).

On foot, head to the Tourist Information Office, which, as well as offering free maps and other information, will also help you book tickets.

OPERA AND CLASSICAL

Students from around the world come to study at the Royal Conservatory of Music, which is the site of the initial rounds of the Concours Musical International Reine Elisabeth de Belgique, one of the most challenging musical contests in the world, which instantly places its winners at the very height of their profession.

The **Théâtre Royal de la Monnaie** *(see p48)* is one of Europe's finest opera houses, and its season runs from September to June. Tickets can be cheap, but beware, many productions sell out months in advance. The **Palais des Beaux-Arts**, the country's most notable cultural venue, is home to the **Belgian National Orchestra** and site of the final rounds of the Concours Musical. Its Art Nouveau hall, Salle Henri LeBoeuf, has recently been renovated, vastly improving the building's acoustics. Its season also runs from September to June.

DANCE

For its size, Belgium is particularly strong in the field of modern dance, with its leading choreographers – above all Anne Teresa de Keersmaeker, Michèle Anne de Mey (www.madm.be) and Wim Vandekeybus (www. ultimavez.com) – having enormous influence internationally. De Keersmaeker is resident at the Brussels opera and director of the world-renowned Rosas company (www.rosas.be).

Venues naturally vary, but the **Théâtre Les Tanneurs**, tucked away in the cobbled streets of the Marolles district, puts dance at the centre of its programme. Another of Belgium's feted dance makers, Michèle Noiret, is its resident choreographer. Tickets prices are reasonable.

JAZZ

Brussels is one of the key cities in the world for jazz, and the leading soloists and groups are sure to include the town in their tour schedules.

Every May, jazz fans from around the world congregate for the **Brussels Jazz Marathon**, which hosts hundreds of gigs in all forms, many of them for free.

The quintessential Brussels jazz venue is the venerable **L'Archiduc**, an Art Deco gem in the centre of town where Miles Davis once popped in to jam. There are regular concerts at weekends and occasionally in the week. For international acts head to **Athanor Studio**, in the basement of the Hotel Arlequin, or classy **Music Village**, which stretches across two 17th-century buildings close to the Grand Place, and features local and international names. Free Tuesday jam sessions pack out **L'Arts-Ô-Bases** across the canal in Molenbeek, and **Sounds** is another popular venue with a prolific agenda of concerts every day except Sunday.

ROCK, FOLK, WORLD AND REGGAE

Brussels is one of the best cities in Europe to catch up-and-coming acts, and ticket prices don't usually go much above €20 for a concert.

The **Forêt-National**, lying southeast of the city centre, is Belgium's top arena for big-name acts. Closer to the centre, Brussels' other venues tend to be more intimate

L'Archiduc, hosting regular jazz concerts in Art Deco surroundings

places, with their own favoured musical genres. **Café Central** favours R&B, blues, bossa nova and ambient. **Cirque Royale** leans towards indie rock, and has a reputation for booking rock and new-wave bands long before they are household names.

The downtown **Ancienne Belgique** has a similar line-up to Cirque Royale, if for more established acts. Flemish student venue **Kultuur Kaffee** at the Vrij Universitiet Brussel (the Dutch-language university) always has a strong line-up of bands and serves the cheapest beer in town. **Recyclart**, showcases avant-garde techno, hardcore, punk and a bit of world music in a refitted abandoned train station. Look out for the old wood-and-brass ticket windows which have been turned into the bar. **Magazin 4** is dedicated to the promotion of French punk and ska. Visit the **Halles de Schaerbeek**, a 19th-century former market,

Logo for rock venue Ancienne Belgique

for a range of different groups, **Vaartkapoen** (also known as **VK Club**) for reggae, the **Beursschouwburg** – the Flemish Cultural Community centre – for Flemish acts, and **La Tentation** for flamenco, salsa and Flemish folk.

Although the city has few noted bands of its own, nearby Liège has quite a strong indie rock scene, centring around the Jaune-Orange label, whose acts often play in Brussels.

THEATRE

There is a substantial English-language theatre scene in Brussels. The city's five English-language troupes – the **American Theater Company**, the **Brussels Light Opera Company**, the **Brussels Shakespeare Society**, the **Irish Theatre Company** and the **English Comedy Club** – are an established part of the Brussels theatre society. Performances are far from amateur and all plays are advertised in the city's listings magazines.

The most important Belgian theatre is the **Théâtre National**, which stages high-quality productions of mainly French classics as well as welcoming visiting companies, such as the Royal Shakespeare Company. Young Belgian playwrights have the opportunity to be showcased at the private **Théâtre Public**, while French 20th-century and burlesque pieces are staged in the glorious and beautifully restored surrounds of the **Théâtre Royal du Parc**.

Le Botanique cultural centre, venue for Les Nuits Botanique festival

CINEMA

For the latest blockbuster films – always in their original language and never dubbed – head to the massive **Kinepolis Laeken**, boasting 28 screens (including IMAX) and free parking. Two central UGC cineplexes will also satisfy most mainstream tastes.

For more intriguing programmes and ambience, try the **Nova** for truly independent films, the **Actors Studio** for foreign and art films and **Arenberg-Galeries**, which has its own eclectically chosen, summer-long festival, "Ecran Total". For mainstream films in Art Deco movie palace surrounds go to **Movy Club**. Tickets cost from €6–7.50.

Brussels has a packed agenda of film festivals for all genres including fantasy (**Brussels International Festival of Fantastic Film**, March), animation (**Anima**, February) and gay (**Belgian Gay and Lesbian Film Festival**, January).

Poster for BIFF film festival, held annually in March

CLUBS AND NIGHTLIFE

Brussels' bright young things start off their weekend in St Géry, a square of trendy cafés and clubs just off the fashion district of Rue Antoine Dansaert. Formerly a run-down quarter surrounding the old grain exchange, the area is now home to latin-flavoured **Mappa Mundo**, popular **Le Roi des Belges** and the elegant **Gecko** bar. The most renowned club in

Latin-inspired Brussels hot spot Mappa Mundo

Brussels, **The Fuse**, has earned a reputation for top-name techno and dance DJs. Once a month it becomes La Demence, a gay night that draws crowds from Germany, France and the Netherlands (www.lademence.com).

Ric's Boat, an actual boat turned nightclub, has a popular Single Friends night the first Friday of the month. **Les Jeux d'Hiver**, in the middle of the Bois de la Cambre woods, attracts an affluent crowd. The loungey Strictly Niceness, on the first Friday of the month at the **Athanor Studio**, is a Brussels institution. In the Marolles, Cuban disco **Havana** stays open until 7am at weekends.

Check www.noctis.com for up-to-date nightlife listings.

MUSIC FESTIVALS

A definite high point on the classical music calender is **Ars Musica**, a festival where composers often premiere their works.

Les Nuits Botanique is a festival of over a hundred concerts, with indie rock, *chanson Française* and rap figuring prominently; it takes over the Botanique for the whole of May. In June, hundreds of free concerts are on offer during the **Fete de la Musique** festival. In the last weekend of the same month, the biggest pop and rock festival in the country comes to the village of Werchter (near Leuven) when the giant **Rock Werchter** festival takes place.

ANTWERP

Antwerp is home to Belgian ballet. The **Royal Ballet of Flanders**, founded in 1969, performs both classical and contemporary works. Tickets start at €15.

The city also claims two opera houses and some fine theatres and jazz venues. Try Art Deco wonder **Buster** for first-rate jazz and jam sessions.

Clubbers from across the country flock to **Café d'Anvers**. The former church, located in Antwerp's red light district, was turned into a house club in 1991. **Petrol Club**, meanwhile, blends electro, hip-hop and rock.

GHENT

For Ghent jazz, the mandatory visit is to Art Nouveau **Damberd Jazz Café**, which has live jazz on Tuesdays. Ghent's popular **Hotsy Totsy** jazz bar also offers occasional stand-up comedy.

The country's most warm-spirited festival, **De Gentse Feesten**, is a centuries-old celebration that lasts for ten days in July. Buskers, street performers, rock and jazz bands compete for the attention of a lively crowd.

BRUGES

Bruges is a real pub-goer's town more than anything, yet jazz lovers have plenty to choose from, notably the family-friendly **De Werf** and **De Versteende Nacht**, with concerts every Wednesday evening.

Logo for the Ars Musica festival

DIRECTORY

OPERA & CLASSICAL

Belgian National Orchestra
Galeries Ravenstein 28.
Map 2 E3.
Tel (02) 552 0460.

Palais des Beaux-Arts
Rue Ravenstein 23.
Map 2 E3.
Tel (02) 507 8200.

Théâtre de la Monnaie
Place de la Monnaie.
Map 2 D2.
Tel (02) 229 1200.
www.lamonnaie.be

DANCE

Théâtre Les Tanneurs
Rue des Tanneurs 75.
Tel (02) 512 1784.
www.lestanneurs.be

JAZZ

Athanor Studio
Rue De La Fourche 17–19.
Tel (02) 514 1615.
Map 2 D2.
www.studio-athanor.be

Brussels Jazz Marathon
www.brusselsjazz
marathon.be

L'Archiduc
Rue Antoine-Dansaert 6.
Map 1 C2.
Tel (02) 512 0652.
www.archiduc.net

L'Arts-Ô-Bases
Rue Ulens 43.
Tel (047) 746 4806.

Sounds
Rue de la Tulipe 28.
Map 2 F5.
Tel (02) 512 9250.
www.soundsjazzclub.be

The Music Village
Rue des Pierres 50.
Map 1 C3.
Tel (02) 513 1345.
www.themusicvillage.com

ROCK, FOLK, WORLD & REGGAE

Ancienne Belgique
Boulevard Anspach 110.
Tel (02) 548 2424.
www.abconcerts.be

Beursschouwburg
A Ortsstraat 20–28.
Tel (02) 550 0350.
www.beursschouwburg.be

Café Central
Rue de Borgval 14.
Tel (02) 513 7308.
www.lecafecentral.com

Cirque Royale
Rue de l'Enseignement 81.
Tel (02) 218 2015.
www.botanique.be

Forêt-National
Avenue Victor Rousseau 208.
Tel (02) 340 2123.
www.forestnational.be

Halles de Schaerbeek
Rue Royale Sainte-Mairie
22b. **Tel** (02) 218 2107.
www.halles.be

Kultuur Kaffee
Boulevard de la Plaine 2.
Tel (02) 629 2325.
www.kultuurkaffee.be

La Tentation
Rue de Laeken 28.
Tel (02) 223 2275.
www.latentation.org

Magasin 4
Rue de Magasin 4.
Tel (02) 223 3474.
www.magasin4.be

Recyclart
Rue des Ursulines 25.
Map 1 C4.
Tel (02) 502 5734.
www.recyclart.be

VK Club
Schoolstraat 76.
www.vkconcerts.be

THEATRE

American Theater Company
www.atc-brussels.com

Brussels Light Opera Company
www.bloc-brussels.be

Brussels Shakespeare Society
www.shaksoc.com

English Comedy Club
Rue Waelhem 73
Tel (02) 675 3702.

Irish Theatre Co
www.irishtheatregroup.be

Théâtre National
Boulevard Emile Jacqmain
111–115.
Tel (02) 203 4155.

Théâtre Le Public
Rue Braemt 64–70.
Tel 0800 94444.

Théâtre Royal du Parc
Rue de la Loi 3.
Tel (02) 505 3040.

CINEMA

Actors Studio
Petite Rue des Bouchers 16.
Tel (02) 512 1696.

Anima
Tel (02) 534 4125.

Arenberg-Galeries
Galerie de la Reine 26.
Tel (02) 512 8063.
www.arenberg.be

Belgian Gay and Lesbian Film Festival
www.fglb.org

Brussels Intl Festival of Fantastic Film
www.bifff.org

Kinepolis Laeken
Bruparck, Boulevard du
Centenaire 20.
Tel 900 00555
www.kinepolis.com

Movy Club
Rue des Moines 21.
Tel (02) 537 6954.

Nova
Rue d'Arenberg 3.
www.nova-cinema.com

CLUBS & NIGHTLIFE

Gecko
Place Saint-Géry 16.
Map 1 C2.
Tel (02) 512 8619.

Havana
Rue de l'Epée 4.
Tel (02) 502 1224.
www.havana-brussels.com

Le Roi des Belges
Rue Jules Van Praet 5.
Tel (02) 503 4300.

Les Jeux d'Hiver
Rue du Pont de la Carpe 2.
Tel (02) 649 0864.
www.jeuxdhiver.be.

Mappa Mundo
Rue du Pont de la Carpe 2.
Tel (02) 513 5116.

Ric's Boat
Quai des Péniches 44.

The Fuse
Rue Blaes 208.
Tel (02) 511 9789.
www.fuse.be

MUSIC FESTIVALS

Ars Musica
www.arsmusica.be

Fete de la Musique
www.conseildelamusique.be

Les Nuits Botanique
www.botanique.be

Rock Werchter
www.rockwerchter.be

ANTWERP

Buster
Kaasrui 1.
Tel (03) 232 5153.

Café d'Anvers
Verversrui 15.
Tel (03) 226 3870.
www.cafe-d-anvers.com

Petrol Club
D'Herbouvillekaai 25.
www.5voor12.be/petrol

Royal Ballet of Flanders
Kattendijkdok-Westkaai 16.
Tel (03) 234 3438.
www.koninklijkballet
vanvlaanderen.be

GHENT

Damberd Jazz Café
Korenmarkt 19.
Map E2.
Tel (09) 329 5337
www.damberd.be

De Gentse Feesten
Tel (047) 490 0431.
www.gentsefeesten.be

Hotsy Totsy
Hoogstraat 1. **Map** D1–2.
Tel (09) 224 2012.
www.hotsytotsy.be

BRUGES

De Versteende Nacht
Langestraat 11. **Map** C3.
Tel (050) 333666.

De Werf
Werfstraat 108.
Tel (050) 330529.
www.dewerf.be

For Ghent and Bruges map references *refer to the inside back cover*

SURVIVAL
GUIDE

PRACTICAL INFORMATION

Although comfortable with its status as a major political and business centre, Brussels has sometimes struggled with its role as a tourist destination. It can be hard to find all but the most obvious sights: the same goes for inexpensive hotels. Both the Upper and Lower Town can easily be negotiated on foot, which might be a relief to those visitors reluctant to take

Guided tour walking group

on the challenging Belgian drivers and roads. Brussels is a very cosmopolitan city, and its residents, many of whom are foreigners themselves, are usually charming and friendly, with most speaking English. The tourist office goes out of its way to help travellers enjoy the city and provides help with everything from finding hidden sights to medical and financial information.

CUSTOMS AND IMMIGRATION

Belgium is one of the 26 EU countries to have signed the 1985 Schengen agreement, which means travellers moving from one Schengen country to another are not subject to border controls. If you enter Belgium from France, Luxembourg, Germany or the Netherlands, you will not have to show your passport, although it is wise to carry it in case of trouble. Bear in mind that it is a legal requirement in Belgium to carry ID on the person at all times. Britain does not belong to Schengen, so travellers coming from the UK must present a valid passport and hold proof of onward passage when entering Belgium. This also applies to US, Australian, Canadian and other Commonwealth citizens.

British travellers no longer benefit from duty-free goods on their journey. Travellers from non-EU countries are still entitled to refunds of VAT (21 per cent on most products) if they spend more than €127 in a single transaction.

TOURIST INFORMATION

Brussels is rarely crowded, so you should not expect to wait at major attractions and museums unless a special event or show is taking place. If you are planning to do extensive sightseeing, the one-day tram and bus pass (*see pp184–5*) is a must. Better still, pick up a Brussels Card from the tourist office (*see below*). Drivers should avoid rush hour (Monday to Friday

from 8am to 9:30am and 5pm to 7pm), although public transport is manageable throughout the day. Many of the city's prestige hotels slash their rates at weekends, when business custom slacks off, so it can be worthwhile timing a short visit around this. Although Brussels' reputation as a rainy city is overplayed, bring a raincoat or waterproof jacket in summer and warm clothing for winter.

The Tourist and Information Office publishes a variety of maps, guides and suggested tours. Available from tourist offices for €33 is the Brussels Card, which includes a three-day travel pass, free access to 25 of the city's museums, discounts for some attractions, restaurants and shops, and a colour guide to the city.

OPENING HOURS

Most shops and businesses are open Mondays to Saturdays from 10am to 6pm, with some local shops closing for an hour during the day.

Supermarkets are usually open from 9am to 8pm. For late-night essentials and alcohol, "night shops" stay open to 1am or 2am. Banking hours usually run on weekdays from 9am to 1pm and 2 to 4pm. Most branches have 24-hour ATMs, and many have Visa or Euro points with Maestro, where foreign cashcards can be used.

Many sights are closed on Mondays. Public museums are usually open on Tuesdays to Sundays from 10am to 5pm.

MUSEUM ADMISSION CHARGES

There was much controversy when the city's major museums, including the Musées des Beaux-Arts and the Musées Royaux d'Art et d'Histoire introduced an admission charge in the mid-1990s. So far the money seems to have been extremely well spent, with the Musée Royaux in particular undergoing much-needed layout improvements. Elsewhere, admission charges

The sculpture court in the Musées Royaux des Beaux-Arts in summer

Visitors taking a break from sightseeing in a pavement café

range from free entry to a daily tariff starting at €5. Reductions for students, children, the unemployed and senior citizens are always given.

TIPPING

A service charge of 16 per cent as well as VAT of 21 per cent are included in restaurant bills (this is marked on the menu as *"Service et TVA compris"*), but most diners round up the bill or add about 10 per cent if the service has been particularly good. Service is also included in taxi fares, although a 10 per cent tip is customary. In other areas, some theatre and cinema ushers expect €0.80 per person, and at nightclubs, you should pay the doormen around €1 if you plan to go back at any point.

In hotels, a small tip for the chambermaid and porter should be given personally to them or left in your vacated room, and you should expect to pay railway porters €1 per bag. Finally, many public toilets – including those in bars, restaurants and even cinemas – have attendants who should be given €0.80.

DISABLED TRAVELLERS

Brussels is not the easiest city for the disabled traveller to negotiate, but the authorities are beginning to recognize that there is significant room for improvement. Most of the more expensive hotels have some rooms designed

specifically for people with disabilities, and most metro stations have lifts. There are also designated parking spaces for disabled drivers, and newer trams provide wheelchair access. The Tourist Office provides information and advice about facilities within the city.

NEWSPAPERS, TV AND RADIO

Most British and American daily newspapers produce international editions, which are on sale at major newsstands. The *Financial Times*, the *International Herald Tribune* and the *Wall Street Journal* are among the most widely available. In addition, **Librairie de Rome, Waterstone's** or **Sterling Books**, among many others, sell English magazines.

Belgium has one of the world's most advanced cable TV networks, with access to more than 40 channels, including both BBC 1 and 2, CNN, NBC, MTV and Arte. The Belgian channels include RTL and RTBF 1 and 2, which are French-speaking, and VTM and Ketnet/Canvas, which are Flemish-speaking. TV listings can be found in the popular English-language magazine *The Bulletin*.

Classical music radio stations include Musique 3 (91.2 FM) and Radio Klara (89.5 FM), whilst internet radio stations, such as StarRadio (www.star-radio. net), offer pop music, as well as news and chat in English.

Personal Security and Health, Banking and Communications

Brussels is one of Europe's safest capitals, with street crime against visitors a relatively rare occurrence. The poorer areas west and north of the city centre, including Anderlecht, Molenbeek and parts of Schaerbeek and St-Josse, have quite a bad reputation, but these areas are perfectly safe during the daytime for everyone except those who flaunt their wealth. After dark, it is sensible not to walk around on your own in these areas. Public transport is usually safe at all hours. Banking follows the European system and is straightforward. In addition, there are hundreds of 24-hour cashpoints located around the city.

LAW ENFORCEMENT

Belgium has a complex policing system, whose overlapping and often contradictory mandates have been criticized in the past. Calls have been made to simplify the judicial structure, a process that is still slowly taking place. Major crimes and motorway offences are handled by the national gendarmerie. However, visitors are most likely to encounter the communal police, who are responsible for law and order in each of the capital's 19 administrative districts. All Brussels police officers must speak French and Flemish.

The main police station for central Brussels is on Rue du Marché au Charbon, close to the Grand Place. If stopped by the police visitors will be asked for identification, so carry your passport at all times. Belgian law classes as a vagrant anyone carrying less than €15 cash. Not using road crossings correctly is also illegal here.

Female police officer

SAFETY GUIDELINES

Most of Brussels' principal tourist attractions are located in safe areas where few precautions are necessary. When driving, make sure car doors are locked and any valuables are kept out of sight. If you are sightseeing on foot, limit the amount of cash you carry and never leave bags unattended. Women should wear handbags with the strap across the shoulder and the clasp facing towards the body. Wallets should be kept in a front, notback, pocket. Hotel guests should keep rooms and suitcases locked and avoid leaving cash or valuables lying around. Rooms often come with a safe; if not, there should be one at reception.

At night, avoid the city's parks, especially at Botanique and Parc Josaphat in Schaerbeek, both of which are favoured haunts of drug-dealers.

LOST PROPERTY

Chances of retrieving property are minimal if it was lost in the street. For insurance purposes, contact the police station for the commune in which the article disappeared. (If you are not sure where that is, contact the central police station on Rue du Marché au Charbon.) Public transport authority **STIB/MIVB** operates a lost-and-found service for the metro, trams and buses. Report items lost in a taxi to the police station nearest your point of departure; quote registration details and the taxi licence number.

TRAVEL AND HEALTH INSURANCE

Travellers from Britain and Ireland are entitled to free healthcare under reciprocal agreements within the EU. British citizens need a EHIC form from a post office, which should be validated before their trip. Europeans should make it clear that they have state insurance, or they may end up with a large bill. While generous, state healthcare subsidies do not cover all problems and it is worth taking out full travel insurance. This can also cover lost property.

DIRECTORY

CRISIS INFORMATION

Police
Tel 101.

Ambulance and fire services
Tel 100.

Central police station
Rue du Marché au Charbon 30, 1000 Brussels. **Map** 1 C3. *Tel (02) 279 7979.*

Medigard Private Doctor Bureau
Tel (02) 479 1818.

Medigard Private Dentist Bureau
Tel (02) 426 1026.

EMERGENCY DEPARTMENTS

Institut Edith Cavell
Rue Edith Cavell 32, 1180 Brussels.
Tel (02) 340 4040.

Hôpital Universitaire Saint Luc
Ave Hippocrate 10, 1200 Brussels. *Tel (02) 764 1602.*

Community Help Service
Tel (02) 647 6780.

LOST PROPERTY

Central police station
Tel (02) 274 1699.

STIB/MIVB
Avenue de la Toison d'Or 15, 1050 Brussels. **Map** 2 D5. *Tel (070) 23 2000.*
www.stib.be
www.mivb.be

LOST CREDIT CARDS

American Express
Tel (02) 676 2121.

MasterCard
Tel 0800 1 5096.

MEDICAL MATTERS

Whether or not you have insurance, doctors in Belgium will usually expect you to settle the bill on the spot – and in cash. Arrange to make a payment by bank transfer (most doctors will accept this if you insist).

Pharmacies are generally open Mondays to Saturdays from 8:30am to 6:30pm, with each commune operating a rota system for late-night, Sunday and national holiday cover. All pharmacies display information about where to find a 24-hour chemist.

Assistants at pharmacies may not speak good English, so when receiving a prescription, make sure the doctor goes through the details before you leave the surgery.

EMERGENCIES

For emergencies requiring police assistance, call 101; for medical or fire services, phone 100. Hospitals with emergency departments include **Institut Edith Cavell** and **Hôpital Universitaire Saint-Luc**. The Community Help Service's (CHS) 24-hour English-language help line is for expatriates, but it may be able to assist tourists.

CURRENCY

Belgium, together with 14 other countries, has replaced its traditional currency with the euro. Austria, Cyprus, Finland, France, Germany, Greece, Ireland, Italy, Luxembourg, Malta, Netherlands, Portugal, Slovenia and Spain also joined the new currency.

Euro bank notes have seven denominations. The 5-euro note (grey) is the smallest, followed by the 10-euro note (pink), 20-euro note (blue), 50-euro note (orange), 100-euro note (green), 200-euro note (yellow) and the 500-euro note (purple). The euro has eight coin denominations: the 1 euro and 2 euros are both silver and gold in colour; the 50-, 20- and 10-cent coins are gold; and the 5-, 2- and 1-cent coins are bronze.

BANKING

Most banks in Brussels are open from 9am–1pm and 2–4pm; some open late on Friday until 4:30 or 5pm, and a few on Saturday mornings.

Banks often offer very competitive exchange rates, and most will happily serve non-clients. Many transactions (especially money transfers) are liable to banking fees, so ask in advance what these rates might be. Most banks will be able to cash traveller's cheques with the signatory's passport or other form of photographic identification. Visitors are usually able to exchange foreign currency, again with valid ID. Many bank attendants speak good English.

CREDIT CARDS

American Express, Diners Club, Mastercard and Visa are widely accepted in Brussels, although it is wise to check in advance if booking a hotel or restaurant. Most hotels will accept a credit card booking. The cardholder may be asked for a credit card imprint at check-in.

POST AND COMMUNICATIONS

Brussels' public payphones are run by former state operator Belgacom. Public phone booths are plentiful but the service information can be difficult to understand; the operator can be contacted by dialling 1380 or directory enquiries in English on 1405. Payphones accept Belgacom phonecards, and both €5 and €10 cards are sold at newsagents, post offices and train stations. Payphones in metro stations accept cash. When using the postal service, addresses should be written in capital letters. A blue "A prior" sticker should ensure swifter delivery on international mail. The ability to use your mobile phone in Belgium depends on your network and it is a

Red Belgian postbox

good idea to ask your provider whether this service is available to you before travelling. Internet cafés are not common in Brussels, but phone shops often have internet access so are worth looking out for.

ATM machine in Brussels

AUTOMATED TELLER MACHINES

Most bank branches have 24-hour cashpoint facilities. Often you will find that there is one machine located in a lobby reserved for members of the bank, while a second ATM on the wall outside is available to everyone. Most ATMs will accept a wide range of cards including those belonging to the Cirrus, Plus, Maestro and Star systems, as well as those from MasterCard and Visa.

BUREAUX DE CHANGE

If you are unable to change money at a bank or to use one of the many cashpoint machines around the city, you may be forced to rely on bureaux de change to obtain euros. These often charge a commission of 3 to 4 per cent and on top of that may have uncompetitive exchange rates. It is therefore worth comparing prices between different bureaux or looking for an alternative. There is a 24-hour automated exchange machine at Grand Place 7, while in the streets around the square there are several bureaux open until 7pm or later. You will also find exchange booths at the city's major stations.

GETTING TO BRUSSELS

Brussels is well suited to both casual and business travellers, with abundant and excellent connections by air, rail and road. The increasing political significance of Brussels in its role as the heart of Europe has led to greater competition between airlines, with many

High-speed Thalys train

operators offering a variety of discounted fares. The Eurostar and Thalys high-speed trains link the city with London, Paris, Amsterdam and Germany, and compare favourably with flying in terms of time. British travellers can use the Channel Tunnel to bring their car with them.

An aeroplane from Belgian carrier Brussels Airlines' fleet

ARRIVING BY AIR

Situated 14 km (8¾ miles) northeast of the city centre, Brussels National Airport is in the Flemish commune of Zaventem (the name by which it is known to most citizens, including taxi drivers). A centre for Belgian carrier Brussels Airlines, the airport is also served by major carriers such as British Airways, American Airlines, Air Canada, Delta and Lufthansa. Among the low-cost operators flying to and from Zaventem are Virgin Express (for London and Europe) and British Midland. A typical journey from London takes 45 minutes. Costs for UK flights range from £60 for a student flight to £270 for a scheduled return flight.

Reaching Brussels from the US can be more expensive than reaching other European cities. Return flights average US $700 for a charter return from New York. Prices from Canada are comparable.

brussels airlines

Logo for Brussels Airlines

The best-value flights from Australia and New Zealand include Singapore Airlines and KLM.

Brussels South-Charleroi Airport has become a second hub, since Ryanair has been operating scheduled flights from various European destinations, including the UK. This is now under review due to a dispute over discounted landing fees. The airport is 55 km (34 miles) from the centre of Brussels and can be reached by train or coach.

AIRPORT FACILITIES

Brussels National Airport has been extensively renovated over the past decade, with a new concourse for intra-EU travel recently completed. Brussels airport features baggage reclaim, customs, car-hire booths, tourist information and ground transport on the lower level. The departure lounge has check-in facilities, ticket and insurance counters and a range of restaurants, bars and shops, before and after the security checkpoints. In addition, there are special lounges for business or first-

class Brussels Airlines passengers, and a corporate meeting centre. On arrival, passengers will also find ATMs, foreign exchange booths and coin- and card-operated payphones.

GETTING INTO TOWN

The cheapest way of getting from Zaventem to the city centre is the express train from the airport to Gare du Nord, Gare Centrale or Gare du Midi. Tickets (about €4) are on sale in the airport complex or, for a small supplementary fee, on the train itself. Three trains run each hour, between 5am and midnight; the journey to Gare Centrale takes 20 minutes.

There is a taxi rank outside the arrivals hall. A one-way fare from here to the centre of Brussels will cost €30–€35 and should take around 20 minutes (though this may be longer at rush hour). If you plan to return by taxi, ask the driver about deals as some companies offer discounts on return fares.

An SNCB/NMBS train runs from Charleroi to Gare du Midi. It takes about 45 minutes to/from the station.

ARRIVING BY TRAIN

Brussels is at the heart of Europe's high-speed train networks, connected to London by the Eurostar service and to Paris, Amsterdam and Cologne by the Thalys network. These trains have a top speed of 300 kph (186 mph) and have slashed journey times between northern Europe's major cities significantly, making them a serious challenge to the supremacy of the airlines.

Eurostar passengers should

book their tickets at least a week in advance, especially to take advantage of reduced fares; they should also arrive at the terminal at least 20 minutes before departure to go through the check-in and customs procedures before boarding. It is possible that you may be refused access to the train if you arrive after this time, although you can often be transferred to the next service at no extra charge.

Trains run hourly between London's St Pancras International station and Brussels

Eurostar train arriving at the Gare du Midi, Brussels

via the Channel Tunnel; the journey takes 1 hour 50 minutes and arrives at the Gare du Midi. Return fares start at around £79/€112. The trains are comfortable, with plenty of legroom, and have two buffet cars, one of which is licensed; first-class passengers receive a meal, free drinks and international newspapers.

Many visitors to Brussels arrive from mainland Europe. The high-speed train company Thalys offers a comfortable journey, with Paris accessible in 1 hour 25 minutes, Amsterdam in around two hours and Cologne in under three.

ARRIVING BY SEA

Belgium can easily be reached from the UK by ferries which arrive several times each day. Cross-Channel ferries run frequently from Dover to Calais and Dunkirk, Ramsgate to Ostend and Hull to Zeebrugge. Services are offered by several companies, including Norfolkline. Foot passengers do not usually need to book, but those with cars should always reserve a space and arrive promptly. Ferry

companies usually offer good child discounts, often with children under 14 years old travelling free.

ARRIVING BY CAR

The opening of the Channel Tunnel has given drivers from Britain a new and faster option for reaching mainland Europe: Le Shuttle (Eurotunnel). This is a car train that takes vehicles from the tunnel entrance near Folkestone direct to Calais, with the journey taking around 35 minutes. From there, Brussels is just a two-hour drive via the A16 motorway, which becomes the E40 when you cross the Franco-Belgian border. Follow signs first to Brugge (Bruges), and then on to Brussels. Those planning to use Eurotunnel should book tickets in advance and try to arrive early. Three trains per hour run between 6:30am and midnight, with one train hourly from midnight to 6:30am. Standard fares start at around £170 return per vehicle, but rise for stays over five days and at popular times. If you book some time in advance, you may be able to take advantage of a number of special offers which are intermittently available.

PASSPORTS AND ENTRY REQUIREMENTS

For visitors from Britain, just a passport is required for a stay of up to 90 days. For a visit of the same length, European nationals should be prepared to produce their identity card. Travellers from the US and Canada will need a full passport. All visitors should, if asked, be able to produce enough money, or proof of access to money, on arrival to pay for their entire stay as well as a return ticket to their home country.

DIRECTORY

BRUSSELS NATIONAL AIRPORT INFORMATION

(www.brusselsairport.be)

Flight Information
Tel 0900 70000.

Disabled Travellers and Special Needs
Tel (02) 753 2212.

Airport Police
Tel (02) 709 6666.

Customs
Tel (02) 753 2910.

AIRLINES

Air Canada
Tel (0871) 220 1111 (UK).
www.aircanada.com

American Airlines
Tel (0845) 778 9789 (UK).
Tel (1 800) 433 7300 (US).
www.aa.com

British Airways
Tel (0870) 850 9850 (UK).
www.britishairways.com

British Midland
Tel (0870) 607 0555 (UK).
www.flybmi.com

Brussels Airlines
Tel (0902) 51600.
www.brusselsairlines.com

Delta
Tel (0800) 414 767 (UK).
Tel (404) 765 5000 (US).
www.delta.com

Lufthansa
Tel (0845) 773 7747 (UK).
www.lufthansa.com

Ryanair
Tel (08701) 569 569 (UK).
www.ryanair.com

Swiss International
Tel (0845) 601 0956 (UK).

TRAIN AND BOAT INFORMATION

Belgian & International Railway Info
www.b-rail.be

Brussels Transport
Tel (02) 515 2000.
www.stib.be

Eurostar
Tel (0870) 535 3535 (UK).
www.eurostar.com

Eurotunnel
Tel (0990) 535 3535 (UK).

Norfolkline
Tel (0870) 870 1020 (UK).

Thalys
Tel (07) 066 7788 (Belgium).

Getting around Brussels

**Metro station
street sign**

Although its public transport system is clean, modern and efficient, Brussels is a city best explored on foot. Most of the key attractions for first-time visitors are within a short walk of the Grand Place, and the Art Nouveau architecture in Ixelles and Saint-Gilles is also best enjoyed on a leisurely stroll. For those anxious to see the main sights in limited time, the tram and metro network covers most of the city at speed, while buses are useful for reaching more out-of-the-way areas. Although expensive, taxis are recommended for late-night journeys. Cycling can be hazardous for the inexperienced.

PLANNING YOUR JOURNEY

If you are seeing Brussels by car, avoid its major roads during rush hours, which run on weekdays from 8–9:30am and 5–7pm as well as Wednesday lunchtimes during the school year, when there is a half day. Tram and bus services run frequently at peak time and are usually not too crowded. However, the small size of Brussels means that walking is usually a viable option.

WALKING IN BRUSSELS

The short distance between sights and the interest in every corner make central Brussels easy to negotiate on foot. Outside the city centre, walking is the only way to appreciate the concentration of Art Nouveau buildings on and around Square Ambiorix, around the district of Ixelles and near St-Gilles Town Hall.

Drivers in Brussels have a bad reputation, and it is important to be alert to traffic while crossing roads. Until 1996, motorists were not obliged to stop at pedestrian crossings: the laws came into effect on April 1 of that year and many drivers still treat them as a seasonal pleasantry. At traffic lights, motorists turning right or left may ignore the walkers' priority. It is essential to be careful even in residential areas.

Blue or white street signs are placed on the walls of buildings at one corner of a street, and can be somewhat hard to locate. Street names

are always in French first, then Flemish, with the name in capital letters and the street type in small letters to the top left and bottom right corners (for example, Rue STEVIN straat).

**Mother and child seeing Brussels'
historic architecture by bicycle**

CYCLING

Compared to the cyclist-friendly cities of Flanders, Brussels can be a frustrating place for pushbike-riders. Car-free zones are few, but the

number of cycle lanes is on the increase. However, on a trip to the suburbs or the Fôret de Soignes, bicycles are the best option and can be cheaply hired from most railway stations (non-Belgians must leave a small deposit).

TRAVELLING BY BUS, TRAM AND METRO

The authority governing Brussels' public transport is the bilingual **STIB/MIVB**, which runs buses, trams and metro services in the capital. Tickets are valid on all three services, which run between 5:30am and 12:30am on weekdays with shorter hours on Sundays and public holidays.

A single ticket, which allows unlimited changes within one hour (excluding the Nato-Brussels Airport line 12), costs €1.50 before boarding or €2 on board. You can also buy a ten-ticket card at €11 or a one-day pass costing €4. The five-ticket card, for €6.70, is not competitively priced but it can be convenient for avoiding repeated queues. There are also combined "STIB/MIVB + Taxi" tickets, a single ticket that offers a reduction on taxi rides.

Single tickets can be bought on buses and trams, and should be stamped in the orange machines next to the exits; you must restamp your ticket if the journey involves a change. On the metro, tickets must be bought and stamped before you reach the platform. Metro ticket offices and most private newsagents sell 10-ticket cards and one-day passes.

Bus at a stop in Brussels city centre

A city tram travelling down Rue Royale towards the city centre

Most stops have clear, comprehensible maps of the city's public transport system, with metros in orange, trams in blue and buses in red. Timetables mark all the stops on each route. Metro stations in the city centre have electronic displays showing where each train is in the system. Those unfamiliar with the tram system will notice the lack of on-board information; there is no indication of what the upcoming stop is, of which many are request stops. Request stops can be made by pressing the yellow buttons by each of the vehicle's exits. Ask the driver to call out the relevant stop. Smoking is banned, as is playing music, although dogs are allowed on both trams and buses.

A few bus services in the capital are run by the Walloon transport group (TEC) or the Flemish operator De Lijn. These services have lettered rather than numbered codes (for instance, the 60 bus is run by STIB/MIVB, the W by De Lijn), but most tickets are valid on all the services.

BRUSSELS BY CAR

It may be a small city, but Brussels has been known to reduce motorists to tears. The seemingly perverse one-way system in many sections of the city centre can swiftly confuse newcomers, while the network of tunnels that

One-day travel pass

bisect the city are notoriously difficult to navigate even for city-dwellers. Belgian drivers, too, have been the butt of jokes from their fellow Europeans for decades. Nonetheless, a car is handy for planning day trips around the rest of the country.

Most international rental agencies have branches here, many at the National Airport in Zaventem or at the Gare du Midi, where the Eurostar and train services arrive.

Like the rest of mainland Europe, Belgium drives on the right, and the "priorité à droite" rule – which means that the driver coming from the right at junctions has absolute priority to pull out unless otherwise indicated – is enforced with sometimes startling regularity. Always watch for vehicles coming from the right, no matter how small the road; some drivers have been known to take their priority even though it means a crash, secure in the knowledge that they are legally correct. Verve and confidence are helpful when driving in a city where many motorists take a flexible approach to road rules. Essential safety precautions, however, should be adhered to at all times. Safety belts are obligatory in all seats, and children under 12 years old are not allowed to sit in the front. Drink-driving is illegal (the limit in Belgium is

Cars and taxis threading their way through the main streets

DIRECTORY

USEFUL NUMBERS

STIB/MIVB
Avenue de la Toison d'Or 15
1050 Brussels. **Map** 2 D5.
Tel (02) 515 2000. www.stib.be

CCN-Service Regional des Taxis et Limousines
Rue du Progrès 80,
1035 Brussels.
Tel (02) 204 2111.

currently 0.5g/l). Speed limits are 50 kph (30 mph) in built-up areas, 120 kph (75 mph) on motorways and dual carriageways and 90 kph (55 mph) on all other roads. Always give way to trams, who will ring their bells should a car be blocking their path. Street parking, usually by meter, is becoming increasingly difficult in the centre of the city.

TAKING A TAXI

Brussels' taxis are among Europe's more expensive, but most journeys are short and cabs are the city's only 24-hour transport service. Service is generally efficient, with most drivers speaking at least a little English, although some people may be surprised at many drivers' lack of familiarity with sections of the city. All taxis have a rooftop sign which is illuminated when the vehicle is vacant. Most cars are either black or white, with Mercedes the make of choice for most companies. It is advisable to find a taxi rank or order a cab by phone, although occasionally drivers will stop if hailed on the street. Passengers ride in the back seat, with the fare meter on the dashboard or just behind the gear-stick. Fares should be posted inside the vehicle. Tips are included in the price, but an extra tip is usually expected.

To make a complaint, write to the **CCN-Service Regional des Taxis et Limousines**, Rue du Progrès 80, 1035 Brussels. Give the taxi's registration number, its make and colour when making the complaint.

Getting around Belgium

As you might expect from a country that is small, modern and predominantly flat, Belgium is an extremely easy place in which to travel. The toll-free motorways compare favourably with any in France, train travel is swift and competitively priced and there are good bus services in those areas not covered by the railway network. Public transport is clean and efficient and the range of touring tickets allows a great deal of freedom and the ability to see the whole country inexpensively. In the level Flemish countryside to the north, hiking and cycling are highly pleasant ways to get around.

Cyclists on a tour of the scenery of Durbuy in the Ardennes

TRAVELLING BY CAR

After the rather enervating traffic in Brussels, driving in the rest of Belgium comes a something of a relief. The motorways are fast, reasonably well maintained and toll-free, while major roads are also excellent. Drivers in cities outside the capital tend to be more relaxed, although the trend in Flanders for car-free city centres can make navigation demanding. The only difficulty most drivers encounter is an occasional absence of clear signs for motorway exits and junctions, which can necessitate taking extra care when approaching junctions (in Flanders, many drivers are confused by signs for "Uitrit". It means exit).

The road rules detailed in the Getting Around Brussels section *(see p185)* hold good for the rest of the country, with speed limits at 50 kph (30 mph) in built-up areas, 120 kph (75 mph) on motorways and dual carriageways and 90 kph (55 mph) on other national roads.

If you break down, three motoring organizations should be able to provide assistance: **Touring Club de Belgique, Royal Automobile Club de Belgique** and **Vlaamse Automobilistenbond** in Flanders. It is worth getting breakdown coverage before you leave, and you must have a valid driving licence (from the EU, US, Australia or Canada) or an International Driving Licence on your person. It is also essential to have comprehensive insurance and/or a Green card, and visitors are expected to carry a first-aid kit and a warning triangle at all times.

All the major rental agencies operate in Belgium, although renting a car can be an expensive business. To rent a vehicle, you must be 21 or over, with a year's driving experience, and have a credit card. A week's rental with unlimited mileage will cost €370 or more but might be reduced on the regular special deals at the big firms. Local agencies may also be cheaper, but be sure to check the terms and conditions. Bicycle hire is available in most Flemish towns with a modest deposit of €15.

TRAVELLING BY TRAIN

Belgium's train network is a more than adequate means of getting to and from major towns and cities. From Brussels, there are direct links to Antwerp, Ghent, Bruges, Ostend, Liège, Mons, Namur and the Ardennes, and even journeys involving a change rarely take more than two hours in total.

Run by **Belgian National Railways** (Société Nationale Chemins de Fer Belges/ Belgische Spoorwegen), the system is clean, modern and efficient, although the quality of rolling stock varies some-what: older carriages have a slightly drab feel, but new

FRENCH/DUTCH PLACE NAMES

One of the most confusing aspects of travel in Belgium is the variation between French and Dutch spellings of town names. On road signs in Brussels, both names are given, while in Flanders only the Dutch and in Wallonia only the French are shown. The following list gives main towns:

French	Dutch	French	Dutch
Anvers	Antwerpen	Malines	Mechelen
Ath	Aat	Mons	Bergen
Bruges	Brugge	Namur	Namen
Bruxelles	Brussel	Ostende	Oostende
Courtrai	Kortrijk	Saint-Trond	Sint-Truiden
Gand	Gent	Tongrès	Tongeren
Liège	Luik	Tournai	Doornik
Louvain	Leuven	Ypres	Ieper

Train travelling through Belgium on a spring evening

models are spacious, very comfortable, and, typically Belgian, offer fine meals and light refreshments.

Fares for standard second-class tickets are calculated by distance, with 100 km (63 miles) costing around €9.40; first-class fares will set you back around 50 per cent more. Because distance is the determining factor in price, return tickets generally offer no saving and are valid only until midnight. Children aged under six travel free, with a maximum of four children allowed per adult, and those aged between six and 11 receive a 50 per cent discount. Several special tariffs are available, including discounts for young adults aged under 26, with weekend tickets and day

Train and motor tour logos

returns reducing the price by up to 40 per cent. The more people travelling, the larger the discount; family members may be eligible for discounts of up to 60 per cent.

A variety of rail passes are on offer for extensive travel. The Railpass costs €65 and allows ten trips within Belgium over one year, while the Benelux Pass is €110 and offers unlimited travel on any five days within one month of purchase on trains in Belgium, the Netherlands and Luxembourg.

TRAVELLING BY BUS

While slower and less comfortable for travelling between major cities, buses come into their own in the more remote or rural areas of the rest of Belgium, as well as in city suburbs. In Flanders, buses are run by the **De Lijn** group; in Wallonia, the network is operated by **TEC**. Fares are calculated according to distance, and are bought from the driver. Bus stops and terminals are generally close to railway stations. Buses have priority on public roads, so journeys are often swift.

SPECIALIST TOURS

Touring can be be a journey full of cultural variety in both Brussels and the rest of the country. In the capital, the Tourist and Information Centre

(see p178) runs a series of over 40 walking and car day tours that cover all the capital and its 19 districts with topics as diverse as "Humanist Brussels" and "Industrial Belgium". The focus is largely on the city's exceptional range of art and architecture, but many diverse themes are covered.

In each major regional city, detailed, multi-lingual private tours are available in the historic town centre; contact the town's main tourist booth for full information.

Away from cities, Belgium also offers hiking and cycling excursions, ranging from one-day adventures to five-day hikes. The Ardennes is a popular destination for hikers, who can appreciate the area's flora and fauna as well as its history. Contact the Wallonia-Brussels tourism promotion office for more details.

A coach full of passengers travelling on a main bus route in Belgium

BRUSSELS STREET FINDER

The page grid superimposed on the area by area grid below shows which parts of Brussels are covered in this *Street Finder*. The central Upper and Lower Town areas are marked in the colours that are also the thumbtab colours throughout the book. The map references for all sights, hotels, restaurants, shopping and entertainment venues

Nymph in Parc de Bruxelles

described in this guide refer to the maps in this section. A street index follows on pp194–6. The key, set out below, indicates the scales of the maps and shows what other features are marked on them, including transport terminals, emergency services and information centres. All the major sights are clearly marked so they are easy to locate. The map on the inside back cover shows public transport routes.

KEY

🟦	Major sight
🟦	Other sight
🟦	Other building
Ⓜ	Metro station
🚆	Train station
🚋	Tram route
🚌	Bus station
🚕	Taxi rank
P	Parking
ℹ	Tourist information
✚	Hospital
🚓	Police station
✝	Church
⊠	Post office
═	Railway line
▦	Pedestrian street

SCALE OF MAPS   1:11,500

0 metres	250
0 yards	250

1

GRAND CHAUSSEE DE GENTSESTEENWEG

QUE DU COMMERCE

BOULEVARD DU KRUIDTUIN

Lower Town

Canal Bruxelles Charleroi

CHAUSSEE DE MONS BERGENSE

BVD DU MIDI ZUID LAAN

RUE DE FRANCE FRANKRIJKSTRAAT

BOULEVARD DE

Façade of La Maison des Ducs de Brabant, Grand Place *(see pp42–3)*

The Triumphal arch in the
Parc du Cinquentenaire, built
in 1905 *(see pp74–5)*

2

3

4

ARDIN BOTANIQUE
AAN

E ROYALE
KONINGSSTRAAT

Upper Town

AVE DE CORTENBERG

BVD BRAND WHITLOCK LAAN

RUE DE LA LOI WETSTRAAT

RUE BELLIARD STRAAT

WATERLOO

AVE DE TERVUREN LAAN

RUE DU TRONE TROONSTRAAT

0 metres   500

0 yards   500

Cathédrale Sts
Michel et Gudule
(see pp70–71)

Street Finder Index

General Index

Acknowledgments

Dorling Kindersley would like to thank the following people whose assistance contributed to the preparation of this book:

Main Contributors
Zoë Hewetson is based in London but works in Brussels as a simultaneous translator for the European Commission. She is also a keen walker and has recently published a guide to walking in Turkey.

Philip Lee lives and works in Nottingham. A veteran travel writer, he has contributed to numerous *Rough Guide* and *Dorling Kindersley Travel Guide* publications, including the *Rough Guide to Belgium*. He frequently writes on travel for British newspapers and magazines.

Zoë Ross is a London-based writer and editor. She has worked on several Dorling Kindersley travel guides, and is now a freelance author.

Sarah Wolff has lived and worked in Brussels for several years. An editor and journalist, she is currently working for *The Bulletin*, Brussels' English-language newsweekly magazine.

Timothy Wright lived in Brussels for most of the 1990s. A successful journalist, he contributed to several English-language magazines published in Brussels and elsewhere in the Benelux countries.

Julia Zyrianova is a freelance journalist and translator. She lived in Brussels and Paris for several years and is now based in London.

Additional Contributors
Antony Mason, Emma Jones, Leigh Phillips.

For Dorling Kindersley
Gillian Allan; Douglas Amrine; Louise Bostock Lang; Vivien Crump; Simon Davis; Rhiannon Furbear; Donald Greig; Marie Ingledew; Carly Madden; Lee Redmond; Marisa Renzullo; Ellen Root; Meredith Smith.

Proofreader
Sam Merrell.

Indexer
Hilary Bird.

Additional Photography
Anthony Cassidy, Steve Gorton, Ian O'Leary, Roger Mapp, Neil Mersh, David Murray, Tim Ridely, Jules Selmes, Anthony Souter, Clive Streeter, Matthew Ward.

Special Assistance
Many thanks for the invaluable help of the following individuals: Joanna at Belgo; Derek Blyth; Christiana Ceulemans at Institut Royal Du Patrimoine Artistique; Charles Dierick at Centre Belge de la Bande Dessinée; Anne at Gaspard de Wit; Elsge Ganssen and Georges Delcart at Rubenshuis; Doctor Janssens at the Domaine de Laeken; Leen de Jong at Koninklijk Museum Voor Schone Kunsten; Antwerpen; Noel at Leonidas; Chantal Pauwert at Stad Brugge Stedelijke Musea; Marie-Hélène van Schonbroek at Cathédrale Sts Michel et Gudule; Elaine de Wilde and Sophie van Vliet at Musées Royaux des Beaux-Arts.

Photography Permissions
Dorling Kindersley would like to thank all the cathedrals, churches, museums, hotels, restaurants, shops, galleries and sights too numerous to thank individually for their assistance and kind permission to photograph at their establishments.

Placement Key - t=top; tl=top left; tlc= top left centre; tc= top centre; trc= top right centre; tr= top right; cla= centre left above; ca= centre above; cra= centre right above; cl = centre left; c= centre; cr= centre right; clb= centre left below; cb = centre below; crb = centre right below; bl=

bottom left; b= bottom; bc= bottom centre; bcl= bottom centre left; br= bottom right; d = detail.

Works of art have been produced with the permission of the following copyright holders: ©Casterman 20 br, Ted Benoit Berceuse Electrique 50clb; ©DACS 2006 18bl, 51t/cra/crb/b, 82tr/cl/cr; ©Dupuis 1999 20tr, 21ca; Sofa Kandissy ©Alessandro Medini 115c; Lucky Luke Licensing ©MORRIS 20br; @Moulinsart SA 4, 20tl/cr/cl/bl, 50tl/tr/cra/crb, 51cla/clb; ©Peyo 1999 - Licensed through I.M.P.S. (Brussels) 21bc; 50cla;

The publishers would like to thank the following individuals, companies, and picture libraries for their kind permission to reproduce their photographs:

AKG, LONDON: 31b, 34t, 36b, 37bl, 37br, 150tr; Galleria Nazdi Cupodimonte 22-3; Erich Lessing 28,/Kunsthistoriches Museum 31t; Musée du Louvre 29b; Musée Royaux d'Arts et d'Histoire, Brussels 35c; Museo de Santa Cruz, Toledo 29t; Museum Deutsche Geschichte, Berlin 31c; Private Collection 150tl; Pushkin Museum 30c; Victoria and Albert Museum, London 32c; Ancienne Belgique ©73c; ALAMY IMAGES: Pat Behnke 149tl, 99bl; Gary Cook 128cl; Ian Dagnall 116cl, 116br; INSADCO Photography/Martin Bobrovsky 148cl; Andre Jenny 78cla; Art Kowalsky 8bl; Angus McComiskey 9br; mediacolor's 78br; Paul Thompson Images/Chris Ballentine 128bc; picturesofeurope.co.uk 149c; Ray Roberts 105br; Joern Sackermann 79br; L'ARCHIDUC: Antoine Huart 173tr; ARS MUSICA: 174cb; ART ARCHIVE: Imperial War Museum, London 109b; AUX ARMES DE BRUXELLES: 144bl.

DUNCAN BAIRD PUBLISHERS: Alan Williams 151br. CH. BASTIN & J. EVRARD: 18tr/cb/bc, 19tr/br, 76br, 86bl/br; 97t, 107t, 118b, 121br; WWW.BRIDGEMAN.CO.UK: Christie's Images, London Peter Paul Rubens (1557–1640) *Self Portrait* 17t; Musée Crozatier, Le Puy-en-Velay, France designed by Berain (c.1725–1730) *Dawn*, Brussels lace 23bl; Private Collection/ Marie-Victoire Jaquotot (1778–1855) *Portrait of the Duke of Wellington* 35b./Max Silbert (b.1871) *The Lacemakers of Ghent* 1913 23t; Private Collection French School (19th century) Louis XIV (1638–1715) of *France in the costume of the Sun King in the ballet 'La Nuit' c.1665* (litho) 32br; Private Collection/ Bonhams, London/Robert Alexander Hillingford (1825–1904) *The Turning Point at Waterloo* (oil on canvas) 34bl; St. Bavo Cathedral, Ghent Hubert Eyck (c.1370–1426) & Jan van Eyck (1390–1441), *Adoration of the Mystic Lamb*, Oil on panel 114bl; Stad Brugge Stedelijke Musea: Groeningemuseum 124ca/cb/b, 125bl; Paul Delveaux *Serenity*, 1970 ©Foundation P. Delveaux – St Idesbald, Belgium 125b; Gruithuis 122t/cb/b, 123c; Gruuthusemuseum 30t; BRÜSEL: 170tl; BRUSSELS AIRLINES: 182bl, 182cla; BRUSSELS INTERNATIONAL FESTIVAL OF FANTASTIC FILM: 174clb.

CAFE COULEUR: 25t; CEPHAS: Nigel Blythe 130-1; TOP/A. Riviere-Lecoeur 150bl; CHIMAY: 150cr; DEMETRIO CARRASCO: 145b; ALAN COPSON: 15bl, 37c; CORBIS: David Bartruff 21cb, 148tr; Jon Hicks 105tr; Wolfgang Kaehler 183c; Ludovic Maisant 145tr; Reuters/Yves Herman 147cr; Patrick Ward 25b.

DAS PHOTO: 172c, 180c, 182t, 186; DRIES VAN NOTEN: 8cr, 169c, 170bc.

ECRAN TOTAL©CINEDIT: 172t.

ROBERT HARDING PICTURE LIBRARY: Charles Bowman 93tr; Julian Pottage 81t, 185b; Roger Somvi 17b, 24t/c; HAVANA: 147c; HEMISPHERES IMAGES: Monde/Suetone Emilio 168bc; HOLLANDSE HOOGTE: 116clb, 117tr; HULTON GETTY COLLECTION: 33t, 34c, 36c, 97b; Keytone 37t.

INSTITUUT ROYAL DU PATRIMOINE ARTISTIQUE/ KONINKLIJK INSTITUUT VOOR HET KUNSTPATRIMONIUM: 22tr, Société des Expositions du Palais des Beaux-Arts de Bruxelles 53tr.

GLENDA KAPSALIS/www.photographersdirect.com: 129bl;
KONINKLIJK MUSEUM VOOR SCHONE KUNSTEN,
ANTWERP: Delvaux *Pink's Bow* ©Foundation P. Delveaux
– St Idesbald, Belgium/DACS, London 2006 100br; J.
Jordaens *As the old sang, the young ones play pipes* 100clb;
R. Magritte *Madame Recamier* ©ADAGP, Paris and DACS,
London 2006 100bl; P.P. Rubens *Adoration of the Magi*
101c; J. Van Eyck *Saint Barbara* 101t; R. Wouters *Woman
Ironing* 101cb.

LEONARDO MEDIABANK: 104tr, 133bl, 135cr;
LONELY PLANET IMAGES: Martin Moos 104cb, 104bl;
Rockoxhuis, Frans Snijders, Fishmarket Antwerp, detail
99ca.

MAPPA MUNDO: 174tr; MODEMUSEUM, Antwerp: 98cl;
MUSEA BRUGGE: Museum of Folklore 129tr; MUSÉE DE
L'ART WALLON DE LA VILLE DE LIÈGE: Legs M. Aristide
Cralle (1884) 35tl; MUSÉES ROYAUX DES BEAUX-ARTS
DE BELGIQUE, BRUXELLES-KONINKLIJKE MUSEA VOOR
SCHONE KUNSTEN VAN BELGIË, Brussel: photo Cussac
6–7, 16t, 34–5, 62clb, 63crb/bl, 64c/b, 64cla; 65tl/tr, 66t,
67b, /©ADAGP, Paris and DACS, London 2006 65br, /©
The Henry Moore Foundation 65c; photo Speltdoorn 16b,
17c, 22c, 63cr, 66b,/©ADAGP, PARIS AND DACS, London
2006 64clb.

DOCUMENT POT: Alain Mathieu 187t.
P&O FERRIES LTD: 183bl; PICTOR: 93t; Robbie Polley:

118b, 122ca, 123b, 124tr, 178t, 181t, 184c/b, 187b;
PRIVATE COLLECTION: 7, 34, 39, 89, 131, 177.

REX FEATURES: 24b, 26c, Action Press 36t.

SCIENCE PHOTO LIBRARY: CNES 1992 Distribution Spot
Image 10; ©STANDAARD STRIPS: 21bl; Sensum.be: 145bl;
NEIL SETCHFIELD: 22tl, 92t, 148c, 169b; SUNDANCER: ©
Moulinsart 20cl.

TELEGRAPH COLOUR LIBRARY: Ian McKinnell 88-9;
ARCHIVES DU THEATRE ROYAL DE LA MONNAIE: 35tr;
TONY STONE IMAGES: Richard Elliott 27; Hideo Kurihara
2–3; ©TOERISME OOOST-VLAANDEREN: 107br;
TOURISM ANTWERP: 95cr; 96clb; 117cl; SERVICE
RELATIONS EXTERIEURES CITY OF TOURNAI: 22b.

ROGER VIOLLET: 32t; Musee San Martino, Naples 33b.

WORLD PICTURES: 26b, 109b.

Jacket
Front - DK IMAGES: Paul Kenward clb; WORLD PICTURES:
main image. Back - DK IMAGES: Demetrio Carrasco tl, clb,
bl; Paul Kenward cla. Spine - DK IMAGES: Demetrio
Carrasco b; WORLD PICTURES t.

All other images ©Dorling Kindersley.
For further information see: www.dkimages.com

Phrase Book

Tips for Pronouncing French

French-speaking Belgians, or Walloons, have a throaty, deep accent noticeably different from French spoken in France. Despite this, there are few changes in the vocabulary used in spoken and written language.

Consonants at the end of words are mostly silent and not pronounced. *Ch* is pronounced *sh*; *th* is *t*; *w* is *v*; and *r* is rolled gutturally. *Ç* is pronounced *s*.

In Emergency

Help!	**Au secours!**	oh sek**oor**
Stop!	**Arrêtez!**	aret-**ay**
Call a doctor!	**Appelez un medecin**	apuh-**lay**un meds**añ**
Call the police!	**Appelez la police**	apuh-**lay** lah pol-**ees**
Call the fire brigade!	**Appelez les pompiers**	apuh-lay leh poñ-**swar** peeyay
Where is the nearest telephone?	**Ou est le téléphone le plus proche**	oo ay luh tehleh**fon** luh ploo prosh
Where is the nearest hospital?	**Ou est l'hôpital le plus proche**	oo ay l'**opeetal** luh ploo **prosh**

Communication Essentials

Yes	**Oui**	wee
No	**Non**	noñ
Please	**S'il vous plait**	seel voo **play**
Thank you	**Merci**	mer-**see**
Excuse me	**Excusez-moi**	exkoo-**zay** mwah
Hello	**Bonjour**	boñ**zhoor**
Goodbye	**Au revoir**	oh ruh-**vwar**
Good night	**Bonne nuit**	boñ-**swar**
morning	**Le matin**	mat**añ**
afternoon	**L'apres-midi**	l'apreh-**meedee**
evening	**Le soir**	swah
yesterday	**Hier**	eeyehr
today	**Aujourd'hui**	oh-zhoor-**dwee**
tomorrow	**Demain**	duh**mañ**
here	**Ici**	ee-**see**
there	**Là bas**	lah bah
What?	**Quel/quelle?**	kel, kel
When?	**Quand?**	koñ
Why?	**Pourquoi?**	poor-**kwah**
Where?	**Où?**	oo
How?	**Comment?**	kom-**moñ**

Useful Phrases

How are you?	**Comment allez vous?**	kom-moñ tal**ay** voo
Very well, thank you.	**Très bien, merci.**	treh byañ, mer-**see**
How do you do?	**Comment ça va?**	kom-moñ sah **vah**
See you soon.	**A bientôt.**	byañ-toh
That's fine	**Ça va bien.**	Sah vah byañ
Where is/are...?	**Où est/sont...?**	ooh ay/soñ
How far is it to...?	**Combien de kilomètres d'ici à...?**	kom-**byañ** duh keelo-**metr** d'ee-see ah
Which way to...?	**Quelle est la direction pour...?**	kel ay lah d**eer**-ek-**syoñ** poor
Do you speak English?	**Parlez-vous Anglais?**	par-**lay** voo oñg-**lay**
I don't understand.	**Je ne comprends pas.**	zhuh nuh kom-**proñ** pah
Could you speak slowly?	**Vous puissez parlez plus lentement?**	voo pwee-say par-lay ploos **loñ**tuh-moñ
I'm sorry.	**Excusez-moi.**	exkoo-**zay** mwah

Useful Words

big	**grand**	groñ
small	**petit**	puh-**tee**
hot	**chaud**	show
cold	**froid**	frwah
good	**bon**	boñ
bad	**mauvais**	moh-**veh**
enough	**assez**	as**say**
well	**bien**	byañ
open	**ouvert**	oo-**ver**
closed	**fermé**	fer-**meh**
left	**gauche**	gohsh
right	**droite**	drawh
straight on	**tout droit**	too drwah
near	**près**	preh
far	**loin**	lwañ
up	**en haut**	oñ **oh**
down	**en bas**	oñ**bah**
early	**tôt**	toh

late	**tard**	tar
entrance	**l'entrée**	l'on-**tray**
exit	**la sortie**	sor-**tee**
toilet	**toilette**	twah-let
occupied	**occupé**	o-koo-**pay**
free (vacant)	**libre**	leebr
free (no charge)	**gratuit**	grah-**twee**

Making a Telephone Call

I would like to place a long-distance telephone call	**Je voudrais faire un interurbain**	zhuh voo-dreh faire uñ añter-oorbañ
I'd like to call collect	**Je voudrais faire un communication PCV**	zhuh voo-**dreh** faire oon kom-oonikah-**syoñ** peh-seh-veh
I will try again later	**Je vais essayer plus tard**	zhuh vay ess-ay-eh ploo tar
Can I leave a message?	**Est-ce que je peux laisser un message?**	es-**keh** zhuh puh les-**say** uñ meh-**sazh**
Could you speak up a little please?	**Pouvez-vous parler un peu plus fort?**	poo-**vay** voo par-**lay** uñ puh ploo for
Local call	**Communication local**	komoonikah-**syoñ** low-kal

Shopping

How much does this cost?	**C'est combien?**	say kom-**byañ**
I would like...	**Je voudrais**	zhuh voo-**dray**
Do you have...	**Est-ce que vous avez...**	es-kuh voo zavay
I'm just looking	**Je regarde seulement**	zhuh ruh**gar** suhl-**moñ**
Do you take credit cards?	**Est-ce que vous acceptez les cartes de crédit**	es-**kuh** voo zaksept-**ay** leh kart duh kreh-**dee**
Do you take travellers' cheques?	**Est-ce que vous acceptez les chèques de voyage**	es-**kuh** voo zak-sept-**ay** lay shek duh vwayazh
What time do you open?	**A quelle heure vous êtes ouvert**	ah kel urr voo zet oo-ver
What time do you close?	**A quelle heure vous êtes fermé**	ah kel urr voo zet fer-**may**
This one	**Celui-ci**	suhl-wee **see**
That one	**Celui-là**	suhl-wee **lah**
expensive	**cher**	shehr
cheap	**pas cher, bon marché**	pah shehr, boñ mar-shay
size, clothes	**la taille**	tye
white	**blanc**	bloñ
black	**noir**	nwahr
red	**rouge**	roozh
yellow	**jaune**	zhownh
green	**vert**	vehr
blue	**bleu**	bluh

Types of Shops

shop	**le magasin**	le maga-**zañ**
bakery	**la boulangerie**	booloñ-**zhuree**
bank	**la banque**	boñk
bookshop	**la librairie**	lee-**brehree**
butcher	**la boucherie**	boo-**shehree**
cake shop	**la pâtisserie**	patee-**sree**
chocolate shop	**le chocolatier**	shok-oh-lah-tyeh
chip stop/stand	**la friterie**	free-tuh-ree
chemist	**la pharmacie**	farmah-**see**
delicatessen	**la charcuterie**	shah-koo-tuh-**ree**
department store	**le grand magasin**	groñ maga-**zañ**
fishmonger	**la poissonerie**	pwasson-**ree**
greengrocer	**le marchand des légumes**	mar-**shoñ** duh lay-**goom**
hairdresser	**le coiffeur**	kwafuhr
market	**le marché**	marsh **ay**
newsagent	**le magasin de journaux/tabac**	maga-**zañ** duh zhoor-no
post office	**le bureau de poste**	boo-**roh** duh pohst
supermarket	**le supermarché**	soo-pehr-**marshay**
travel agent	**l'agence de voyage**	azhons duh vwayazh

Sightseeing

art gallery	**la galérie d'art**	galer-**ree** dart
bus station	**la gare routière**	gahr roo-tee-yehr

cathedral	la cathédrale	katay-**dral**
church	l'église	ayg**leez**
closed on public holidays	fermeture jour ferié	fehrmeh-tur zhoor fehree-ay
garden	le jardin	zhah-**dañ**
library	la bibliothèque	beeb**leeo**-tek
museum	le musée	moo-**zay**
railway station	la gare (SNCF)	gahr (es-en-say-ef)
tourist office	les informations	layz uñ-for-mah-syoñ
town hall	l'hôtel de ville	oh**tel** duh vil
train	le train	trañ

Staying in a Hotel

Do you have a vacant room?	est-ce que vous avez une chambre?	es-kuh voo zavay oon shambr
double room with double bed	la chambre à deux personnes, avec un grand lit	la shambr uh duh per-**son** uh-vek uñ groñ lee
twin room	la chambre à deux lits	la shambr ah duh lee
single room	la chambre à une personne	la shambr ah oon pehr-**son**
room with a bath	la chambre avec salle de bain	shambr ah-vek sal duh bañ
shower	une douche	doosh
I have a reservation	J'ai fait une reservation	zhay fay oon ray-zehrva-**syoñ**

Eating Out

Have you got a table?	Avez vous une table libre?	avay-**voo** oon tahbl leebr
I would like to reserve a table.	Je voudrais réserver une table.	zhuh voo-dray rayzehr-**vay** oon tahbl
The bill, please.	L'addition, s'il vous plait.	l'adee-**syoñ** voo **play**
I am a vegetarian.	Je suis végétarien.	zhuh swee vezhay-**tehryañ**
waitress/waiter	Monsieur, Mademoiselle	gah-sohn/ mad-uh-mwah-zel
menu	le menu	men-**oo**
cover charge	le couvert	luh koo-**vehr**
wine list	la carte des vins	lah **kart**-deh vañ
glass	verre	vehr
bottle	la bouteille	boo-**tay**
knife	le couteau	koo-**toh**
fork	la fourchette	for-**shet**
spoon	la cuillère	kwee-**yehr**
breakfast	le petit déjeuner	puh-**tee** day-**zhuh-nay**
lunch	le déjeuner	day-**zhuh-nay**
dinner	le dîner	dee-**nay**
main course	le grand plat	groñ plah
starter	l'hors d'oeuvres	or duhvr
dessert	le dessert	duh-zehrt
dish of the day	le plat du jour	plah doo joor
bar	le bar	bah
cafe	le café	ka-**fay**
rare	saignant	say-nyoñ
medium	à point	ah **pwañ**
well done	bien cuit	byañ **kwee**

Numbers

0	zero	zeh-**roh**
1	un	uñ, oon
2	deux	duh
3	trois	trwah
4	quatre	katr
5	cinq	sañk
6	six	sees
7	sept	set
8	huit	weet
9	neuf	nerf
10	dix	dees
11	onze	oñz
12	douze	dooz
13	treize	trehz
14	quatorze	ka**torz**
15	quinze	kañz
16	seize	sehz
17	dix-sept	dees-**set**
18	dix-huit	dees-**zweet**
19	dix-neuf	dees-**znerf**
20	vingt	vañ
21	vingt-et-un	vañ ay uhn
30	trente	tront
40	quarante	karoñt
50	cinquante	sañkoñt

60	soixante	swahsoñt
70	septante	septoñt
80	quatre-vingt	katr-**vañ**
90	quatre-vingt-dix/ nonante	katr vañ **dees** nonañ
100	cent	soñ
1000	mille	meel
1,000,000	million	miyoñ

Time

What is the time?	Quelle heure?	kel uhr
one minute	une minute	oon mee-**noot**
one hour	une heure	oon uhr
half an hour	une demi-heure	oon **duh-mee** uhr
half past one	une heure et demi	uhr ay duh-mee
a day	un jour	zhuhr
a week	une semaine	suh-mehn
a month	un mois	mwah
a year	une année	annay
Monday	lundi	luñ-**dee**
Tuesday	mardi	mah-**dee**
Wednesday	mercredi	mehrkruh-**dee**
Thursday	jeudi	zhuh-**dee**
Friday	vendredi	voñdruh-**dee**
Saturday	samedi	sam-**dee**
Sunday	dimanche	dee-**moñsh**

Belgian Beer and Food

fish	poisson	pwah-**ssoñ**
bass	bar/loup de mer	bah/loo duh mare
herring	hareng	ah-**roñ**
lobster	homard	oh-ma
monkfish	lotte	lot
mussel	moule	mool
oyster	huitre	weetr
pike	brochet	brosh-ay
salmon	saumon	soh-moñ
scallop	coquille Saint-Jacques	kok-eel sañ jak
sea bream	dorade/daurade	doh-rad
prawn	crevette	kreh-vet
skate	raie	ray
trout	truite	trweet
tuna	thon	toñ

Meat

meat	viande	vee-**yand**
beef	boeuf	buhf
chicken	poulet	poo-**lay**
duck	canard	kanar
lamb	agneau	ah**yoh**
pheasant	faisant	feh-zoñ
pork	porc	por
veal	veau	voh
venison	cerf/chevreuil	surf/shev-roy

Vegetables

vegetables	légumes	lay-**goom**
asparagus	asperges	ahs-pehrj
Belgian endive /chicory	chicon	shee-koñ
Brussels sprouts	choux de bruxelles	shoo duh broocksell
garlic	ail	eye
green beans	haricots verts	arrykoh vehr
haricot beans	haricots	arrykoh
potatoes	pommes de terre	pom-duh **tehr**
spinach	epinard	aypeenar
truffle	truffe	troof

Desserts

pancake	crêpe	crayp
waffle	gauffre	gohfr
fruit	fruits	frwee

Drinks

coffee	café	kah-**fay**
white coffee	café au lait	kah-**fay** oh lay
milky coffee	caffe latte	kah-**fay** lat-uh
hot chocolate	chocolat chaud	shok-oh-lah shoh
tea	thé	tay
water	l'eau	oh
mineral water	l'eau minérale	l'oh meenay-ral
lemonade	limonade	lee-moh-nad
orange juice	jus d'orange	zhoo doh-ronj
wine	le vin	vañ
house wine	vin maison	vañ may-sañ
beer	une bière	byahr

Tips for Pronouncing Dutch

The Dutch language is pronounced in largely the same way as English, although many vowels, particularly double vowels, are pronounced as long sounds. *J* is the equivalent of the English *y*, *v* is pronounced *f*, and *w* is *v*.

In Emergency

Help!	**Help!**	help
Stop!	**Stop!**	stop
Call a doctor!	**Haal een dokter!**	Haal uhn **dok**-tur
Call the police!	**Roep de politie!**	Roop duh poe-**leet**-see
Call the fire brigade!	**Roep de brandweer!**	Roop duh **brahnt**-vheer
Where is the nearest telephone?	**Waar ist de dichtsbijzijnde telefoon?**	Vhaar iss duh **dikst**-baiy-zaiyn-duh-tay-luh-**foan**
Where is the nearest hospital?	**Waar ist het dichtsbijzijande ziekenhuis**	Vhaar iss het **dikst**-baiy-zaiyn-duh **zee**-kuh-hows

Communication Essentials

Yes	**Ja**	yaa
No	**Nee**	nay
Please	**Alstublieft**	ahls-tew-**bleeft**
Thank you	**Dank u**	dhank-ew
Excuse me	**Pardon**	pahr-**don**
Hello	**Goed dag**	ghoot dahgh
Goodbye	**Tot ziens**	tot zins
Good night	**Slaap lekker**	slap **lek**-kah
morning	**Morgen**	**mor**-ghugh
afternoon	**Middag**	**mid**-dahgh
evening	**Avond**	**av**-vohnd
yesterday	**Gisteren**	**ghis**-tern
today	**Vandaag**	van-**daagh**
tomorrow	**Morgen**	**mor**-ghugh
here	**Hier**	heer
there	**Daar**	daar
What?	**Wat?**	vhat
When?	**Wanneer?**	vhan-**eer**
Why?	**Waarom?**	vhaar-**om**
Where?	**Waar?**	vhaar
How?	**Hoe?**	hoo

Useful Phrases

How are you?	**Hoe gaat het ermee?**	Hoo ghaat het er-**may**
Very well, thank you	**Heel goed, dank u**	Hayl ghoot, **dhank ew**
How do you do?	**Hoe maakt u het?**	Hoo maakt ew het
See you soon	**Tot ziens**	Tot zeens
That's fine	**Prima**	**Pree**-mah
Where is/are...?	**Waar is/zijn...?**	vhaar iss/zayn
How far is it to...?	**Hoe ver is het naar...?**	Hoo vehr iss het nar
How do I get to...?	**Hoe kom ik naar...?**	Hoo kom ik nar
Do you speak English?	**Spreekt u engels?**	Spraykt uw **eng**-uhls
I don't understand	**Ik snap het niet**	Ik snahp het neet
Could you speak slowly?	**Kunt u langzamer praten?**	Kuhnt ew **lahng**-zarmer-praat-tuh
I'm sorry	**Sorry**	sorry

Useful Words

big	**groot**	ghroat
small	**klein**	klaiyn
hot	**warm**	vharm
cold	**koud**	khowt
good	**goed**	ghoot
bad	**slecht**	slekht
enough	**genoeg**	ghuh-**noohkh**
well	**goed**	ghoot
open	**open**	open
closed	**gesloten**	ghuh-**slow**-tuh
left	**links**	links
right	**rechts**	rekhts
straight on	**rechtdoor**	rehkht dohr
near	**dichtbij**	dikht baiy
far	**ver weg**	vehr vhekh
up	**omhoog**	om-**hoakh**
down	**naar beneden**	naar buh **nay**-duh
early	**vroeg**	vrookh

late	**laat**	laat
entrance	**ingang**	**in**-ghang
exit	**uitgang**	**ouht**-ghang
toilet	**wc**	vhay-say
occupied	**bezet**	buh-**zett**
free (vacant)	**vrij**	vraiy
free (no charge)	**gratis**	**ghraah**-tiss

Making a Telephone Call

I'd like to place a long-distance telephone call	**Ik wil graag interlokal telefoneren**	ik vhil ghraakh **inter**-loh-kaal tay-luh-foh-**neh**-ruh
I'd like to call "collect"	**Ik wil "collect" bellen**	ik vhil " collect call" **bel**-luh
I will try again later	**Ik probeer het later nog wel eens**	ik pro-**beer** het later laater nokh vhel ayns
Can I leave a message?	**Kunt u een boodschap doorgeven?**	kuhnt ew uhn **boat**-skhahp **dohr**-ghay-vuh
Could you speak up a little please?	**Wilt u wat harder praten?**	vhilt ew vhat **hahr**-der **praat**-ew
Local call	**Lokaal gesprek**	low-**kaahl** ghuh-**sprek**

Shopping

How much does this cost?	**Hoeveel kost dit?**	hoo-**vayl** kost dit
I would like...	**Ik wil graag...**	ik vhil ghraakh
Do you have...?	**Heeft u...?**	hayft ew
I'm just looking	**Ik kijk alleen even**	ik kaiyk alleyn **ay**-vuh
Do you take credit cards?	**Neemt u credit cards aan?**	naymt ew credit cards aan?
Do you take travellers' cheques?	**Neemt u reischeques aan?**	naymt ew **raiys**-sheks aan
What time do you open?	**Hoe laat gaat u open?**	hoo laat ghaat ew opuh
What time do you close?	**Hoe laat gaat u dicht?**	hoo laat ghaat ew dikht
This one	**Deze**	**day**-zuh
That one	**Die**	dee
expensive	**duur**	dewr
cheap	**goedkoop**	ghoot-**koap**
size	**maat**	maat
white	**wit**	vhit
black	**zwart**	zvhahrt
red	**rood**	roat
yellow	**geel**	ghayl
green	**groen**	ghroon
blue	**blauw**	blah-ew

Types of Shops

antique shop	**antiekwinkel**	ahn-**teek**-vhin-kul
bakery	**bakker**	**bah**-ker-aiy
bank	**bank**	bahnk
bookshop	**boekwinkel**	**book**-vhin-kul
butcher	**slager**	slaakh-er-aiy
cake shop	**banketbakkerij**	bahnk-**et**-bahk-er-aiy
chip stop/stand	**patatzaak**	pah-**taht**-zak
chemist/drugstore	**apotheek**	ah-poe-**taiyk**
delicatessen	**delicatessen**	daylee-kah-**tes**-suh
department store	**warenhuis**	**vhaah**-uh-houws
fishmonger	**viswinkel**	**viss**-vhin-kul
greengrocer	**groenteboer**	**ghroon**-tuh-boor
hairdresser	**kapper**	**kah**-per
market	**markt**	mahrkt
newsagent	**krantenwinkel**	**krahn**-tuh-vhin-kul
post office	**postkantoor**	**pohst**-kahn-tor
supermarket	**supermarkt**	**sew**-per-mahrkt
tobacconist	**sigarenwinkel**	see-**ghaa**-ruh-vhin-kul
travel agent	**reisburo**	**raiys**-bew-roa

Sightseeing

art gallery	**gallerie**	ghaller-ee
bus station	**busstation**	**buhs**-stah-shown
bus ticket	**strippenkaart**	**strip**-puh-kaart
cathedral	**kathedraal**	kah-tuh-**draal**
church	**kerk**	kehrk
closed on public holidays	**op feestdagen gesloten**	op **fayst**-daa-ghuh ghuh-slow-**tuh**
day return	**dagretour**	**dahgh**-ruh-tour
garden	**tuin**	touwn
library	**bibliotheek**	bee-bee-yo-tayk
museum	**museum**	mew-**zay**-um

railway station	station	stah-**shown**
return ticket	retourtje	ruh-**tour**-tyuh
single journey	enkeltje	eng-**kuhl**-tyuh
tourist information	dienst voor tourisme	deenst vor tor-ism
town hall	stadhuis	staht-houws
train	trein	traiyn

Staying in a Hotel

Do you have a vacant room?	Zijn er nog kamers vrij?	zaiyn er nokh kaa-mers vray
double room with double bed	een twees persoons-kamer met een twee persoonsbed	uhn tvhay per-**soans**-ka-mer met uhn **tvhay** per-**soans** beht
twin room	een kamer met een lits-jumeaux	uhn **kaa**-mer met uhn lee-zjoo-**moh**
single room	eenpersoons-kamer	ayn-per-**soans** kaa-mer
room with a bath/shower	kaamer met bad/douche	**kaa**-mer met baht/doosh
I have a reservation	Ik heb gereserveerd	ik hep ghuh-ray-sehr-**veert**

Eating Out

Have you got table?	Is er een tafel vrij?	iss ehr uhn **tah**-fuhl vraiy
I would like to reserve a table	Ik wil een tafel reserveren	ik vhil uhn **tah**-fel ray sehr-**veer**-uh
The bill, please	Mag ik afrekenen	muhk ik **ahf**-ray-kuh-nuh
I am a vegetarian	Ik ben vegetariër	ik ben fay-ghun-**taahr**-ee-er
waitress/waiter	serveerster/ober	sehr-**veer**-ster/**oh**-ber
menu	de kaart	duh kaahrt
cover charge	het couvert	het koo-**vehr**
wine list	de wijnkaart	duh **vhaiyn**-kart
glass	het glass	het ghlahss
bottle	de fles	duh fless
knife	het mes	het mess
fork	de vork	duh fork
spoon	de lepel	duh **lay**-pul
breakfast	het ontbijt	het ont-**baiyt**
lunch	de lunch	duh lernsh
dinner	het diner	het dee-**nay**
main course	het hoofdgerecht	het **hoaft**-ghuh-rekht
starter, first course	het voorgerecht	het **vhor**-ghuh-rekht
dessert	het nagerecht	het **naa**-ghuh-rekht
dish of the day	het dagmenu	het **dahg**-munh-ew
bar	het cafe	het kaa-**fay**
café	het eetcafe	het **ayt**-kaa-**fay**
rare	rare	'rare'
medium	medium	'medium'
well done	doorbakken	door-**bah**-kuh

Numbers

1	een	ayn
2	twee	tvhay
3	drie	dree
4	vier	feer
5	vijf	faiyf
6	zes	zess
7	zeven	**zay**-vuh
8	acht	ahkht
9	negen	**nay**-guh
10	tien	teen
11	elf	elf
12	twaalf	tvhaalf
13	dertien	**dehr**-teen
14	veertien	**feer**-teen
15	vijftien	**faiyf**-teen
16	zestien	**zess**-teen
17	zeventien	**zayvuh**-teen
18	achtien	**ahkh**-teen
19	negentien	**nay**-**ghuh**-tien
20	twintig	**tvhin**-tukh
21	eenentwintig	aynuh-tvhin-tukh
30	dertig	**dehr**-tukh
40	veertig	**feer**-tukh
50	vijftig	**faiyf**-tukh
60	zestig	**zess**-tukh
70	zeventig	**zay**-vuh-tukh
80	tachtig	**tahkh**-tukh
90	negentig	**nayguh**-tukh

100	honderd	**hohn**-durt
1000	duizend	douw-zuhnt
1,000,000	miljoen	mill-**yoon**

Time

one minute	een minuut	uhn meen-**ewt**
one hour	een uur	uhn ewr
half an hour	een half uur	een hahlf uhr
half past one	half twee	hahlf twee
a day	een dag	uhn dahgh
a week	een week	uhn vhayk
a month	een maand	uhn maant
a year	een jaar	uhn jaar
Monday	maandag	**maan**-dahgh
Tuesday	dinsdag	**dins**-dahgh
Wednesday	woensdag	**vhoons**-dahgh
Thursday	donderdag	**donder**-dahgh
Friday	vrijdag	**vraiy**-dahgh
Saturday	zaterdag	**zaater**-dahgh
Sunday	zondag	**zon**-dahgh

Belgian Beer and Food
Fish

Fish	vis	fiss
bass	zeebars	see-buhr
herring	haring	**haa**-ring
lobster	kreeft	krayft
monkfish	lotte/zeeduivel	lot/seafuhdul
mussel	mossel	moss-uhl
oyster	oester	**ouhs**-tuh
pike	snoek	snook
prawn	garnaal	gar-nall
salmon	zalm	sahlm
scallop	Sint-Jacoboester/ Jacobsschelp	sind-yakob-ouhs-tuh/yakob-scuhlp
sea bream	dorade/zeebrasem	doh-rard
skate	rog	rog
trout	forel	foh-ruhl
tuna	tonijn	tuhn-een

Meat

meat	vlees	flayss
beef	rundvlees	**ruhnt**-flayss
chicken	kip	kip
duck	eend	aynt
lamb	lamsvlees	**lahms**-flayss
pheasant	fazant	**fay**-zanh
pork	varkensvlees	**vahr**-kuhns-flayss
veal	kalfsvlees	**karfs**-flayss
venison	ree (bok)	ray

Vegetables

vegetables	groenten	**ghroon**-tuh
asparagus	asperges	as-puhj
Belgian endive/ chicory	witloof	vit-lurf
Brussels sprouts	spruitjes	spruhr-tyuhs
garlic	knoflook	**knoff**-loak
green beans	princesbonen	prins-ess-buh-nun
haricot beans	snijbonen	snee-buh-nun
potatoes	aardappels	**aard**-uppuhls
spinach	spinazie	spin-a-jee
truffle	truffel	truh-fuhl

Desserts

fruit	fruit/vruchten	vroot/vrooh-tuh
pancake	pannekoek	**pah**-nuh-kook
waffle	wafel	vaff-uhl

Drinks

beer	bier	beeh
coffee	koffie	coffee
fresh orange juice	verse jus	**vehr**-suh zjhew
hot chocolate	chocola	sho-koh-**laa**
mineral water	mineraalwater	meener-**aahl**-vhaater
tea	thee	tay
water	water	vhaa-ter
wine	wijn	vhaiyn

Bruges City Map
(see pp118-129)